CONTENTS

BSO

00019945

DATE DUE			
- 5 FEB 2015			
			PRINTED IN U.S.A.

VAL

ANI

An I

and

Peter A. Fa   Attig

PRENTICE-HALL, INC., Englewood Cliffs, New Jersey 07632

Library of Congress Cataloging in Publication Data

FACIONE, PETER A
    Values and society.

    Includes index.
    1. Ethics.   I. Scherer, Donald, joint author.
II. Attig, Thomas, joint author.   III. Title
BJ1025.F15   170   77-21995
ISBN 0-13-940338-8

© 1978 by Prentice-Hall, Inc., Englewood Cliffs, N.J. 07632

All rights reserved. No part of this book
may be reproduced in any form or
by any means without permission in writing
from the publisher.

Printed in the United States of America

10 9 8 7 6 5 4 3 2 1

Prentice-Hall International, Inc., *London*
Prentice-Hall of Australia Pty. Limited, *Sydney*
Prentice-Hall of Canada, Ltd., *Toronto*
Prentice-Hall of India Private Limited, *New Delhi*
Prentice-Hall of Japan, Inc., *Tokyo*
Prentice-Hall of Southeast Asia Pte. Ltd. *Singapore*
Whitehall Books Limited, *Wellington, New Zealand*

PREFACE

Every day we make evaluations, judgments, and decisions. Among the most common and important in our lives are decisions concerning goals, judgments concerning ways to achieve what we wish to achieve, and evaluations of what ought to be done. Individuals make these evaluations as they reflect on what they should or should not do. Corporations, institutions, and communities make them concerning both their communal or institutional goals and the methods used to achieve them. Legislative bodies, judges, and government officials make them as they determine the direction of society, frame its laws, administer its policies, and adjudicate its conflicts. Often it is not easy for us to decide what we ought to do, what is right and what is wrong, where our obligations, responsibilities, rights and duties lie. Yet these decisions are a necessary and essential part of our lives. Whatever we do amounts to some sort of decision concerning our goals, actions, responsibilities, and life styles.

This book's purpose is to help you come to grips with these questions. It offers serious, philosophical reflections and analyses of the values that people have found most important in guiding their individual and social choices. In so doing it focuses on the importance of such values as self-interest, social utility, human freedom, individual rights and duties, justice, community, and law as these affect decisions. The book also offers you the conceptual tools and philosophical skills necessary to understand what values are operating in specific moral issues and how rationally to resolve the moral problems that grow out of diverging or conflicting personal or social values.

To accomplish its purpose the book is divided into three parts. Part I provides you with the preliminary conceptual tools you will need to deal effectively with value questions. It also develops the techniques necessary for discussing value-related questions logically. The concepts distinctions, and techniques presented in Part I are used throughout the rest of the book. Part II presents analyses of seven basic topic areas in ethics and social philosophy: egoism, utilitarianism, freedom, rights and duties, justice, society, and law. The discussions include a treatment of the central ideas and philosophical issues of each area, presenting and analyzing the positions of different philosophers. The discussions in Part II offer clarifications and critiques of the thoughts that dominate the philosophical tradition of Western civilization on each topic. Part III provides you with the strategies used in rationally resolving the value conflicts that arise between the theories and normative principles discussed in Part II. Having learned these strategies, you can apply them to specific moral issues that arise in either personal ethics or social philosophy.

Beyond presenting the basic philosophical issues as clearly and concisely as possible, and beyond using applied elementary logic and conceptual analysis to further clarify and discuss these philosophical issues, the book includes several features that should make it more useful to both teachers and students. For example, the text is presented in small instructional units, which we call "modules." Each module begins by stating what you should learn by studying it. These learning goals, or instructional objectives, should serve as guides to your study of a particular module. The modules then present a case study—a story that illustrates the ideas or techniques being developed. The explanatory text draws out theoretical points and describes philosophical techniques both abstractly and by appeal to the case study and other examples. Each module ends with a set of exercises, asking you to apply the ideas and the tools you are learning. The exercises should serve to reinforce your understanding of what you read about in the text of the module. Answers are provided, and you are referred back to specific sections of the module, so that if you have difficulty with any exercise you can immediately review the relevant text. Some modules also contain a brief biography of a notable philosopher. These biographies serve as supplemental reference points, indicating the historical development of philosophical thought. We have drawn together modules that deal with a specific topic area into the chapter-sized groupings we call "clusters."

Although this book was designed for a variety of possible uses, its primary employment is as a main text of a first course in ethics or in social philosophy. A variety of paths can be taken through the text. We suggest that you begin with Part I, which presents the conceptual tools. You have several alternatives when you move into Part II, depending upon your interests and goals in the study of ethics and/or social philosophy. May we recommend a couple of patterns for you? If your interest is primarily in ethics, you will probably want to focus on (a) Cluster Two, Self-Interest, (b) Modules 7 and 8 of Cluster Three, Utility, (c) Cluster Four, Freedom (possibly omitting the discussion of punishment in Module 12), (d) Cluster Five, Rights and Duties, and (e) Cluster Six, Justice. On the other hand, if you are interested in focusing on social philosophy, you might select (a) Cluster Three, Utility, (b) Cluster Four, Freedom (possibly omitting the discussion of autonomy in Module 11), (c) Cluster Five, Rights and Duties (possibly omitting the discussion of foundations of deontology in Module 16), (d) Cluster Six, Justice, (e) Cluster Seven, Society, and (f) Cluster Eight, Law.

The clusters in Part II are designed to be used independently. You can select whatever combination or ordering of clusters best suits your particular goals. After you have worked through the material you select in Part II, move to Part III to learn the strategies for rationally resolving value conflicts. If your focus has been on ethics, you will want to read the preliminary note to Cluster Nine and then study Modules 25 and 27; if your emphasis has been social philosophy, you will want to study Modules 26 and 27 after you have read the preliminary note in Cluster Nine.

This book can also be used as a supplementary text. For example, it can be used as background reading or as a text in a more specialized course that integrates theoretical studies of ethics and social philosophy with specific normative issues. It can accompany an anthology on normative issues or be used in conjunction with a text devoted to some specific set of normative problems, such as problems in medical ethics. It can be used in introductory philosophy courses to introduce the ethics and social philosophy component of the philosophical enterprise. The book has also been designed with the independent reader in mind; thus it is suitable for use in any of a variety of self-instruction settings.

Our aim has been to present concepts and theories in ethics and social philosophy as well as the philosophical tools for dealing with normative questions. We have presumed that most readers will have had no previous experience with philosophy and will be interested primarily in acquiring practical as well as theoretical knowledge of ethics or social philosophy. Thus the book can be used not only in the undergraduate philosophy courses mentioned above but also in continuing education programs, community colleges, and elsewhere, as long as one's aim is to introduce students to ethics or social philosophy for the first time. The presentation of material is compatible with a large variety of teaching approaches, ranging from the more conventional lectures and discussions to methods relying on individualized instruction and self-paced learning.

We are most grateful for the help so many people have given us with this project. We thank our students at Bowling Green State University who have used earlier versions of this text and who have worked through the exercises. We also thank our reviewers. Tom Beauchamp, Kenneth Kipnis, and Donald Morris, and editors at Prentice-Hall, Inc., for their constructive and directive comments. We thank Pat Bressler and our other typists and proofreaders for their care and attention to detail.

We welcome, and would be most grateful for, any comments and suggestions that you might wish to offer.

PETER A. FACIONE
DONALD SCHERER
THOMAS ATTIG

PART I

CONCEPTUAL
TOOLS

Cluster One

THE STARTING POINT

Success in any serious activity begins with the mastery of certain basic skills and ideas. You should bring to your study of ethics and social philosophy a number of cognitive skills, including the abilities to (a) formulate assertions expressing normative points of view, (b) use conceptual analysis to clarify and interpret normative assertions, and (c) use critical thinking to support these claims. You probably already have these skills (even if you do not recognize the terminology we use). The educational goal of this cluster is to help you further develop and perfect these abilities. We will introduce you to the concerns of ethics and social philosophy, helping you to understand the concepts and to develop the necessary practical skills to study any of a variety of topic areas. You will learn how to identify normative issues, classify value judgments into broad general categories, and formulate arguments that support normative conclusions.

MODULE 1
NORMATIVE CONCERNS

This module explains what ethics and social philosophy are all about. It clarifies the distinction between facts and values, then focuses on assertions that express value judgments about how people ought or ought not to behave, either individually or collectively. Such assertions are called normative statements, and the matters of human behavior they refer to are the principal concerns of the normative disciplines of ethics and social philosophy. After reading Module 1, you should be able to

- Distinguish normative statements from other assertions.
- Give examples of normative and non-normative statements.
- State points of comparison and contrast between value judgments and fact judgments.
- Describe ethics and social philosophy in terms of their normative concerns.
- Contrast the concerns of ethics and social philosophy with the similar yet different concerns of the social sciences, values-clarification, behavioral modification, and counselling.

THE CASE OF THE AMBIGUOUS ASSIGNMENT

There had been racial tensions at the school all during the spring. Mr. Hartpang, the social science teacher, decided that one way to keep the lines of communication open between various groups of students was to frankly discuss the racial issues in class. He gave the students the following assignment as a preliminary to the class discussion: "Write a paragraph of about fifty words on the topic 'Racism Today.'" Two of the papers were selected to be read in class.

"Racism Today" by Judith Harris: "Everybody says that it's wrong to be prejudiced but people have been prejudiced for centuries. Lots of people try to hide their racism in public; but at home they let it out. Kids see their parents' racism and so they learn to be prejudiced too. They learn it so well that they don't even know they are racists."

"Racism Today" by Louis Ross: "People should stop being racists. Racism is immoral because it leads to violence which leads to injury and destroyed property. It's not fair to treat some people one way and other people other ways just because they are different colors. Racism should be rooted out of today's society."

1:1.1 Normative vs. Non-Normative Statements.   ~~Normative state-~~ ~~ments are assertions that express our value judgments.[1] Accordingly,~~ ~~every normative statement says or implies that something is good or bad~~,

[1] Numbers starting paragraphs are coded as follows: The first number indicates the module number. The number after the colon indicates the section and subsection of the module. So, for example, 8:3.4 means section 3, subsection 4, of Module 8.

better or worse, ought to be or ought not to be. All of the statements that Louis Ross made in the case study above are normative statements. Some normative statements, such as "The crimson leaves of a red maple are most beautiful during an autumn sunset," are about aesthetic concerns. Some normative statements express value judgments about logical concerns—for example, "Aristotle's argument is not acceptable." Some normative statements, such as "Arrows are better weapons than are spears," express value judgments that do not necessarily have immediate behavioral implications. Others, such as "Informed consent laws should be revised," do have immediate behavioral implications about what should or should not be done. As we shall see in 1:3.1, a broad spectrum of such statements with immediate behavioral implications express the concerns of ethics and social philosophy. Here are some additional examples of normative assertions:

> The rock-opera *Tommy* is delightful.
> Picasso's "Guernica" is magnificent.
> The administration building is an abomination.
> You have drawn the wrong conclusions from your data sample.
> Your inference is invalid.
> Public nudity should be legalized.
> Environmental conservation is the responsibility of everyone.
> Violence in children's television should be eliminated.
> Everyone has the right to adequate health care.
> Adultery is a sin.

1:1.2   Non-normative statements are statements that are value-neutral, ones that do not express (or are not intended to express) value judgments. Non-normative statements include reports, descriptions, or assertions either true or false used to express matters of empirical or logical fact. For example:

> In 1976 Americans celebrated their bicentennial.
> Triangles have three sides.
> Many people value fair play.
> •People usually do what they are told.
> Violence is a socially disruptive force.
> Many people have religious beliefs.
> Alcoholism is a widespread disease.
> Small children enjoy being told stories.
> • Competition leads to decreased productivity.
> Erma thinks Pearl Buck is a great writer.

All of these statements express judgments about facts, either empirical facts or conceptual (logical) facts. As you can see from the last example in the list, there can be factual judgments about what other people value. We can make factual claims about values and about a person's value judgments.

Further examples of non-normative statements occur in the Judith Harris paragraph in the case study. Her essay on racism today is composed exclusively of non-normative, value-neutral statements.

1:1.3   If you contrast what Harris wrote with Ross's essay, you will see why this case is called "The Case of the Ambiguous Assignment." Both Ross and Harris followed the instructions, yet they came up with quite different essays. Harris wrote a non-normative essay that relied on her understanding of various scientific theories and facts. Ross wrote a totally normative essay aimed at treating racism today as a normative problem with social dimensions.

Many issues can be treated from both the normative and non-normative points of view. Consider alcoholism, for example. Normative statements can be made:

> Drinking is wrong.
> Don't drink and drive.
> Beer and wine should be made illegal.
> It's all right to use alcohol in moderation.

Non-normative statements also can be made:

> Legal prohibition contributes to increased drinking.
> Nero was an alcoholic.
> Alcoholism among the aristocracy contributed to Rome's fall.
> There are more alcoholics today than there were last year.
> Teenage alcoholism is increasing.
> Alcohol is physically addictive.
> Alcohol is destructive of normal liver function.

1:1.4   Some statements are, at first glance, difficult to categorize as either normative or non-normative. Consider, for example:

> Gerald is lazy.
> Brenda is industrious.

On the one hand, each of these statements seems to be non-normative in describing how eager some person is to work. In part, the assertions report that Gerald is not eager to work and that Brenda is. Yet clearly each says more than that. Gerald is being evaluated lowly, and Brenda is commended. "Lazy" does not simply mean "inclined to do a little." A negative evaluation of that inclination is involved in the meaning of the term. Notice the similar situation with "industrious." Throughout the text, we shall treat statements that have both descriptive components and evaluative components as normative statements. The principle we will be following is that a statement should be considered normative whenever it says or implies that something is good or bad, better or worse, for being the way it is.

1:2.1 Comparing Normative and Non-Normative Statements. Non-normative statements can be appraised as true or false. They can be used as the premises or conclusions of arguments. And, most importantly, non-normative statements are amenable to being argued for and thus having their truth (or falsity) demonstrated by rational proof and appeal to relevant information. To argue in support of a non-normative statement one appeals to empirical and possibly logical information. For example, to show that alcohol is physically addictive one must appeal to biochemistry and medicine. One can run experiments and marshal evidence in order to confirm or disconfirm such non-normative statements. A descriptive study reveals what is needed to support non-normative or value-neutral statements.

We have elected to treat normative claims or assertions as statements, although we recognize that this is a matter of some dispute. Many would argue that normative claims cannot be appraised as true or false; they would deny that normative assertions are statements at all. On the other hand, many others would contend that normative claims are like statements of the non-normative variety. We will continue to speak of normative claims as statements that can reasonably be called true or false because of certain practices relating to how people commonly treat them. First, as with other statements, people do, from time to time, offer arguments in support of normative claims. Second, people evaluate the adequacy of these kinds of arguments, calling some reasons offered in support of normative claims better and some weaker. Third, people recognize that certain combinations or sets of normative assertions are consistent, whereas other sets are not. We will have more to say on this feature in Module 3, when we talk about universalizability. So, whatever the precise status of normative claims, whatever the exact character of their possible truth or falsity, there are certain important similarities between them and non-normative statements. These similarities warrant our treating normative claims as statements.

Normative claims can often be supported by argumentation and appeal to relevant information. Some normative studies, such as logic, are rather rigorous and fully developed, so that there is considerable confidence in the normative statements they support. If the techniques of logic tell us that a particular argument is valid, there is little reason to doubt the truth of that normative conclusion. Other normative studies, such as aesthetics, are less fully developed or less rigorous in their procedures. Nonetheless, one can still make reasonable arguments to the effect that one piece of sculpture is more beautiful or better than another. The normative studies, ethics and social philosophy, fall someplace between aesthetics and logic in terms of how fully they are developed and how rigorously established (and widely accepted) their conclusions are.

1:2.2   Arguments in support of normative statements attempt to demonstrate, in nontrivial and nonfallacious ways, that their normative conclusions are true. Proofs offered in support of statements, either normative or non-normative, are basically arguments; their premises can be listed, they can be examined for logical correctness, their premises can be evaluated as true or false. Let us look at two examples. First, we have the argument that Louis Ross offered in support of his normative statement that racism is immoral.

(1) Racism leads to violence.
(2) Violence leads to injury and destruction.
(3) Anything that leads to injury and destruction is immoral.

(4) So, racism is immoral.

Premise (3) is needed (unspoken but implicit) in the original passage. It provides the value dimension Ross implicitly relies on to support his normative conclusion. Contrast this with an argument that Harris makes:

(1) People express their racism where it is seen by their children.
(2) Children imitate and learn from their parents.

(3) So, children learn from their parents to be racist.

Premise (2) is an unspoken premise in Harris' argument. Notice that neither it nor premise (1) is normative. Rightly so, for one need not use normative assertions to support non-normative claims.

1:2.3   It is customary to distinguish statements of fact from expressions of opinion. While this distinction is quite legitimate, it is important that you realize the difference between it and the normative/non-normative distinction we have been discussing. When we distinguish statements of fact from matters of opinion, we have in mind that the statements of fact are known to be true whereas the matters of opinion are statements that nobody is now in a position to know. For example, someone might believe that soccer will have more fans in the year 2000 than football will. Since no one today can know whether this will prove true, this assertion about the future popularity of soccer is a matter of opinion.

Whether a given normative statement should be regarded as a matter of opinion is, in the first place, a question of whether any reasons can be given in support of it. If a person asserts a normative statement without having any reasons for it, the assertion might be called a matter of opinion. Normative assertions, however, can be backed by reasons. Moreover, there are several well-accepted standards by which the relevance and the strength of those reasons can be evaluated. Ethics and social philosophy are in large part attempts to define the relevance and strength clearly. Accordingly, we should not assign all normative statements to the category of matters of opinion. In contrast to normative opinions we should be aware of reasoned, normative assertions. Standards for normative reasoning are discussed more fully in Module 3.

1:3.1 Concerns of Ethics and Social Philosophy. As indicated in 1:1.1, ethics and social philosophy focus upon concerns expressed in normative statements that have immediate implications for human conduct. Thus, they are concerned with the value judgments appropriate to human behavior. Yet, not all such judgments are correctly understood as having ethical or social philosophical significance. The following normative statements would not ordinarily be understood as having such significance:

Brush your teeth after every meal.
Excuse yourself before leaving the table.
Allow your coffee to cool before drinking it.
Don't use a standard screwdriver in a Phillips screw.

Though these statements have immediate behavior implications, they concern what is prudent, what is good etiquette, or what is good technique. In ordinary circumstances, such matters lack a certain seriousness or weightiness that attaches to the concerns of the ethicist or social philosopher: behavior that either entails significant harm or benefit for others or for oneself, is in accord with or in violation of duties, or involves respect or disrespect for human or moral rights. Examples of statements expressing such concerns are the following:

Murder is wrong.
Self-mutilation is immoral.
You should almost always respond to a cry for help.
Wealth should be distributed equitably.
Promises should be kept.
One must never tell a lie.

The right to live is most fundamental.

The state has no right to tax citizens without representation.

How, then, are ethics and social philosophy to be distinguished? Ethics is the normative study of individual conduct, and social philosophy is the normative study of communal conduct. If the question of euthanasia is treated as one about the possible behavior of an individual, as in "Would it be right for me to perform a mercy killing?", then the problem is one of personal ethics. On the other hand, if the normative issue is a possible communal act, as in "Should euthanasia be legalized?", then the problem is one of social philosophy. In terms of content, then, there is a considerable overlap between ethics and social philosophy.

1:3.2   Ethics and social philosophy are both disciplined studies. They approach normative problems from a rational, intellectual point of view. Their aim is to arrive at reasonable resolutions of normative issues through the use of rational argumentation and careful consideration of relevant information. In other words, they strive for well-thought-out value judgments.

In pursuing these normative questions, ethics and social philosophy bridge the gap between theory and practice. Obviously it is desirable to reach a reasonable resolution to the moral problem presented by a given situation. There are practical concerns such as determining the obligations or responsibilities of people and groups: "What should I do?" and "What should we do?" But there is also the theoretical concern for finding the more general principles or the more universal moral standards that can be relied upon in a variety of situations: theories of moral obligation, theories of praise and blame, and theories about the meaning of individual good and social well-being.

1:3.3   Ethics and social philosophy have a very practical side, and yet they are not to be confused with other practical human activities that are also concerned with human behavior. Ethics is not advising; it is not counselling. Ethics is not concerned with telling people what is best for them; it is not concerned directly with helping people to deal in a more emotionally stable way with their personal problems. Ethics is not values-clarification. Values-clarification techniques can help people find out what they value or prize. The concern of ethics, however, is not with what one *does* value but with what one *should* value. Ethics should not be confused with behavior modification, which aims to alter how a person acts—often through the use of rewards and punishments to reinforce behavior, or even through drug therapy. Ethics does not concern itself with forcing, causing, or encouraging people to act in certain ways. Its immediate goal is knowledge. This knowledge can serve as a guide to one's behavior, but it does not program that behavior.

1:3.4   Just as there are similar yet different concerns on the practical side, there are also similar yet different concerns on the theoretical side. Ethics and social philosophy are not to be confused with the social or behavioral sciences. Unlike sociology or anthropology, the concern is not with describing the values, norms, or customs of a given community. Unlike psychology, the concern is not with discovering motivations nor with explaining and predicting human behavior. Unlike history, economics, or political science, the concern is not with understanding the causes or factors that contributed to economic, social, or political phenomena past or present. The primary concern of the scientist is to tell how the world is, why the world is that way, and how it is likely to be in the future. In contrast, the primary concern of the ethicist or social philosopher is with how the world *should* be, what will make it *better*, how one *ought* to live.

1:3.5   The problems of ethics and social philosophy are problems about "conduct." They are problems about what people *should do, how they ought to behave.* They may be questions about goals, such as "Should legislation be passed to support the maxim of equal pay for equal work?" They may be questions about the means to a goal, such as "Is price fixing for higher profits justified in today's market?" Whether they concern goals or means, they remain questions about human behavior and whether or not it is moral, justified, or right.

Exercises for Module 1: Normative Statements

1.   Which of the following are normative statements? (1:1.1–1:1.3)

 a. Murder is wrong.
 b. A person shot through the heart will likely die.
 c. Racism is a function of ignorance.
 d. American foreign policy is a product of political compromise.
 e. Given two equally qualified candidates for a job, one a woman and the other a man, we should hire the woman.
 f. Always obey your parents.
 g. Individual autonomy ought to be respected at all costs.
 h. There is nothing more important than human life.
 i. Polygamy is no longer practiced in New York.
 j. Life under communist rule is not worth living.

2.   Below is a set of statements. If a statement is purely descriptive, mark it *PD*. If the statement is a normative statement that has descriptive implications, mark it *N* for normative and then state its descriptive implication. (1:1.4)

 a. The architecture of the church is gothic.

b. Terry is rude.

c. Gerald is clever.

d. The government is oppressive.

e. The union is conducting a membership drive.

f. Videotape machines for private use are still unreliable.

g. Fluorescent light is cool light.

h. The cooler a light, the less wasteful it is of energy.

In the above statements knowledge of the meanings of the terms involved is sufficient to determine if the statement is purely descriptive or if it has an evaluative component. The meaning of some words, however, is sufficiently unclear that reasonable persons might disagree about whether some statements using them were purely descriptive or contained an evaluative component. The following are examples:

i. Norma is healthy.

j. Centralized government is inefficient.

k. Herbert manipulates people.

l. Susan is an alcoholic.

3. Which of the following specific directives would properly fall within the scope of ethics or social philosophy? (1:3.1, 1:3.2, 1:3.5)

   a. Use plutonium if you wish to build effective atomic weapons.

   b. An antiabortion amendment should be added to the U.S. Constitution.

   c. Bribery of foreign officials by international corporations should be prohibited.

   d. Good grooming is a good idea.

   e. When bowling, only one's waist should bend.

   f. Nuclear warfare kills innocent people and is, therefore, wrong.

   g. Never break promises.

   h. Do not use company funds for your own advantage.

   i. Put savings aside regularly.

   j. Funds should be set aside for nonfossil fuel development.

4. Which of the following expresses a general concern of ethics or social philosophy? (1:3.3–1:3.5)

   a. A concern to determine whether a particular act is right or wrong.

   b. A concern to list the values held by a given community.

   c. A concern to help people learn what motivates their activity.

   d. A concern to encourage people to act ethically.

   e. A concern to discover standards or principles that justify moral evaluations.

f. A concern to describe how people behave in society.

g. A concern to determine how people ought to behave.

h. A concern to protect human life.

i. A concern to replace religion with humanism.

5. Write two normative statements and two non-normative statements about each of the following. (1:1.3)

   a. National elections.   *e*. Defense spending
   b. Consumerism.   *f*. Genetic control.
   c. Liberal education   *g*. Pornography.
   d. American funeral practices.   *h*. Suicide.

   At least one of the normative statements in each set should express a concern of ethics or social philosophy.

6. Compare and contrast normative statements that express value judgments with non-normative statements expressing factual judgments. (1:1.1, 1:1.2, 1:2.1)

7. Briefly state the chief concerns of ethics and social philosophy. Give examples of the problems they would treat. (1:3.1, 1:3.2, 1:3.5)

8. Explain how ethics and social philosophy differ from both the behavioral sciences and counselling techniques. (1:3.1, 1:3.4)

Selected Answers to Exercises for Module 1

1. The normative statements are *a, e, f, g, h, j*.
2. *a*. *PD*.
   b. *N:* Terry's behavior offends people.
   c. *N:* Gerald figures things out.
   d. *N:* The government restricts persons.
   e. *PD*.
   f. *N:* The videotape machine either breaks or fails to produce the desired product rather frequently.
   g. *PD*.
   h. *N:* Cool lights use less energy than hot lights to produce the same amount of light.
3. The questions of ethics and social philosophy are *b, c, f, g, h, j*.
4. The question of ethics and social philosophy are *a, e, g*.
5. Here are some examples of correct answers.
   a. Non-Normative: Voter registration is declining.
                     Few people today value their right to vote.
      Normative: Good citizens should vote for the candidates of their choice.

		Presidential campaigning should be carefully regulated.
c. Non-Normative:		Fewer students today value a liberal education.
		Critics are currently questioning the worth of the liberal arts.
Normative:		There is nothing more fulfilling than liberal education.
		Liberal education is a waste of time.
f. Non-Normative:		We still know little about genetic control.
		The prospects of influencing character through genetic control frighten many.
Normative:		We should not tamper with nature's genetic code.
		Genetic manipulation should be used to prevent birth defects.
h. Non-Normative:		Suicide is increasing in New York.
		Addicts frequently commit suicide.
Normative:		Self-sacrificing suicide is permissible.
		All suicide is wrong.

MODULE 2
ANALYSIS OF NORMATIVE STATEMENTS

In Module 1 we introduced the distinction between normative and non-normative statements. In this module we will introduce procedures of conceptual analysis that are useful in distinguishing some of the possible meanings normative statements can have. After reading Module 2, you should be able to

- Distinguish subjectivist and objectivist interpretations of normative statements.
- Distinguish interpretations of normative statements as being about intrinsic or instrumental values.
- Distinguish interpretations of normative statements as being about absolute or relative values.
- Give examples of each of the types of normative statement listed above.
- Describe the role of conceptual analysis in the interpretation of normative statements.

THE CASE OF THE SUGAR MOGUL

C. J. Mogle, the executive vice-president of Boyce Sugar Enterprises, was asked to speak on the corporation's position on trade agreements with Cuba. After his speech he agreed to a television interview with Anita Vantage.

VANTAGE: What do you think about the proposed legislation to permit sugar importation from Cuba?

MOGLE: It's a good policy.

VANTAGE: What do you mean, sir?

MOGLE: I mean I like it.

VANTAGE: Why? Do you believe it will help the balance of trade or lower domestic sugar prices?

MOGLE: No. I like it because I generally favor legislative activity designed to help international businesses.

VANTAGE: Are there any other reasons why you think the legislation is good?

MOGLE: Yes. I expect it will benefit Boyce Enterprises.

VANTAGE: Do you mean that what is good for Boyce Sugar Enterprises is good for the country?

MOGLE: No, I didn't say it was good for the country. I said it was good for us at Boyce Sugar.

VANTAGE: Do you feel that legislation should serve the public good or the good of only a few?

MOGLE: Why, the public good, of course, unless it puts certain businesses at a disadvantage in the international market.

VANTAGE: In your view, if the pending sugar legislation fails, will it disadvantage Boyce Enterprises in the international market?

MOGLE: Why yes, its failure would cut into our projected profits.

VANTAGE: But then, it would be to the advantage of domestic producers to keep Cuban sugar out of the U.S. market.

MOGLE: Yes, it would help the domestic companies, but that is no concern of ours. The sooner we put those small domestic sugar producers out of business, the sooner we can more carefully regulate the sugar industry.

VANTAGE: What do you mean, Mr. Mogle? What regulations are needed?

MOGLE: Oh, I don't mean regulations in the sense of "laws"; I mean we can control production, distribution, and ultimately prices.

VANTAGE: May I ask you a more personal question? What would you say if a domestic producer tried to put Boyce out of business?

MOGLE: Why, that should be illegal!

2:1.1 Alternative Interpretations and Conceptual Analysis. In the case study Anita Vantage tries to interpret Mogle's claim that the proposed legislation is good. She offers two interpretations, namely that the legislation will benefit the balance of trade and that it will bring down domestic prices. The implications are first that these are desirable goals and second that all policies that help to achieve these goals are, thereby, good. Mogle, on the other hand, rejects these reasons and offers an alternative interpretation of his claim. He asserts that when he said the policy was good he meant simply that he liked it. Vantage, not satisfied with that answer, presses him for reasons. Only then does Mogle explain that he favors the policy because it would benefit his corporation. The interview illustrates that a normative claim such as "X is good" can be interpreted in a variety of ways.

In seeking to assess the truth of normative claims, our first task is to short-circuit the disagreements that can arise over how normative statements such as "X is good" are to be understood. We must begin, as Vantage did, by locating the speaker's intended interpretation of his or her normative claims. Only then can we assess the strength of the reasons offered in support of those claims.

2:1.2   To discover how Mogle intends his normative claim to be interpreted, Vantage presses him three times to clarify what he means. Slowly he reveals his position. As Vantage realizes, the simple claim "It's a good policy" can be difficult to interpret correctly. It is ambiguous in the ways we suggested in 2:1.1.

One of the chief tools used by philosophers to secure the needed clarification of vague or ambiguous assertions is _conceptual analysis_. Conceptual analysis is the methodical examination of words, ideas, and concepts with a view toward clarifying their meaning. By examining various nuances of usage and meaning we can isolate the precise sense of a vague or ambiguous concept and so identify the exact meaning of a particular statement. For example, suppose we are presented with the claim "Public nudity is obscene." It is not clear whether or not this is a normative or non-normative claim. "Obscene" may be used here to mean "unchaste," the implication being that public nudity is undesirable. Or "obscene" may be used here in a non-normative sense, as in "found to be offensive by at least 60 percent of the population." In this case the claim that public nudity is obscene becomes the non-normative sociological claim that at least 60 percent of the population finds public nudity offensive.

2:1.3   Philosophers believe that it is often possible to remove problematic vagueness and ambiguity by analyzing complex, unfamiliar, and difficult concepts or ideas into their simpler, more familiar, better-understood constituent ideas. For example, the concept "hexagon" can be analyzed into the familiar ideas "being a closed figure," "having straight sides," "having sides of equal length," and "having exactly six sides." The hope is that through such analysis the original concept will be clarified. Often the fruits of a systematic and complete conceptual analysis are presented in the form of a definition. For example:

> "*A* is a bachelor at time *t*" is definitionally equivalent to "*A* is a male, *A* is an adult, *A* is not married at time *t*, and there is no time *t'* such that *t'* is earlier than *t* and *A* was married at *t'*."

The conditions set forth in the definition are usually viewed as those that must be met if the term being defined is to be used correctly. Each of the conditions is seen to be a necessary prerequisite; the group of conditions taken together is seen to be sufficient for the proper use of the term. For example, you cannot be a bachelor unless you satisfy all four of the conditions given, and further, you are a bachelor if you do satisfy all four.

This mode of conceptual analysis is used to clarify concepts in ethics and social philosophy as well. Here is an example of the analysis of the concept of a "supererogatory virtuous act" in terms of simpler component ideas:

> "*A* performs a supererogatory virtuous act by doing *X* at time *t*" is definitionally equivalent to "*A* performs *X* at time *t*, *X* is a virtuous act, and the performance of *X* by *A* at *t* is over and above any of *A*'s duties at time *t*."

Besides being used to relate complex ideas to their simpler constituents, conceptual analysis is used to relate two equally complex ideas to each other. This can be done by tracing each of the complex ideas back to their common conceptual roots and, so, establishing their connection to each other. For example, one might ask whether or not it is possible to be free in an unjust society. The concepts of freedom and justice are both relatively complex. However, we can establish a connection between these ideas using conceptual analysis. We can, thereby, argue that genuine freedom cannot exist in a completely unjust society. To prove this we would have to show that there is a conceptual inconsistency between genuine freedom and total injustice. The primary data in this proof would not be the empirical information that can be gained through social psychology. Rather it would be the conceptual information available through a careful analysis of the two concepts.

2:1.4.   To better use conceptual analysis you should learn the range of possible meanings that certain crucially problematic words can have. Normative words, such as "good," are particularly problematic. Through the study of ethics and social philosophy you will encounter a large number of normative words, cover a variety of justifications that can be offered for normative claims, and study the typical pros and cons of a variety of normative positions. This study should help you be aware of the major strengths and weaknesses of normative positions, because you will already have an understanding of the twists and turns of thought that most positions typically take.

2:2.1 Subjectivist and Objectivist Interpretations. One important step in understanding normative statements is to find out whether a particular claim is meant to be taken subjectively or objectively. The conceptual analysis undertaken by Vantage, as noted in 2:1.1, is directed toward determining whether Mogle's position is *subjectivist or objectivist.* The interpretations she offers, in terms of promoting trade and lowering prices, are objectivist. In general, an objectivist interpretation of "X is good" is that X possesses some characteristic that makes it worthy of preference, desire, or value, independently of the actual preferences or desires of the speaker. One can express the objectivist interpretation using statements such as "X is a worthy goal," "X is really the just thing to do even though we would not like it," "X is our duty." *On the objectivist interpretation a normative claim becomes a statement about what in or about X makes it worthy of being preferred independently of the speaker's actual personal preferences or feelings concerning* X. Mogle, however, finds neither of the interpretations offered by Vantage to his liking, and instead he offers a subjectivist interpretation of his position. The subjectivist interpretation of "X is good" is that the speaker prefers or values X. This preference can be expressed in many ways—for example, "I like X," "I approve of X," "I favor X." *On the subjectivist interpretation a normative claim becomes a claim about what is in fact desired or preferred by the speaker.*

2:2.2   Here is another case study. We will be using it momentarily to illustrate how one can further interpret normative claims by noting the kinds of values they appeal to. As you read it, you can also be asking yourself whether the normative claims made are to be given subjectivist or objectivist interpretations.

THE CASE OF THE IN-CAR TELEVISION

The meeting room quieted as the sales executive, Ms. Galoti, began to speak. "I would like to recommend that a new luxury option be made available, a mini-television set installed in the dashboard directly in front of the passenger seat. I believe this option will greatly increase the pleasure of the passenger, especially on long, otherwise boring, car trips."

"I'm not sure," said Mr. Harris, the marketing executive. "I cannot see any practical use for such a device. It could actually hinder safe driving by distracting the driver. So, it is not only useless, it could be dangerous, too."

"No," came the reply from Ms. Galoti. "It does have uses. Just like a radio it can pick up important weather alerts and also it can serve to keep the driver awake late at night. In these ways it might even lead to fewer accidents."

"I have to agree with Harris on this one," said the systems consultant, Ruth Kirby. "Television is a lot more visually distracting than radio. With that tube in the dash board the driver would have most of his or her attention focused toward the right. Chances are the driver will check the left side mirror less often, and will probably not turn around to check the left blind spot at all. So, as long as we build the basic American car, putting a television in front of the passenger will be a bad idea."

"That's it!" said Galoti. "We can either redesign the basic car so that no passengers are riding up front with the driver, or, better yet, we can offer television as a back-seat-only option. What do you think?"

2:3.1 Intrinsic vs. Instrumental Values. Many normative statements give reasons why things are desirable or undesirable. Generally speaking, people have classified most things into those which are desirable (undesirable) in and of themselves and those which are desirable (undesirable) as a means to some other end. Those which are desirable or undesirable in and of themselves are said to be *intrinsically* good or bad. For example, people have generally thought of things such as pleasure, honor, wisdom, intelligence, virtue, life, liberty, and harmony as intrinsically desirable. Intrinsically undesirable things might include pain, ignorance, boredom, frustration, terror, infamy, and discord. Things that are viewed as desirable (undesirable) because they are useful as means to further ends are called *instrumentally* good or bad. Money is often considered to be the chief instrumental good (asset), and poverty, therefore, the greatest instrumental evil (liability). The same item can be both an asset and a liability, depending on your goals. Some things, such as health, peace, and wisdom, can be viewed in terms of both their intrinsic and instrumental values.

2:3.2 Let us turn to the case study in 2:2.2 for some examples. Galoti argued for the proposal by appealing to the pleasure the television would bring to the passenger and to its ability to dispel boredom. The justifications at work might be reconstructed as: (1) "Pleasure is intrinsically desirable. The television will increase the pleasure of the passenger. So, we should approve the proposal." (2) "Boredom is intrinsically undesirable. The television will dispel the boredom of the passenger. So, we should approve the proposal." Harris, in the case study, argued that the proposal should be rejected. His argument was that the television was not instrumentally desirable. In reply Galoti pointed to the possibility of using it to hear weather news and of using it to keep the driver awake as two instrumental assets. Harris also argued that the television was an instrumental liability because it could distract the driver from the goal of driving safely. Harris's argument that the television was instrumentally dysfunctional might be reconstructed as follows. "Safe driving is desirable. Anything that distracts the driver hinders the goal of safe driving. The television will distract. So, the proposal should not be approved."

2:4.1 Absolute vs. Relative Values. Driving safely is something most people in our society regard as desirable in an absolute sense. In order to achieve this in America we have adopted a convention of driving on the right side of the road. In other countries, such as Great Britain, the convention is to drive on the left side of the road. In America, then, driving on the right is desirable. It is a relative good; that is, it is good relative to American convention. In Great Britain driving on the right is undesirable.

It is generally thought desirable that dinner guests show courtesy and gratefulness to their host. In Western civilizations this is done by following the convention of sampling all of the foods offered and being sure to eat everything that one takes. In Eastern civilizations this is done by following the convention of taking only a portion of what is served and by always leaving some food uneaten. In the West we show how good the food is by consuming it; in the East we show how bountiful the meal is by leaving some food uneaten. Eating all of one's meal can be viewed as both desirable and undesirable relative to the two contrary conventions. However, the conventions that elicit different behavior both aim at the same absolute value—that is, expressing respect for the other person, in this case one's host.

In the case study Kirby argues that the television idea is poor relative to how cars are constructed right now. This leads Galoti to challenge the designing of cars with a passenger riding next to the driver. This is not, she seems to suggest, an absolute good. Ultimately, however, she decides not to redesign cars but to propose that the television be located in the back seat, where it would not be a visual distraction. Her final recommendation accepts current design practices and avoids what is instrumentally undesirable relative to these practices.

2:4.2 Following the conventions of one's society becomes a relative good. It is desirable to follow conventions not because they are intrinsically desirable in themselves but because they are instrumentally desirable. They are the ways a given society or community has arrived at for achieving its further social or communal ends, which ends it views as absolutely desirable. Some of a society's absolute goals may be common to all or most civilized communities. Avoiding harm, maximizing individual liberty, respecting persons, promoting communal security—these values or goals seem to be very widely shared. There are, however, vast differences in the conventions established by various communities as they try to pursue even these widely shared goals. That the conventions vary is an empirical fact. Whether there are basic human values that transcend all these various conventions is a question we have not tried to settle here. We also have not touched the question of why a society has selected its absolute goals. But it is clear that they have been selected. In our society, for example, safe, efficient, and fast transportation appears as an absolute value along with maximizing individual liberty, preserving a rule of law, respecting other persons, and respecting property rights.

2:4.3   When we call something relatively good or bad, one meaning is that it is good or bad relative to an established social convention for achieving some goal. The concept of *relative* value also has meaning when no conventions are involved. This occurs when instrumental value is being judged. The same means (say, starting on a trip at 11:00 A.M.) may be good relative to one goal (getting all our work done before we leave) yet bad relative to another (reaching our destination before the storm strikes). This *relative* value should not be called "conventional," since no conventions for starting trips are involved. Thus we see that relative value may be either conventional or nonconventional.

2:4.4   Discussion of the relative desirability or undesirability of various practices suggests an interesting problem: *Are ethical principles themselves relative?* This could be taken as a non-normative question: "Are there differences in the moral standards of various communities or societies?" The affirmative answer to this empirical question is called "sociological relativism." In one sense sociological relativism is obviously true. We have cited examples confirming it. In another sense it is as yet unresolved. If it is taken as a question about there being cultural differences in basic underlying human values, what we have called absolute values, then maybe the answer will turn out to be "No."

The question, however, could be taken as a normative rather than empirical question. We might be asking, "Is it desirable that there should be differences in the moral standards of different communities or societies?" Here, too, there is ambiguity. We may want to say "Yes" to ethical relativism if we are only agreeing that within one's society it is better to follow its conventions rather than those of another society. One could argue that social stability and security are the intrinsic goods promoted by conformity to established conventions. However, we may want to reject ethical relativism if it means that there should be differences in the most basic moral principles of human communities.

To accept ethical relativism in its strongest sense is to say that there should be differences in the basic moral standards of different communities—for example, that persons should be respected in some societies but not in others. This view would involve certain difficulties. It would be hard to argue for it, because there would be no moral principles beyond those of a given society to which we could appeal. We would also have some trouble deciding how many members (or what percentage of the members) of a group would have to accept a moral principle for it to become operative for that group. We would have a hard time justifying the desirability of any changes in the society's existing standards. Improvements would seem impossible, for the possibility of an improvement implies a standard outside the community against which those of the community are being judged.

2:4.5 *Ethical nihilists* are people who believe that any claim that something is or is not desirable is a meaningless claim. *Ethical skeptics* are those who think that normative claims make sense but simply cannot be justified. *Ethical relativists* believe that they make sense and that they can be justified, but that the justification does not extend beyond the society in which one lives. A person who maintained that one's duty was always to live by the conventions of one's society would be an ethical relativist in one sense of the term. Someone who believed that from time to time a person should strive to challenge, improve, or reform the moral standards of one's society would not be an ethical relativist in the strongest sense of the term, for a relativist must hold that the established standards are *correct,* in which case there is no reason why they should be changed.

Exercises for Module 2: Analysis of Normative Statements

1. What is conceptual analysis? From what you have learned so far, state how it functions in ethics and social philosophy. (2:1.1, 2:1.4)

2. Provide subjective reasons that might be offered in support of each of the following normative claims. (2:2.1)

   a. Cigarette smoking in public places should be prohibited by law.
   b. It is wrong for public officials to take bribes.
   c. Keep off the grass.
   d. Prostitution should be legalized.
   e. Premarital sex is bad.

f. Avenge injuries done to you.

g. Never harm another—even in self-defense.

3. Provide objectivist reasons that might be offered in support of each of the normative claims in Exercise 2. (2:2.1)

4. What is the difference between subjectivist and objectivist interpretations of normative claims? (2:2.1)

5. Recall the listing in 2:3.1 of things that many have thought of as being intrinsically valuable: pleasure, honor, wisdom, intelligence, virtue, life, liberty, and harmony. Provide normative statements that give expression to the intrinsic value (or lack of it) of each of these things. (2:3.1)

6. Working with the list of things thought to be intrinsically valuable in Exercise 5, provide normative statements that express the instrumental value (or lack of it) of other things that may be thought of as means to those desirable ends. (2:3.1)

7. What is the difference between something intrinsically desirable and something instrumentally desirable? (2:3.1)

8. Suppose that justice, respect for persons, health, and safety are held to be of absolute value. Provide for each of these two conventions that might be adopted in different societies that may be understood as promoting these values in differing ways. (2:4.1, 2:4.2)

9. Here are five arguments. Classify the normative principle operative in each as an appeal to absolute or relative normative concerns. (2:4.1, 2:4.2)

    a. Reverse discrimination procedures should be enacted into law because with proper safeguards they promote justice.

    b. Polygamy should be considered seriously in circumstances where through warfare the male population has been severely reduced.

    c. International corporations should respect the sovereignty of the states in which they do business lest international harmony be undermined.

    d. Involuntary euthanasia should never be condoned, for it can never take appropriate account of the wishes of the person who is to die.

    e. I exposed the corpse of my dead husband to the elements because that was the custom of the tribe with whom we were living.

10. What is the difference between something that is absolutely desirable and something that is relatively desirable in a given society? Give three examples of each. (2:4.1, 2:4.2)

11. Define ethical relativism and distinguish it from ethical nihilism and ethical skepticism. (2:4.4, 2:4.5)

Selected Answers to Exercises for Module 2

2. Here are some examples of correct answers.
   a. I don't like to have to put up with the foul odor.
   b. I don't like trampled lawns.
   f. I approve of manly responses.
3. Here are some examples of correct answers.
   a. Such smoking poses a serious threat to public health.
   e. Such activity may well lead to serious guilt feelings following marriage.
   g. A world where this was accepted would be more peaceful.
5. Here are some examples of such statements.
   a. Only pleasure is a good in itself.
   d. Wisdom is its own satisfaction.
   e. Intelligence in and of itself is worth little. It has value only as a means to the good life.
6. Here are some examples of such statements.
   b. Suicide is wrong because it is dishonorable.
   e. Discipline is valuable in promoting the development of virtues.
   g. Sex-role socialization is morally objectionable to the extent that it inhibits the free development of human potential.
8. Here are some examples of such conventions.
   a. Justice: (1) Presume that the accused is innocent until proven guilty. (2) Presume that the accused is guilty unless proven innocent.
   c. Health: (1) Provide emergency care first for those in greatest danger of death. (2) Provide emergency care first for those whom one has the best chance to aid.
   d. Safety: (1) To prevent accidents with pedestrians require that bicyclists ride in the street. (2) To prevent accidents with cars require that bicyclists ride on the sidewalks.
9. In argument b the value of polygamy changes with the circumstances of the need to insure the future of the species. In e the exposing of the corpse is valued because it was the custom of the tribe with which the widow lived.
10. Here are some examples: (1) In Eskimo society exposing the elderly to the cold so that they might die was thought to be the best means of promoting the survival of the most members of the community. (2) In our society we value absolutely the health of mothers of newborn children. When medical knowledge was less developed than today, this absolute value was promoted by the custom of confining new mothers to bed for extended periods of time.

Module 3
ASSESSING NORMATIVE ARGUMENTS

People can supply several types of reasons on behalf of their normative claims. In Module 3 we will consider why it is important to strive for reasoned support of normative claims. We will distinguish justification from pseudo-justification. We will then focus upon genuine attempts at justification and outline several ways in which such justifications in ethics and social philosophy are susceptible to rational criticism. After reading this module, you should be able to

- Compare and contrast offering a justification for a normative claim and doing any of the following: stating one's motivations, appealing to someone's emotions as a means to elicit certain behavior, rationalizing one's position, and offering excuses.
- Give examples of each of the above.
- Distinguish ways in which attempted justification for a normative claim can fail, including use of false, irrelevant, or inconclusive factual support and citation of normative principles that are not universalizable.
- Give examples of each of the above.

3:1.1 Seeking Reasons. An important step toward understanding what people mean by their normative claims is to ask for reasons why we should accept their normative views. Vantage challenged Mogle in precisely this way in the case study at the beginning of Module 2. She tried to make Mogle reveal his reasons for preferring the pending sugar legislation. Besides offering us further insights into what people mean, hearing their arguments and reasons often helps us take some position on their normative claims ourselves. For example, one of Mogle's reasons for favoring the legislation was that it "was good for Boyce Sugar." We may not share the desire to help out Boyce Enterprises; we may even be tempted to view that reason as grounds to reject the legislation. However, until we hear a person's reasons, it is very hard to stake out our own rational response to his or her normative statements. Neither uninformed assent, blind trust, nor conservative obstructionism is an adequate substitute for seeking the proper interpretation of the normative claims and a listing of the reasons offered in support of those claims.

3:1.2 The goal of presenting reasons for normative claims is to develop arguments that support their truth or establish their wisdom. We should strive for reasons that would persuade unbiased, informed, rational people that our normative positions are, beyond any reasonable doubt, correct. We shall call such reasons *justifications.* In the case study Vantage suggests some possible arguments in support of the view that the legislation is desirable for the country. Her arguments can be reconstructed as follows:

A. (1) Whatever improves the balance of trade is good for the country.
(2) The pending legislation would improve the balance of trade.

---

(3) So, it is good for the country.

B. (1) Whatever lowers domestic prices is good for the country.
   (2) The legislation would lead to lower domestic sugar prices, and, in turn, to generally lower domestic prices.

   _____

   (3) So, it is good for the country.

C. (1) Whatever is good for Boyce Enterprises is good for the country.
   (2) The legislation, according to Mogle, is good for Boyce.

   _____

   (3) So, it is good for the country.

As you study ethics and social philosophy, you will encounter a wide variety of arguments. Not all of them will be structured like the three examples above. Actually there is considerable variation in the structure of arguments people offer as proofs in support of their normative claims. However, it is reasonable to ask (a) whether that which is offered in support of a normative claim is in fact a justification or merely a pseudo-justification and (b) whether a purported justification meets the minimum adequacy requirements applicable in ethics and social philosophy.

3:2.1 Justification and Pseudo-Justification. There are a number of things that people confuse with giving reasons in ethics and social philosophy. You should note them, so that you can avoid confusion as you attempt to support your own views and to understand and evaluate the support that others offer for their views. You should beware, moreover, that the temptation to confusion derives in part from the common desires to defend one's pet prejudices and to avoid taking full responsibility for one's actions.

3:2.2 *Justification* is not the same as giving one's *motivations.* People are motivated to act by such things as ambition, anger, desperation, fear, friendship, grief, hope, jealousy, and love. It is possible to answer the question, "Why did you do X?" by citing one's motivations. For example, one might say, "I did it because I loved them," or, "I did it because I was afraid." Such a listing of one's motivations for acting is not to be confused, however, with giving reasons that justify normative claims. To give such reasons is to answer the question, "Why did you do X?" by citing the normative considerations that support the belief that the action is correct. The contrast is that between providing an account of facts about oneself that led one to act and presenting the justification itself. A governor may be motivated out of political self-interest to sign an important bill. Be that as it may, the governor cannot justify signing the bill by appeal to his or her personal motivation. The justification has to be in terms of reasons why the bill should be signed. It should be noted here that appealing to one's good intentions is not obviously equivalent to establishing that one's action is normatively correct.

3:2.3 *Appeals to emotion* aimed at directly bringing about action do not constitute justification. To justify a normative claim is to argue that it should be accepted. To prove a statement true is to argue that it should be believed. However, believing a statement or accepting a normative claim is not always the same as engaging in some immediate activity. We can accept the view that military intervention is warranted without running out to join the Army. An emotional appeal aimed at getting someone to act a certain way is not a justification of the normative claim that the person should act that way. It usually bypasses justification altogether. Patriotic music, speeches appealing to our national pride, vivid pictures illustrating the enemy threat to the safety of our homes and families—these are the tools used to play on our feelings and to get us to join up.

Some philosophers would argue that there is a sense in which a justification can also be an appeal to one's feelings. One might regard one's sense of fair play or one's conscience as at least akin to the sentiments or emotions referred to above. So, an appeal to our sense of justice, say, might be made as a way of justifying a normative claim. We shall distinguish this sort of appeal from regular appeals to emotion. A regular appeal to emotion aims directly at bringing about an action by appealing to an attitude or arousing a feeling, whereas, whatever emotion is involved in an ethical argument, a justification aims at showing that a normative assertion is true by appealing to a universalizable principle. (Universalizability is discussed in 3:5.1.)

3:2.4 *Rationalization* is not justification. To rationalize is to choose first and look for reasons later. In rationalizing one accepts or rejects reasons because they respectively do or do not support one's predetermined choice. A clear example would be former President Nixon's Watergate cover-up. Motivated by what looks like personal political ambition, he moved to cover up the Watergate break-in. Later, when the news came out, he realized he needed a justification. He and his aides met in order to cook up a likely-sounding story, which they hoped they could present as the justification. They invented the "national security" story. They rationalized what they had done. Notice that Nixon not only *chose* first, he also acted, and only afterwards did he and his aides try to find a normative principle that they could portray as their justification. Acting before seeking reasons, however, is not essential to rationalizing; one is rationalizing when one *chooses* first, whether one acts before or after seeking reasons.

3:2.5 *Excuses* are not justifications. When we do something wrong but we wish not to be held responsible, we offer an excuse. For example, we failed to make the car payment because we forgot what day it was, or we missed the important meeting because we were sick. A successful excuse gets us off the hook, it provides a reason why we should not *be held accountable,* blamed, or punished. It does not, however, change the ethical quality of what we did. It does not justify failing to make the car payment or missing the meeting. Nixon might have offered excuses for his cover-up. He could have said, "I realize it was wrong but I was under severe pressure and I did not, at that time, regard the Watergate affair as a very significant event." Perhaps no one would have accepted the excuses, but perhaps some would have. Accepting an excuse is far different from accepting a justification. To accept Nixon's rationalization as a justification is to say he did right. To accept an excuse would be to say he did wrong but should not be held fully responsible for the error.

3:3.1 Rational Criticism of Normative Arguments. Having clarified the differences between several varieties of pseudo-justification and genuine attempts at justification, let us now turn to consider how the latter may be susceptible to rational criticism. The arguments offered in defense of normative claims may be more or less adequate to the task. For example, normative arguments can be fallacious or nonfallacious. Perusal of any standard textbook on logic should acquaint you with the wide variety of fallacies to which normative arguments are subject. Thus, contradicting those who hold that in ethics and social philosophy any opinion is as solid as any other, we shall now indicate how normative arguments can fail to meet minimal requirements of rationality. We shall devote our attention here to the need to properly marshal factual support where it is appropriate and to argue from universalizable moral principles.

3:4.1 The Need for Factual Support. Providing adequate factual support is often crucial in ethics and social philosophy. Simply not providing such support where it is appropriate is itself a failure to meet a minimal requirement in reasoning about normative concerns. Let us briefly, though not exhaustively, note some of the circumstances where such support is pertinent.

(a) Normative reasoning commonly involves the evaluation of agents, actions, or practices in terms of normative principles. A fundamental prerequisite for the success of such evaluation is, then, the establishment of the fact that the agents, actions, or practices are of the types covered by the principles. Thus, for example, to argue that a particular person should not be appointed to a particular position because in general liars should not be so appointed requires that one establish that the person in question is indeed a liar. Or to argue that a particular act of disconnecting a human being from a life-support system is wrong because it is an act of willful homicide requires, in part, that one establish that the human being was not in fact dead prior to being removed from the machine.

(b) In seeking to justify actions or policies appeal is frequently made to their purported consequences. Data supporting the predictions of consequences would then be vitally important. Thus, if one were to argue that lying to a particular person would prevent his or her suffering unnecessarily, one would have to provide information about his or her personality to show that he or she was susceptible to being hurt by the truth in question. Or if one were to attempt to justify rehabilitation rather than punishment as a response to criminal behavior because it reduces the rate of recidivism, one would have to supply information concerning the rates of return to crime of those who had been treated in the different manners in question.

(c) Many questions in ethics and social philosophy concern the distribution of benefits and burdens; that is, they are matters of distributive justice. Facts about actual past or present distributions as well as accurate predictions of future distributions often are crucial in assessing the fairness of the distributions in question. For example, establishing the injustice of American slavery depends, in part, upon an accounting of the disproportionate distribution of benefits and burdens in slave states. In deciding how benefits and burdens ought to be distributed, it is generally agreed that they ought to be dispersed in proportion to the deserts of the persons involved. There is much disagreement over what makes a person deserving—whether it is, for example, his ability, actual contribution, effort, or need. In any case, facts pertaining to actual ability, contribution, effort, or need would have to be provided in order to justify distribution proportionate to any of them.

(d) In assessing responsibility and supporting claims that persons are deserving of praise or reward, blame or punishment, factual considerations are central in at least two ways. First, facts about the agent are important. Was the agent in fact free to do otherwise, or was he or she coerced or otherwise not at liberty? Was the agent of sound mind and in command of his or her faculties so that it is even appropriate to consider him or her a responsible agent? Second, facts about what actually was done are crucial. Who in fact did the deed in question? What exactly was done?

3:4.2 Thus far we have shown how one can fall short of the minimal requirement in reasoning about normative concerns by not providing factual support where it is appropriate. One can also perceive the need for factual support for normative claims and yet fail in defending one's view by presenting *inadequate factual support*—factual claims that are either false, irrelevant, or inconclusive.

No support is provided for a normative statement by descriptive statements that are simply false. Thus, in the example of rehabilitation vs. punishment, if it turned out to be simply false that recidivism is reduced by rehabilitation procedures, then making that false claim would lend no support to the argument that rehabilitation is preferable. Similarly, for all of the above-cited varieties of cases where citation of factual support is crucial, if the factual claims at the base of the arguments for such normative statements are false, the conclusions are left in need of support. This is not to say that other factual support could not be provided, only that it has not been provided.

One could offer exclusively true factual statements in defense of a normative claim and yet fail to support the claim adequately if one were to offer information that is irrelevant to the point at issue. Subsection 3:4.1 illustrates several important contexts and ways in which citation of fact is relevant in supporting normative claims. Facts cited that did not serve to establish or disestablish what was at issue there would be irrelevant.

There is one common species of irrelevant appeal against which you should be on guard. It is the citation of facts about the sources of the views that are being defended. However true it may be that a belief has the endorsement of parents, scripture, political authority, custom, and public opinion or is an outgrowth of strong feeling or emotion, citation of such facts about the origins of views is not equivalent to citation of reasons in support of their truth. Disclosing how one came to be a defender of a view is not relevant to the task of displaying a sound justification. For example, while parents may well be the typical source for a belief that lying is wrong, it is implausible to suppose that lying is wrong *because* parents say it is. Or, while it may well be that strong feeling contributes to the growth of antiracist belief, it is no clearer that antiracism is correct *because* of the strong feeling out of which it grows than it is clear that its opposite, racism, is correct *because* of the strong feeling out of which it grows.

There is one more way in which citation of factual support for a normative claim can be inadequate. It is possible to cite both true and relevant information that is nevertheless not conclusive in deciding the issue at hand, though it is taken to be so. Thus, for example, in the debate over euthanasia it might be suggested that physicians would suffer greatly if they regularly had to inform patients of the availability of euthanasia procedures. While this may well be true, and while it is fairly clear that suffering on the part of one of the parties involved is a relevant consideration, it would be a mistake to take this factual information alone as decisive in the matter. Surely there are other matters to be put in the balance, including the value of each human life and the prospects of suffering for the one for whom euthanasia might be an option.

3:5.1 Universalizability. One additional requirement exists for reasoning used in ethics and social philosophy: the *universalizability* requirement. This is a demand for consistency in the reasons people give in order to justify their normative claims. It can be stated as follows: (UR) If R counts as a reason in favor of person A's doing X in situation S, then R also counts as a reason for a similar person to perform a similar act in similar circumstances. For example, suppose Mrs. Jones breaks the speed laws in order to drive her injured child to the hospital. Suppose, further, that she gives as her reason that she was obligated by parental duty and her own love to see to it that her injured child received swift attention. Her reason would satisfy the universalizability requirement (UR) only if it counted as a reason for something like this: Mr. Smith fails to come to a complete stop at stop signs in order to rush his injured child to the doctor's office.

The UR requires that reasons be generalizable in three ways: they must apply to *similar agents* performing *similar acts* in *similar circumstances*. Mrs. Jones's reason applies to Mr. Smith because all three of the similarities are present. However, her reason does not apply to any of these:

(1) A nine-year-old child's driving the family car to take an injured brother or sister to the hospital.

(2) Mrs. Jones's leaving her other preschool children in dangerous circumstances in order to drive her injured child to the hospital.

(3) Mrs. Jones's breaking the speed laws in order to drive her well child to the doctor for a routine examination.

In (1) the *agent* is changed from an adult who presumably knows how to drive and is licensed to a child who does not know how to operate a car. In (2) the *act* was changed from the violation of traffic laws to a case of dangerous parental neglect. In (3) the *circumstances* were changed: the child was not in need of swift emergency treatment.

Exercises for Module 3: Assessing Normative Arguments

1. Explain the difference between giving a justification and each of the following. (3:2.5, 3:2.4, 3:2.3, 3:2.2)

   a. Offering an excuse.
   b. Rationalizing one's activities.
   c. Appealing to emotions in order to influence behavior.
   d. Stating one's motivations.

2. Suppose Mrs. Karloski drove from Madison, Wisconsin, to Milwaukee, regularly exceeding the speed limit by 10 miles per hour. Give two examples of each of the following:

      a. Offering an excuse for her speeding.
      b. Rationalizing her speeding.
      c. Stating her motivations for speeding.

3. Suppose Mrs. Borbonne wanted to persuade her husband to punish their son for lying to her. Give two examples of each of the following:

      a. Appealing to her husband's emotions to get him to punish their son.
      b. Appealing to universalized principles.

4. The citizens of your home town are debating whether to double the size of their recreational lands. Describe how justification might fail because of each of the following:

      a. No factual support is marshaled.
      b. False statements are offered.
      c. Irrelevant truths are presented.
      d. Inconclusive truths are presented.

Selected Answers to Exercises for Module 3

2. Possible answers might be:
      a. "I thought the speed limit was 65, not 55."
      b. "More cars passed me than I passed."
      "I got there safely, so there couldn't have been anything too wrong in my speed."
      c. "I get very bored on long drives."
      "I was excited about getting home for the reunion."
3.   *a*. "Aren't you ashamed to have a liar for a son?"
      "You don't want your son embarrassing his mother, do you?"
      b. "Lying should never go unpunished."
      "A child ought to follow the norms his parents propose for him."
4.   *a*. If the debate disintegrated to repeated insistence that the recreational area should or should not be acquired, factual support would be missing.
      c. Most facts about your town's climate and the education and religion of its citizens, for example, would be irrelevant to the question at issue, although they all might be relevant to the kind of recreational land appropriate for the town.
      d. Any of the following *by itself* would be inconclusive, but each might have some relevance: population size, population growth, present park locations, who now uses parks, who would use expanded areas, costs of area development and maintenance, and who would pay the costs.

PART II

BASIC NORMATIVE CONCEPTS

SELF-INTEREST

Can people ever act out of motives other than those of self-interest? If they cannot, what can be the point of normative theories that recommend that they do? Even if people can be otherwise motivated, should they act on those motives, or would that be foolish? If being moral entails that at some times people must act in ways other than in pursuit of their self-interest, then what reasons can there be for being moral? This cluster on egoism addresses these question. They are questions of fact, of normative theory, and of the viability of normative theorizing itself. Addressing these questions are two theories: *psychological egoism,* an empirical theory about what in fact *does* motivate human action, and *ethical egoism,* a normative theory about what *should* motivate human conduct. We will discuss these answers by means of conceptual analysis of "acting self-interestedly." We will carefully separate the factual, conceptual, and normative issues involved. We will explore the variety of motives out of which persons may act. Module 4 explains what may or may not be involved in the pursuit of self-interest; it then contrasts that pursuit with others. Module 5 draws the distinction between psychological and ethical egoism as these theories relate to the pursuit of self-interest, and it carefully examines the argument in support of psychological egoism. Module 6 examines the relationship between psychological and ethical egoism, and it addresses the central question of ethical egoism: "Should people act exclusively out of self-interest?" The educational goal of the cluster is for you to understand the views of psychological and ethical egoists on motivation and conduct.

Module 4
EGOISM AND SELF-INTEREST

Egoistic theories focus upon the pursuit of self-interest in human conduct. In this module we shall clarify the concept of "acting self-interestedly" by considering (a) the contrast between unenlightened and enlightened self-interested conduct, (b) the varieties of things it might be in one's interest to pursue, (c) the compatibility of cooperation with others and pursuit of one's own interest, and (d) the relation of "acting self-interestedly," "acting in one's own interest," and "doing as one pleases." After reading Module 4, you should be able to

- Characterize unenlightened and enlightened pursuit of self-interest.
- Contrast self-interested and non-self-interested reasons for cooperation.
- Distinguish between the subject and the object of interest.
- Explain the importance of the subject-object distinction for the analysis of "acting self-interestedly."

THE CASE OF THE DEFERENTIAL HOUSEWIFE

"Look, Olga," said Ginger, "here comes Maria. Does she ever look glum today! I wonder what her trouble is."

"Drink your coffee, Ginger. Let's mind our own business. Her problems are her own. Okay?"

"Sure, but I bet she's the one who brings up her troubles. You watch . . . Oh, good morning, Maria. Sit down for a coffee break. What's new?"

"G'morning Ginger, Olga. Nothing's new. Just the same old story. No matter what I do for Manuel and the kids, it's never enough. Clean this, fix that, settle this fight, fix that meal—over and over till my back hurts. And then what do they do? I'll tell ya'! Nothin! Not a 'thank you'; not even a grunt of appreciation. Nothin' at all."

"Look, Maria," said Ginger, "there's more to it than that. Think! What are *you* getting out of all of that effort? Please yourself sometimes, make the situation work for you!"

"Oh, Ginger, I couldn't. It sounds so selfish, so shortsighted! You know. I can't just neglect them. They need me; and, well, I need them. I care for them. I'm not an island—I can't live without them and without doing the things they need."

"No, Maria, you missed my point. I didn't say that you should drop everything and live like you're the only woman alive today."

"Well, what did you mean then?"

"I meant that everyone who is married got married because of what it offers. Face it, dear, you didn't marry Manuel out of love. You love him not for himself but for what he represents to you. He provides security, affection, and attention. Sorry, I hate to disillusion you, honey, but we all act that way. What I'm saying is face that fact. Deal with it. Use it to your advantage."

"How, 'honey'?" hissed Maria.

"Come now, Maria, I'm not trying to be patronizing, just realistic. I'm taking this terrific 'Complete Womanhood' course at the Y. It's taught me a lot about how I can get my family to do things for me. There are lots of little tricks I've learned. I use some on John to keep him, shall we say, 'interested' in me—and he never even suspects. I've got a little surprise outfit to wear tonight when he gets home from the office. I'll bet it earns me a night of fun and maybe even that vacation to Sun Valley I've been working on. Why don't you come to class with me tomorrow? You can pick up a few practical hints to use on ol' Manuel. There's enough in that course to last a smart girl a lifetime!"

"No thanks, Ginger, I don't have trouble keeping Manuel 'interested.' Besides, it doesn't seem, well, 'right' for me and Manuel."

"What does that mean, Maria?"

"I think she means that she feels she would be lying to Manuel, tricking him, toying with him. You know, not being honest and sincere," broke in Olga. "And, too, what about your own self-respect?"

"That's it, Olga. It seems devious and selfish."

"Look, Ginger," said Olga, "these little tricks of yours, they can hurt a marriage. . . . Well, I don't know, but with Bill and me, well, we have something special. At least I think so, anyway. I would feel that I had lost my self-respect if I had to lie to Bill or trick him just to gratify myself. Don't you think it's possible? I mean, don't you think one person can care for another for the sake of that other person rather than simply as a tool to be used to satisfy his or her own desires? I do."

"I do too, Olga. And more than that, Ginger, I feel it's part of my duty as a wife and mother, as a woman, to care for others and put aside my desires."

"Really now, I cannot believe you, Maria," said Ginger. "Don't you see, you're unhappy because you always try to put others first. People always do what they want to do. People, at least as I see them, always serve old 'number one' first. Maria, did you ever ask Manuel why he married you? Who do you think he was trying to please? You can bet it wasn't you, sweetie. Look, you will just never be happy until you own up to the fact that you, yes you, have always been pursuing your own interests—you are no different from any of the rest of us. I believe that nobody can want others to be happy at their own expense. You can't and you shouldn't try to. It's self-defeating. Besides, who deserves to have their desires met more than you? Put yourself first, Maria, or you'll suffer right to the end."

"Oh, Ginger, I am sometimes very confused by you," said Olga. "Do you want Maria to improve her own life or do you just want her to do what she wants to do? I cannot tell which it is."

"I'm confused too, Ginger. And I do care for my family no matter what you think."

"Don't let me upset you, Maria; I was only trying to explain your problem. . . ."

Olga interrupted, "Yes we know, but Maria does not have to swing all the way over from total self-sacrifice to using other people only to serve her personal interests. Why can't she stop in the middle—be an equal with her children and with Manuel? Look, Ginger, Maria says she does care for her husband and family. She should not lose her own self-respect in an effort to please them. But neither should she neglect them to please herself."

"Well, Olga, Ginger, while you two analyze my troubles and prescribe a cure, I've got to be going. The kids are due home from school in a few minutes."

"Ginger, I've got to run too; I have a client to meet in twenty minutes."

"Well, have fun you two, I'm off to the store to use some of John's wonderful money on wine for him—and for me! You know what I mean?"

4:1.1 Unenlightened and Enlightened Self-Interest. The case study focuses on whether Maria is or ought to be *selfish*. Selfishness, however, has many distinct meanings. Throughout this module our discussion of self-interest is meant to clarify these distinct meanings. The first distinction arises between what has come to be called unenlightened and enlightened self-interest. This difference has traditionally been characterized in terms of shortsighted and farsighted planning for one's own benefit. An unenlightened view of self-interest would define it in terms of acting on the basis of present feelings and impulses with no thought of long-term consequences or feelings. The enlightened pursuit of self-interest would, in contrast, be more subtle, more restrained, and more refined as well as farsighted. For example, even if another martini were appealing, an enlightened egoist would consider the extra danger in traveling home and the increased hangover on the morning afterward. Similarly, an enlightened egoist would recognize that blatantly self-interested behavior, especially behavior that obviously harms or endangers others, will likely bring more grief than reward in the long run. The enlightened egoist recognizes that it cannot be in one's self-interest to live in such a way as to miss out on possible future happiness that could be one's own with a little restraint.

In the case study, Maria expresses initial skepticism about Ginger's recommendation that she think of her own interests more. Part of her skepticism arises out of her belief that pursuit of self-interest requires one to be obvious and possibly even obnoxious. This strikes her as short-sighted, and she worries about the possible long-range consequences of losing her family and the advantages it offers her. Ginger, enlightened as she is, immediately reassures Maria that pursuit of self-interest can be farsighted and subtle. She hopes the course on "Complete Womanhood" can enable her to "win the game" of marriage for a lifetime.

EPICURUS (341–270 B.C.)

One of the earliest advocates of enlightened self-interest was Epicurus. By the age of thirty-four he had developed enough originality, intellectual maturity, and reputation to establish his own community in Athens called the Garden. There he and his followers devoted themselves to cultivating friendship and pleasure. They were one of the first societies to admit women and slaves as members.

Epicurus taught that human beings come to exist simply as parts of nature. They have no divine creator nor any particular fate. Like other natural things, humans seek their own self-interest. Epicurus saw this as both natural and desirable. He identified self-interest with pleasure. He then offered guidance to those who wished to undertake the pursuit of pleasure in an enlightened way.

He recommended that people come to understand their natural condition and in so doing conquer their fears of death and mythological deities. He taught that true pleasure is achieved in peace of mind. Other things, such as wealth, political power, or fame, really cannot guarantee pleasure. The ideal is "the good life," in which one's physical and psychological needs are met.

4:1.2 Notice that the contrast between unenlightened and enlightened pursuit of self-interest need not be characterized solely in terms of a shortsighted vs. farsighted contrast. One can also be relatively enlightened about the varieties of things it can be in one's interest to pursue. Thus, in the case study Ginger stresses creature comfort and material goods, as for example the vacation to Sun Valley, as worthy of pursuit. Olga mentions additional goods that it might be in one's self-interest to pursue, such as self-respect, integrity, and satisfying, close relationships with another person. Such goods are not simply materialistic, and one does not have to be as competitively oriented as one pursues them.

4:2.1 Cooperation and Self-Interest. It might be thought that cooperation with others and pursuit of self-interest are mutually exclusive. This view assumes that what is in the interest of one person is necessarily not in another person's interest—in fact is probably contrary to it. This view would mean that people should, if they would pursue their self-interest, live isolated, lonely, competitive, and likely combative lives. A view more in line with the reality of human interaction, however, recognizes that the avoidance of the tensions and insecurities that would result from such isolated living is itself in the self-interest of each individual. Moreover, there are abundant examples of situations where individuals engaged in helping others benefit in the long run. There are also cases where individuals involved in cooperative endeavors stand to gain personally from the effort in ways that would be impossible without the cooperation.

A crude example of self-interested helping of another would be a person's bringing hot meals to a rich but bedridden widow with the end in view of being written into her will. Other human practices are analogous to this, although the variations are usually more subtle. Business partnerships can be conceived as grounded in the pursuit of self-interest by each of the partners. They pool their resources and use the common means of their investment for achieving the distinct ends of the personal profit and well-being of each. In social philosophy it is possible to conceive of the establishment of government as rooted in each citizen's recognizing the long-term benefits of mutual security and the protection of property that can be afforded by community strength. Each cooperates to insure the functioning of the state, not directly for the sake of the harmony the cooperation brings, but rather for the sake of the more effective pursuit of self-interest that the harmony promotes. (For a more detailed statement of the "Social Contract," see Module 21.)

In the case study, Ginger maintains that people get married only to more effectively pursue their self-interest. In her view the cooperation that marriage entails is worth the trouble in the long run. Manuel and the children are obviously reaping the rewards of Maria's undying devotion and attention to their needs. Ginger is simply suggesting to Maria that she must realize this and that she should see to it that she gets her share of the rewards marriage has to offer. Indeed, in Ginger's view it is quite appropriate for Maria to continue to serve the interests of her family, although those interests are not to be taken as intrinsically valuable. Ginger is convinced that playing an apparently self-sacrificing role only makes sense if in doing so one can effectively pursue one's own interest.

4:3.1 Self-Interest and Doing What One Wants.   There is a difference between the *subject* of interests and wants, or *who* has the interests or wants, and the *object* of the interests or wants, or *what* is desired by the person in question. Thus, to say "People do what they want to do" can be true in a trivial way if it only means "All *subjects* act upon the interests and desires they have." That is one sense of the expression "acting in one's own interest." That sense is not the same as saying that the principal *object* of those interests is the well-being of the person who has the interests. The idea that *I* want to give you a million dollars is clearly distinct from the idea that it is to my own advantage for me to give it to you. Thus, "acting in one's own interest" can mean "acting in the interest of furthering one's own well-being." This is the truly self-interested sense of the expression. What makes an interest or want one of *self*-interest is not that the self has the interest but rather that benefit for the self is the principal goal of the action.

People who pursue their own interest, or do what they want, in the self-interested sense noted above, act neither out of a sense of duty nor out of a sense of the value of serving the interests of others for the others' sake. Rather, they act with the ultimate objective of improving their own lot in life. Thus, to say that people are acting self-interestedly is not simply to say that they are acting on interests or wants that they have. Rather, it is to say that from among the logically possible objects of interest or want, the people assign first priority to their own welfare.

4:3.2 This analysis enables us to distinguish conceptual and empirical matters. We have argued that "doing what one wants" and "acting self-interestedly" are conceptually distinct. Thus, it is an empirical question whether people ever want or are motivated by anything other than goals that are discernibly self-interested.

The points of this analysis are illustrated in the case study. Ginger responds to Maria's and Olga's skepticism about the "Complete Womanhood" course with an argument that confuses acting out of wants that are one's own and always wanting one's own benefit. She says that people always do what they want to do, and she speculates about Manuel's reasons for marrying Maria. Ginger suggests that Maria should acknowledge that she has really been concerned primarily with her own welfare all along, though she has been careless in pursuing it. Olga then observes that Ginger is guilty of the very confusion that our conceptual analysis discloses. In speaking of "Maria's genuine interest in the welfare of her family," Olga seems both to be recognizing that Maria is the subject of such an interest—she has these wants—and yet suggesting that the "genuineness" of her interest consists in her having the welfare of her family for its own sake as the object of her interest.

Exercises for Module 4: Egoism and Self-Interest

1. How should the pursuit of self-interest be described? What does it involve, and what does it exclude? Moreover, how is the enlightened pursuit of self-interest distinguished from its unenlightened pursuit? Below is a list of characteristics. If any characteristic is essential to both pursuits, mark it *B;* if it fits only the pursuit of enlightened self-interest, mark it *E;* if it fits only the pursuit of unenlightened self-interest, mark it *U;* if it fits neither, mark it *N*. (4:1.1, 4:1.2)

    _____ *a*. Always being aware of my own wants.
    _____ *b*. Always trying to determine the likely consequences for myself of any possible action.
    _____ *c*. Always doing whatever the majority wants.
    _____ *d*. Always doing whatever I want at a given moment.
    _____ *e*. Always obeying the dictates of legitimate authorities.
    _____ *f*. Always disobeying the dictates of legitimate authorities.
    _____ *g*. Always acting so as to please others.
    _____ *h*. Never frustrating others by my actions if the likely consequence of such frustration is that I shall, over the course of time, be less able to gain my desires.
    _____ *i*. Always trying to develop my capacities to the greatest possible extent.
    _____ *j*. Gaining the greatest possible pleasure for myself.
    _____ *k*. Cooperating with others only when such cooperation satisfies my interests more than any other line of action seems to satisfy them.

2. Below is a set of reasons for acting cooperatively. Some are self-interested reasons, some are non-self-interested. Mark the self-interested reasons *S* and the non-self-interested reasons *N*. (4:2.1, 4:3.1)

_____ *a* . If I cooperate with her, we will accomplish what I want.

_____ *b* . If I cooperate with her, she will succeed in her desires.

_____ *c* . If I cooperate with her, many people will get what they want.

_____ *d* . If I cooperate with her, she will give me what I want.

_____ *e* . If I cooperate with her, the greatest percentage of people will be satisfied.

_____ *f* . If I cooperate with her, she will be very receptive to my future requests.

_____ *g* . If I am to avoid being frustrated, I must cooperate with her.

_____ *h* . If I cooperate with her, I will be keeping my promise to help her.

_____ *i* . If I cooperate with her, others will benefit me because of the favor with which they view my cooperation.

3. Below is a series of statements. Some state who has a given interest, want, or desire; mark those *S*. Others state whose interest would (or would not) be served by a course of action; mark those *O*. (4:3.1)

_____ *a* . Only Marcia wanted to go to the circus.

_____ *b* . Marcia would be very unhappy seeing a circus of such poor quality.

_____ *c* . Everybody likes ice cream.

_____ *d* . Ice cream contains too much cholesterol to be healthy for many persons.

_____ *e* . Jones wants to cooperate.

_____ *f* . Maria wants to please Manuel.

_____ *g* . Manuel is pleased by Maria's actions.

_____ *h* . Pacifists want peace, regardless of the cost.

_____ *i* . Everybody would be better off if there were peace at any price.

4. Now check your responses for Exercises 2 and 3 against the answers. If you have made any errors, be sure you understand the correct answers before proceeding. When you understand, test your understanding by stating the characteristics of self-interested reasons that distinguish them from reasons not based on self-interest.

5. Review the work you have done in Exercises 1–4. Together they should clarify for you what it means to say that a person acts in his own enlightened self-interest. To test your understanding further, you should now draw upon your work in the preceding three exercises to provide a definition of each of the components of this concept, and to incorporate these into a definition of the concept of a person's acting in his own enlightened self-interest. Your definition

should clarify (a) the concept of the *object* of interest (Exercise 3), (b) how cooperation is possible, provided that it is self-interested (Exercise 2), and (c) what makes the pursuit of self-interest enlightened, rather than unenlightened (Exercise 1).

Answers to Exercises for Module 4

1. *a. B.*   *b. E.*   *c. N.*   *d. U.*

   e. N: According to the egoist my actions are concerned only with my self-interest. So whether an action has been dictated by an authority matters only if *my interest* is enhanced or frustrated by its being dictated.

   f. N: The pursuit of one's self-interest may on occasion involve disobeying authorities, and the pursuit of one's self-interest may involve obeying. But neither obeying nor disobeying is conceptually related to pursuing self-interest.

   g. N.

   h. E: Notice that as long as the ultimate concern of action is with the consequences for one's self, the action is self-interested.

   i. N: The analysis of pursuing one's self-interest involves no statement about whether it is, or is not, essentially in one's self-interest to develop one's capacities.

   j. N: Same reason as *i*. The analysis of acting in one's own self-interest does not involve essentially any statement about pleasure.

   k. B: As in *h,* the ultimate concern here is with one's own benefit.

2. *a. S.*   *b. N.*   *c. N.*   *d. S.*   *e. N.*   *f. S.*   *g. S.*   *h. N.*

   i. S : Compare this to *h* and *k* in Exercise 1.

3. *a. S.*   *b. O.*   *c. S.*   *d. O.*   *e. S.*   *f. S.*   *g. O.*   *h. S.*

   i. O.

4. Being motivated by reasons of self-interest means having as one's basic concern one's own interest and the extent to which that interest is accomplished or frustrated by a given action. Any means, including cooperation, that is compatible with my self-interest and that is effective in accomplishing it is acceptable. If one's ultimate concern is with the interests of any person or persons other than one's self, then one's reasons are not self-interested. Moreover, if one's stated reasons do not mention the interests of any person or persons other than one's self, then one's reasons are not self-interested. Moreover, if one's stated reasons do not mention the interests of any parties, speaking instead in terms of finding favor with God, developing aesthetic capacities, exercising certain virtues, or doing one's duty, then these are not reasons of interest at all, either self-interest or the interest of others.

5. Your answer should be drawn from the summary statements in each section of the module and from the answer provided to Exercise 4.

MODULE 5
EGOISM—PSYCHOLOGICAL AND ETHICAL

Psychological egoism is the view that human conduct *is* motivated exclusively by self-interest. *Ethical egoism* is the view that human conduct *should be* based exclusively on self-interest. In this module we will contrast these two theories. We will contrast ethical egoism with alternative views of the relative importance of one's own interests and the interests of others—namely, altruism, and egalitarianism. We will examine the argument that bases psychological egoism on the origins of socially useful desires in presocial selfishness. We will argue that this support is undercut by its reliance on the "genetic fallacy" and on the questionable assumption that human nature is fixed and unchangeable. After reading Module 5, you should be able to

- Compare and contrast psychological egoism and ethical egoism, giving examples of how each theory either explains or would direct conduct.
- Compare and contrast ethical egoism with altruism and with egalitarianism, giving examples of how each would direct conduct.
- Characterize the genetic fallacy.
- Present the case for psychological egoism based on an examination of the origins of socially useful desires in presocial selfishness.
- Describe how the above-cited case for psychological egoism commits the genetic fallacy.

THE CASE OF THE DEFERENTIAL HOUSEWIFE, PART II

Dear Olga,

Hi, how are you? How is your family?

John and I are here at Sun Valley, we are having a super time. Wish you and Bill could be here with us. Oh well.

I've been thinking a lot about what you were saying. You remember?—when Maria, you and I met for coffee a few weeks ago. You were talking about how Maria should not go from one extreme to the other, how she should respect both herself and her family, how she should treat everyone like an equal. Well, I'm not persuaded.

The way I see it, when you get right down to it everyone is selfish.

What I cannot understand is how people ever got together in communities or nations in the first place. It must be because they thought that in the long run they were better off if they could avoid the daily worry of being stabbed in the back by their neighbor. Sure, dear, people cooperate. They even get married and try to live—or survive—together. But let me tell you, honey, the beginning of all that cooperation is good old self-interest. It's the only thing that keeps people together. Why, look at children; they first have to learn that they get punished for not being cooperative. Then they start to behave.

Oh, I know you, Olga, you are probably already thinking about how I'm being illogical. You always are accusing me of that, aren't you? Well, I don't much care about that. Even if you can't say how people end up thinking about cooperation by looking at how they started out, I still will go on knowing that people are, at bottom, motivated by self-interest. That will never change 'cause that's just how people are.

My gosh, how I've run on! I only meant to say "hello." Guess I got carried away. Well, I shall not let this disagreement spoil my vacation or my friendship. You know my motto: "Keep number one, number one!" I really do wish you and Bill could fly up to join us—say for the weekend? I so enjoy your company. Keep in touch.

Love,
Ginger

5:1.1 Psychological Egoism and Ethical Egoism.   *Psychological egoism* is the view that people cannot and do not act except out of self-interest. It is an empirical claim about the invariable presence of a single motivation behind all that people do. There is no value judgment here, but rather a factual claim about the nature of human motives. This factual claim extends to all human beings and to all human actions without exception. The view is that although some actions may not appear to be self-interested—for example, actions that involve helping or cooperating with others—all actions really are self-interested on close inspection. In other words, it is held that in all their actions people are ultimately motivated by concern for their own well-being, not for the well-being of anyone else.

Ethical egoism is the view that people should act only out of self-interest. It is a *normative* claim about the best way to lead a life and about what makes human actions right or wrong. The right thing to do is always to pursue self-interest. Although it may be possible, contrary to psychological egoism, to act out of concern for something other than self-interest, the view here is that it would always be wrong to do so. People should help or cooperate with others only when it is reasonable to expect that their self-interest will be best served by doing so.

This distinction between psychological egoism and ethical egoism is illustrated in the case study for Module 4. Ginger holds both positions. When she speculates about the reasons why Manuel got married, why Maria entered into such a relationship, and why people in general do what they do, she invariably points to what she believes to be their self-interested motivation. In the case study for the present module Ginger reveals herself as a convinced psychological egoist who subscribes to the factual belief that people do what they do to improve their own well-being.

In her motto "Keep number one, number one," Ginger is recommending that people should always put themselves first; she is making the claim of ethical egoism. Even if people could be motivated by concerns other than self-interest, Ginger would recommend that they never act on those motives. She holds to the normative view that right action consists in the pursuit of self-interest. Earlier she recommended the course on "Complete Womanhood" to Maria, because she believed it would help Maria to better pursue her self-interest and because she believed it was right for Maria to do precisely that. Ginger believes that a person can never be happy until she or he realizes the centrality of the pursuit of self-interest to living the good life.

5:1.2   Several views are possible on the relative importance of one's own well-being and that of others. It is important to recognize this in order not to be taken in by a possible argument in defense of ethical egoism. An ethical egoist might well argue that even if a person can pursue the interests of others for their own sake, surely others are not more deserving than the self of having their interests pursued. From this the egoist might wish us to conclude that, therefore, one should not pursue the interests of others but should rather pursue one's own self-interest. Even if the premise of this argument is conceded—that others are not more deserving than the self—its conclusion does not follow. An underlying presupposition is that one must choose between always putting self-interest first, the egoist's position, and always putting the interests of others first, the position known as *altruism*. This presupposition is faulty, for there is at least a third possible position. One can hold that the interests of every person are equally deserving of attention. This position has been called *egalitarianism*. If there is some mistake in the view that one should always be self-sacrificing, it does not immediately follow that one should always be self-interested. There are three alternatives here: egoism, altruism, and egalitarianism.

In the case study Ginger recalls how Olga had pointed out an egalitarian position between the two extremes of egoism and altruism. Not being a psychological egoist, Olga had credited Maria with genuine concern for the well-being of her family, and she would not have her misconstrue that concern as the pursuit of self-interest that Ginger recommends. Moreover, Olga had suggested that if Maria wished to be less compromised in effectively serving the needs of her family, she might have to recover self-respect and the respect of Manuel and the children as an equal in the relationships involved. Olga defended mutual concern and respect as an alternative to both deference and selfishness. But it is clear from her letter that Ginger will not move from her acceptance of both ethical and psychological egoism.

5:2.1 Psychological Egoism and the Origins of Social Concern. What argument can be offered in support of psychological egoism? One central defense begins with the claim that in the history of human society and in the histories of individual persons social concern originates in motives of self-interest. Only out of self-interest do people band together in societies in the first place, and only out of self-interest can children be motivated to interact as social beings. The view is that presocial (uncivilized) persons are moved exclusively by self-interest. From this premise it is argued that any new behaviors that persons develop as members of social groups must fundamentally be explained as arising out of those same presocial and egoistic impulses. What originated in selfishness must itself be and remain selfish. Ginger used this argument in her letter to Olga.

5:2.2   In order to evaluate an argument such as this, it is necessary both to examine the plausibility of the premises and underlying presuppositions on which it is based and to determine whether the conclusion follows from those ideas. There is at least room to question the truth of the premise about the origins of society and socially functional behavior. How firmly established is the belief that society grows out of enlightened self-interest, either in human history taken as a whole or in the history of each individual? While it may be reasonable to admit that one of the motives for social behavior is self-interest, how has it been (or could it be) established that self-interest is the only motive? Surely it is an empirical matter, since it is at least conceptually possible that social behavior originates in part from non-self-interested motivation.

5:2.3   Fortunately, we need not concern ourselves with whether the empirical evidence about the beginnings of civilization or the development of social concern in the child weighs more heavily in favor of, or against, the psychological egoist's premise here. Even if it were established beyond dispute that all social concern originates in self-interest, it simply does not follow that all social concern *must remain* self-interested forever after.

It is not generally logical to move from premises about how something originates to beliefs about how it remains in all of its subsequent states. Physically, chemically, and biologically, things may be found originally in one state and then later in another. It is clear that things change. Things do not retain for their entire existence all of the properties they had in their original states. Development brings changes in kind as well as changes in degree. As examples, consider the differences between water and ice; between hydrogen, sulphur, and oxygen separately and H_2SO_4 (sulphuric acid); and between tadpoles and frogs. While it might be argued that this is to trivialize the claim of the psychological egoist, that he or she is after all talking about a psychological and not simply a physical, chemical, or biological matter, it remains to be established that psychological transformations never occur. Surely it is an empirical and not merely a conceptual matter whether the change from self-interest to another motivation is possible. Is it true, for example, that whatever one's motives are in entering a conversation, they remain constant as the conversation progresses? Perhaps you enter a conversation for the fun of some good-natured teasing. But if you perceive the depth of the other's feelings, you may abandon this motivation.

Similarly, it is fallacious to assume that all events and actions are adequately explained by original states or situations. This fallacy, called the *genetic fallacy,* rests on the dubious assumptions that references to origins are by themselves adequate to explain later events and actions, and that intervening transformations never make origins irrelevant to the explanations of later events and actions. Are adult motivations uniformly childlike, appearances to the contrary? Or, to put the question more directly, need all adult actions be motivated by self-interest, even if the actions of children always are? It is not logically necessary that this be so; hence the psychological egoist's argument is seriously faulty. If it is to be established that all adult motives are self-interested, this must be done by empirical investigation of the motives present in adult living and not by the fallacious argument based on beliefs about the child's initial motives.

5:2.4   One final underlying presupposition (or assumption) of the psychological egoist's argument must be examined. The view that social behavior originates in self-interest and, therefore, remains self-interested throughout its history is rooted in the assumption that human nature is fixed and unchanging. Although we cannot settle this issue here, it is fair to say that this view is not widely held among contemporary thinkers. Philosophers whose thinking otherwise differs greatly, such as existentialist Jean Paul Sartre and behaviorist B. F. Skinner, agree that there is no such thing as a fixed, stable, and determined human nature. Thus the psychological egoist's contention that human personality could never admit of motives that would lead people to act out of concern for duty or a concern for the well-being of others for their own sake needs a great deal of independent support if the argument about the origins of social concern is to carry much weight. In her letter Ginger shows that she believes human nature cannot change. She also commits the genetic fallacy discussed in 5:2.3. Although her beliefs are strong, her case for psychological egoism is weak.

Exercises for Module 5: Egoism—Psychological and Ethical

1. *a.* Describe a case in which some person acts in a self-interested way.
   b. Would the psychological, or the ethical, egoist tend to regard this action as predictable?
   c. How would a psychological egoist explain an action that did not apparently serve the agent's interest?
   d. If an ethical egoist heard of the case you described, what would his or her attitude be toward the action and toward the agent?
   e. If psychological egoism were true, what sense could be attached to the advice, "Follow your own interest"? (5:1.1)
2. Make up and describe a situation in which one person, Mona, may act either egoistically or altruistically in relation to another, Lisa. (5:1.2)
3. Describe a second situation in which Mona may act either egoistically or egalitarianistically on behalf of a group to which she belongs. (5:1.2)
4. *a.* Characterize the genetic fallacy, providing an example not drawn from psychological egoism. (5:2.3)
   b. State the grounds on which a typical psychological egoist would defend his or her view.
   c. State the conclusion the psychological egoist then draws.
   d. Match the characteristics of the genetic fallacy with features of the psychological egoist's defense of his or her view.

Answers to Exercises for Module 5

1. *b.* The psychological egoist would tend to regard the action as predictable, since he or she asserts that people always act in such a way as to pursue what they think is in their own best interest.

c. According to the psychological egoist, a person's action might fail to be in his own best interest only if the person made a mistake in trying to figure out what his own best interest would be or appearances were deceiving.

d. The ethical egoist would *approve* of the action and would be inclined to *commend* the agent. He or she would not assume that persons always try to act in their best interest. According to him, they might both attempt and succeed in doing something contrary to their own interests.

e. If psychological egoism were true, everyone would always *try* to follow his own best interest, so the advice would seem superfluous. The only sense the advice could have would be to encourage people to be careful not to make mistakes in calculating what action would best serve their interests.

2. A correctly stated situation will include statements of what is in Mona's interest and what is in Lisa's interest. Moreover, somehow Mona's interest should be contrary to, or at least clearly distinct from, Lisa's, so that the actions pursuing the one interest will be different from those pursuing the other. Check your description for each of these characteristics.

3. You should be able to infer the characteristics of a correct answer to this question from those of a correct answer to Exercise 2. Look at each characteristic stated there and infer the corresponding one that should be included here; then check to see that you have included it.

4. a. The genetic fallacy is a form of argument. Its premise is that in its *origin* or in its initial form something is characterized by certain properties. The conclusion is that the thing thereafter *remains* characterizable by those same properties.

b. Two sorts of grounds are given: (1) the presocial behavior of human children is entirely selfish, and (2) the presocial and precivilized behavior of human beings is entirely selfish.

c. From these grounds the psychological egoist concludes: all human behavior is selfish.

d. Both the individual (1) and human history (2) are considered. In each case the (supposedly) earliest form of behavior is characterized (as selfish). The conclusion is then drawn that all human behavior must, therefore, retain that characteristic.

MODULE 6
EGOISM SCRUTINIZED

In this module we shall explore the relation of psychological egoism to ethical egoism by considering how the truth or falsity of the empirical theory relates to the plausibility of the normative theory about how people ought to live their lives. We shall then address directly the basic question of ethical egoism: Should people act exclusively out of self-interest? In so doing we shall be treating two possible responses to the question, "Why should I be moral?" After reading Module 6, you should be able to

- Explain the meaning of *"Ought* implies *can."*
- Discuss the relation of psychological egoism and ethical egoism in terms of "Ought implies can."
- Show how the falsity of psychological egoism entails that the ethical egoist advises people not to act on some of their concerns.
- Contrast the potential meaningfulness of egoistic and nonegoistic living in different societies and in the light of human mortality.
- Show how the falsity of psychological egoism and considerations of human mortality suggest answers to the question, "Why should I be moral?"

THE CASE OF THE DEFERENTIAL HOUSEWIFE, PART III

"Look, Olga," said Maria, "here comes Ginger. She must be just back from vacation. Look at her tan."

Olga and Maria continued their lunch as Ginger approached. She pulled up a chair from a nearby table and sat down. "Mind if I join you two? Did I ever miss our little lunchtime chats. How have you two been, anyway? I just loved my little trip to Sun Valley. I told you that looking out for number one pays off."

"Oh, I'm so pleased you had fun, Ginger," said Maria. "And, your tan— how deep and rich you look."

"Like I say, Maria, people are selfish, so they might as well act that way."

"Ginger," said Olga, "how can we help being selfish if what you say, that self-interest is always our motive, is true? So why bother to tell us to wise up?"

"Yes, Olga, it would be silly of me to tell you to act out of duty or out of a concern for others. That's impossible! But telling people to be self-interested is another matter. It's consciousness-raising, honey. Why, that course I told you about raised my consciousness and it showed me plenty of useful tricks, too. I sure get a lot more out of life now than I did before."

"Maybe so, Ginger. But I do not believe that my concern for Manuel and the children is basically a selfish one. I love them. I really am thrilled and happy for them when they do well or when something I do pleases them. That's how I feel even when I don't see anything in it for me."

"Now, Maria, there's got to be a selfish motive in there, even if you can't see it or refuse to admit it. There's a selfish motive for everything."

"Really, Ginger, you are being tiresome," said Olga. "Tell me, is there anything you are willing to count as counterevidence? Don't be so stubborn. When Maria says she loves her family and she is moved by their needs, why don't you believe her? Must you keep trying to explain her love away? You keep trying to tell us that behind everything there lurks some selfish motive that even you can't put your finger on. Why can't you take Maria's word?"

"No Olga, dear, Maria is either confused or dishonest—sorry, Maria, but that's life—I didn't mean to hurt you. Olga, I cannot imagine a case when people are not acting selfishly. Maria, you should take a harder look at yourself. Be honest with yourself and with us. Come on now, what's the real story, honey?"

"Wait, Maria. Look, Ginger. I think Maria is genuinely concerned for her family. If so, then to put self-interest first, as you would have it, actually means that she should stop doing what she really wants to do. She wants to meet their needs!"

"I can see that you are the stubborn one, Olga. Look, Maria, as a friend I'm telling you, you're a fool to work for your family if you don't get anything out of it. Believe me sweetheart, it's true."

"Sorry, Ginger, I think Olga has said it, but I'll tell you myself—I will not be happy if I take care of my family only so as to gratify my own desires. Helping them is its own reward, Ginger. I won't feel right if I neglect them. Why do you want me to stop anyway? I'm not married today just for what I can get out of it. People can have a sense of obligation to others. They can, Ginger. They should and they do have that sense of—well, call it responsibility."

"Ginger, someday I won't be around, but my kids will. I want them to be happy, and I believe that the way I raise them will help them to be happy their whole lives. Vacations are nice, but I also have the future to think about—the future of my children not just while I'm with them but even after I'm not around to see how things turn out."

"Well, have it your way, Maria, honey. I've got to run off now. John's off on a business trip and I have to meet someone for . . . ah . . . lunch. Goodbye, girls."

6:1.1 The Relation of Psychological Egoism and Ethical Egoism. How does the truth or falsity of a theory about how people *do* behave lead directly to any conclusion about how people *ought* to behave? It is clear that ethical egoism would not follow as a strict logical consequence of the truth of psychological egoism. In other words, psychological egoism could be true and ethical egoism false. On the other hand, it is also clear that ethical egoism could be held as a normative theory even by those who believed psychological egoism to be false. In other words, psychological egoism could be false and ethical egoism true.

6:1.2   This, however, is not all that can and should be said about the relation of the two theories, for there is a closer connection. You can understand it by understanding what philosophers have meant by the expression, *"Ought* implies *can."* Imagine a simple case where a little girl, Jenny, tells you that she wants to play with her building blocks. "Well," you say, "go get them off the shelf and play with them. That is what you ought to do." But Jenny tells you the blocks are too heavy for her to lift down, so she cannot do as you say. This example suggests that it is pointless to tell someone that she or he ought to do something if she or he is not able to do it. Thus, part of the meaning of *"Ought* implies *can"* is, "If a person ought to do something, then doing it is within his or her power."

In the case study Ginger argues that it would be foolish to recommend that people act non-egoistically, since it is impossible for them to do so. It would seem wrong and cruel to punish a person for not being twelve feet tall; but if it is a law of human nature that human beings always act self-interestedly, then they can no more avoid self-interested action than they can manage to be twelve feet tall.

6:1.3   The very compact expression *"Ought* implies *can"* has a further meaning. It also means that saying that a person ought to do something implies that the person *is capable of not doing*—or, if you will, able to fail to do—what he or she ought to do. It makes sense to charge a person with a duty or obligation, with something that he or she ought to do, only when it is possible for him or her not to do as he or she ought. To tell a person, for example, that she or he must refrain from cutting the tall grasses where the pheasants nest presupposes not only that she or he can refrain, but also that she or he has the ability to cut the grass. The person might, for example, not have adequate lawn-mowing equipment or might be too busy.

The idea of a normative theory is to provide reasoning in favor of one course of action where several alternatives are available. Thus, if psychological egoism is true, and people cannot help but be self-interested, then it is not obvious that ethical egoism has the normative field to itself, for there is serious question whether there is a normative field at all. Olga challenges Ginger in precisely this fashion by suggesting that in Ginger's view people must automatically be egoists, whether or not Ginger ever recommends that they become so.

6:1.4   There is one possible way around the argument of the preceding paragraph. Perhaps there is a point in recommending that people become ethical egoists even if psychological egoism is true. It could be that one can be more or less careless about the pursuit of self-interest. If this is so, then ethical egoism can be understood as nonsuperfluous, given that there is a range of alternative ways of pursuing self-interest more or less successfully. Following the ethical egoist's recommendation, then, would involve a significant change in one's life to the extent that it involved a person's becoming enlightened in pursuit of self-interest. Ginger, in responding to Olga's objection, recognizes that this is the only reasonable position for her to take.

6:2.1 Psychological Egoism as an Empirical Theory.   Psychological egoism is presented as an empirical theory that offers the most satisfactory account of carefully observed human behavior and its motivation. In supporting this theory, psychological egoists point to obviously self-interested actions and argue that many apparently non-self-interested actions turn out on closer inspection to be based on self-interest after all. These theorists may, for example, detect self-interested motivation in cases of apparent heroism and self-sacrifice as further evidence for the theory.

Although psychological egoists may succeed in showing that *some* seemingly unselfish acts are selfishly motivated, they must, if the theory is to be established, show that *all* are. But even the most convinced psychological egoist concedes that there are cases where the self-interested motive is not clearly detectable. In such cases these theorists may say that the actions in question are instances of self-deception (persons are deceived in not recognizing their self-interests) or that there are unconscious self-interested motivations at work. At this point the psychological egoist is maintaining that, empirical evidence to the contrary, there simply *must be* a self-interested motive present. Ginger takes this position in the case study. For her, no testimony, no evidence, can dislodge the theory.

6:2.2   It may be suggested that at this point a supposedly empirical theory of human motivation has become a nonempirical, or *a priori*, theory, which is held to be true in spite of empirical evidence to the contrary. The very conception of the nature of the theory has shifted. While there may be some cases, perhaps all too frequent, where self-interest is masked by apparent concern for duty or the well-being of others, the detection of this appearance, and ultimately the underlying self-interested reality, is presumably an empirical matter. Moreover, while there may be some such cases, this does not suffice to establish the truth of the empirical theory of psychological egoism. The psychological egoist must show that self-interest is in reality the underlying motive in *all* cases where people seem to act in non-self-interested ways. Recourse to claims about self-deception or unconscious self-interest as universally present may, for many, be founded more on an undying faith in psychological egoism (as an *a priori* theory) than on hard factual evidence.

In such cases psychological egoism is held more as a *postulate* for explaining human actions than as a *hypothesis* to be confirmed or falsified by observation. When the advocate of the theory admits, as Ginger did, that no human action could ever convince him or her that non-self-interested behavior is possible, the shift from factually based hypothesis to *a priori* postulate has occurred. Olga focuses on this shift in Ginger's views. When confronted with Maria's apparent self-sacrificing behavior, Ginger remains convinced that there must be self-interested motivation at its base. Although Maria ultimately may be deceiving herself, this remains to be shown by some empirical means. Ginger has become an advocate of an *a priori* version of psychological egoism that could scarcely be confirmed or disconfirmed by observation of human behavior. Olga, by contrast, prefers to take Maria's apparent self-sacrificing motivation at face value, at least until there is some good factual reason not to.

6:3.1 Ethical Egoism and Pursuit of One's Own Interests. Let us consider now the principal question of ethical egoism: "Should persons act exclusively out of self-interest?" Since there is reason to doubt that psychological egoism is a true empirical theory of human motivation, it seems plausible to suppose that human interests may range beyond those of self-interest. That is, there is some reason to believe that persons are both capable of and interested in behaving in non-egoistic ways. The ethical egoist is, then, recommending that people act on only some of the interests they have: those of self-interest. Is this a reasonable recommendation?

Some challenge ethical egoism with this argument: People are generally happiest when they do what they want to do, and their happiness is diminished when their acting on their wants is frustrated. Often people want to do things that amount to their acting out of concern for duty or the well-being of others. Ethical egoism recommends that people not act out of those motives, so it recommends that people sometimes not do what they want to do. Ethical egoism, therefore, recommends a restricted range of motives for action. This, for some, would diminish the happiness generally arising from doing what one wants to do. The argument urges that any recommendation that diminishes happiness without compensation is unreasonable and should be rejected.

Olga uses this argument in responding to Ginger. She believes that

Maria's concern for her family is genuine, and she argues against Ginger's ethical egoism by suggesting that Maria would not be as happy as she might be if she were to stop acting out of a sense of duty and concern for the well-being of the members of her family for their own sake. Maria's life would be diminished to the extent that she was encouraged no longer to derive pleasure from pleasing Manuel and the children except when she could see something in it all for herself.

6:3.2   The line of reasoning above is tantamount to a response to the question, "Why should I be moral?" One possible reading of the question is, "Why should I base my behavior upon concern for persons, rather than acting exclusively out of my self-interest?" Being moral is contrasted to being prudent about one's self-interests as an enlightened egoist might be. If human motivation extends beyond the limits described by psychological egoism, then persons already have among their concerns those of respecting persons by honoring duties toward them and looking toward their well-being. Why should people base their behavior upon such concerns? Simply because they have the concerns. It is not as if they were being asked to introduce moral concern into their lives where such concern was foreign to them and obviously odious. If one has these interests already, then there already is concern to be moral.

6:4.1 Ethical Egoism and Human Happiness.   There are two additional perspectives some have adopted in evaluating the ethical egoist's recommendation that self-interest is the way to happiness. In the first we are invited to consider the social environments within which persons might pursue their egoistic course. On the one hand, imagine a society in which enlightened egoism is universally encouraged. Indeed, some social philosophers have recommended that society should be so conceived and that legislators should write laws on the assumption that those governed by the laws will and should behave as enlightened egoists. Within such a society cooperation and friendship would be encouraged and supported only to the extent that they were useful to the individuals involved. Anyone who valued harmony or the like for its own sake would be frustrated and thought foolish. In such a social environment the convinced ethical egoist would find his or her greatest happiness—though, if the argument in 6:3.1 is correct, he or she would be encouraged to suppress wants and interests that were his or her own but that were not self-interested. Whatever the constraints on the ethical egoist's happiness, the non-ethical egoist could be very frustrated by this social environment. For with most people regularly pursuing this self-interest, the non-egoist might well tend to be misunderstood. Appearing to follow egalitarian or altruistic motives, people might easily regard him or her as deceitful. They might be disgusted that non-egoists would think them so gullible as to be taken in! Moreover, the non-egoist might be moved toward despair by the general lack of appreciation of non-self-interested pursuits.

On the other hand, imagine a society where cooperation, friendship, trust, and harmony were valued for their own sake. Within such a society an egoist who professed his or her egoism might well experience frustration and even be ostracized. It would clearly be in the interest of the egoist to live hypocritically. He or she would always be at risk of being exposed and would have to expend much energy upon deception and manipulation. In such an environment the life of an egoist would not likely be a very happy one.

6:4:2   In these considerations about social environment we find the most ambiguous answer to the question, "Why should I be moral?" For the suggestion is that a life of self-interested prudence is likely to yield more happiness and less frustration in a society oriented toward pursuit of self-interest, while the "moral life" will yield more satisfaction within a society of egalitarian and altruistic persons.

6:4.3   This brings us to the second perspective mentioned in 6:4.1. The sort of life that will provide a person the greatest happiness varies not only with the environment in which he or she must live but also with the kind of person he or she is and the values he or she holds dear. As it happens, some people attach great significance to, and derive their happiness from, a belief that they are leading lives of lasting value or that will leave a mark or make a difference after they have died. People do have the idea that things that are more enduring, things that can go on and have significance independent of them, are more valuable. When contemplating their own mortality, such persons often yearn to live their lives in such a way as to make a difference, or a contribution, to something of greater permanence than their own lives. Thus, many people are concerned to influence and contribute to the lives of others who may live on after them. This concern to contribute to the well-being of others can be and often is a motivation for entering into and sustaining friendship and family relations. On a broader scale, many people believe their lives to be more meaningful or fulfilling to the extent that they perceive themselves as making some contribution, however small or great, to the maintenance of growth of movements, societies, cultures, and traditions. By comparison, it is possible for people to perceive their own self-interest as fleeting and less capable of sustaining a sense that they are leading meaningful lives. The meaning of a life dominated by the pursuit of self-interest can be perceived as less substantial to the extent that it is tied to the individual's still being alive to experience and value it. If a person's interests range in such ways beyond self-interest, then the egoist's recommendation of self-interest would be rejected as precluding meaningful and, therefore, happy living.

Toward the end of the case study Maria responds to Ginger in these terms. Maria suggests that she values making a significant contribution to the lives of those for whom she cares. Even though she might not live to see her children live out their lifetimes, she derives meaning in her life from helping to shape their, and not merely her, future.

6:4.4 Implicit in this section is yet another possible response to the question, "Why should I be moral?" If a person wishes to lead a meaningful life, and if he or she believes that meaning in life can and does in part depend upon making significant contributions to or influencing for the better the lives of others, then being moral can be understood as an integral part of leading a meaningful life. Thus, valuing the well-being of others and acting out of a sense of responsibility for or duty to them may be understood as more meaningful than leading an egoistic life limited to pursuit of self-interest.

Exercises for Module 6: Egoism Scrutinized

1. *a.* Ethical theorists have been concerned about the implication that it is not possible for a person to do a certain action. In saying "Ought implies can," part of their meaning has been that persons cannot be held responsible for what they cannot do. Suppose that a necklace could be saved only if Sam Swimmer (a random bystander) were to swim under water for at least six minutes—longer than any person could survive without air. What implication would follow concerning Sam's responsibility for saving the necklace?

    b. How does this illustrate "Ought implies can"?

    c. Describe two further examples in which the impossibility of doing something would show a person's not being responsible for doing it.

    d. In the light of *b,* what is problematic about the assertion, "Psychological egoism is true, but people ought to be egalitarian"? (6:1.1, 6:1.2)

2. *a.* Describe three situations in which a person acts, perhaps, virtuously or dutifully, but under some constraint or force such that he or she had no choice but to act as he or she did.

    b. What would be problematic about asserting that any person who gets into such a situation *ought* to act in the ways you have just described?

    c. How does this illustrate "Ought implies can"?

      d. In the light of *c,* what is problematic about the assertion, "Psychological egoism is true, and people ought to be egoistic in their actions"? (6:1.3)

3.   *a.* Characterize the human motivations that must exist if psychological egoism is false. (5:1.2)

      b. Characterize the human motivations upon which ethical egoism exhorts people to act. (5:1.1)

      c. If we assume that people tend to be happiest when they ao what they want to do, explain why the ethical egoist is advocating a view that does not maximize human happiness, assuming that psychological egoism is false. (6:3.1)

      d. What connection does the text draw between the falsity of psychological egoism and the tendency to be moral? (6:3.2)

4.   *a.* State the frustrations of an ethical egoist in a society in which non-egoistic behavior is the expected rule.

      b. State the frustrations of an altruist or an egalitarian in a society in which egoistic behavior is the expected rule. (6:4.1)

      c. State the satisfactions of an ethical egoist in a society in which egoistic behavior is the expected rule.

      d. State the satisfactions of an altruist or an egalitarian in a society in which non-egoistic behavior is the expected rule.

5.   Begin with the premise: "What is fleeting is less valuable than what is permanent; and what is longer lasting is, in that regard and to that extent, more valuable than what passes more quickly." Use it to construct an argument that ethical egoism is false. (6:4.4)

Selected Answers to Exercises for Module 6

1.   *a.* It would follow that it is not the case that Sam ought to save the necklace. In other words Sam is not responsible for saving the necklace.

      b. If *ought* implies *can,* then if it is false that someone can do something, it is also false that he or she ought to do it.

      d. If psychological egoism is true, then people cannot pursue egalitarian interests. Accordingly, if it is not the case that they can pursue these interests, then it is not the case that they ought to pursue them.

2.   *b.* If, for example, a person is pushed in such a way that he or she falls, helplessly, down a flight of stairs, then even if he or she was not hurt, it would be wrong to assert that another person in such circumstances ought to fall that way, because this would imply that the person could control how he or she fell, whereas we began by assuming that the original person fell helplessly.

    c. This illustrates the point that saying a person ought to do a certain action assumes that not doing it is within his or her power.

    d. If psychological egoism is true, then the assertion, "People ought to be egoistic in their actions," involves the false assumption that people could try to act other than egoistically. Note, however, that they could still fail to act egoistically.

3. *a*. Some human motivations must exist that are non-self-interested. They might, for example, be altruistic or egalitarian.

    b. Ethical egoism exhorts people to act on self-interested motivations.

    c. If psychological egoism is false, people have non-self-interested motivations. If people tend to be happiest when they act on their own motivations, then people will tend to be happiest if they sometimes act on non-self-interested motivations. Since ethical egoism exhorts people not to act on non-self-interested motives, people will tend, on the above assumptions, to be less happy following the ethical egoist's advice.

    d. The falsity of psychological egoism entails that people do already have nonegoistic concerns.

4. *a*. The ethical egoist will be suspected and distrusted by his fellows, and their distrust will constrain him or her from successfully pursuing his or her self-interest. On the other hand, if his or her egoism is not known to others, he or she will be constrained from the direct pursuit of other interests by his or her instrumental interest, in such a society, in concealing his or her egoism in order to prevent distrust.

    b. The ethical altruist or egalitarian will either be suspected of deceit or be taken as sincere. If suspected of deceit, he or she will be rebuffed and will not gain the cooperation and friendship of others. If taken as sincere, then others will systematically use him or her to their own ends, ignoring any consideration for his or her own good.

5. (i) What is fleeting is less valuable than what is permanent; and what is longer lasting is, in that regard and to that extent, more valuable than what passes more quickly. (ii) Nothing is in a person's interest after he or she is dead. (iii) Hence to act for the sake of advancing one's own interest is to act for the sake of something without permanent worth. (iv) The interests of one's descendants and of society are more lasting than those of the self. (v) Hence, ethical egoism is false; one ought to pursue the more lasting interests of one's descendants and one's society, rather than one's own more fleeting interests.

UTILITY

Utilitarianism is an ethical theory. As such it tries to answer the question: What makes an action or a practice right or wrong? Historically, the hope of the classical utilitarians Jeremy Bentham and John Stuart Mill was to provide an objective means for making value judgments. In particular they were concerned about objectively judging alternative social policies and alternative pieces of legislation confronting nineteenth-century England. Accordingly, many democratic ideals operative in English political philosophy are assumed in their theories. The educational goal of this cluster is for you to understand and be able to discuss classical utilitarian thought and outline the development of the concept of utility in twentieth-century Western society. Module 7 explains how utilitarians would have us evaluate the consequences of our actions. Module 8 discusses how, on utilitarian theory, we should evaluate the rightness or wrongness of our actions themselves. Module 9 shows the utilitarian response to complications often advanced against their theory.

MODULE 7
THE EVALUATION OF CONSEQUENCES

Utilitarianism is to be understood, in part, as a response to a felt need to find a common ground for agreement about what actions or practices are right or wrong. In this module we shall examine the utilitarians' starting point: that the best means to achieving such agreement is to evaluate the consequences of actions or practices. The utilitarians chose this starting point out of the conviction that many or all aspects of these consequences could be defined objectively, because they could be counted or measured. They sought such quantifiable judgments out of the conviction that judgments about quantities would be judgments on which all persons could agree. Agreement between persons, or intersubjective agreement as it is frequently called, is obviously a desirable characteristic of evaluations, especially in a democratic society. We will discuss the classical utilitarian view that the consequences for anyone who might be affected by an action or practice are to count as of equal normative significance. We will introduce the four objective characteristics of these consequent states of affairs that utilitarians would have us take into account: their intensity, duration, propinquity, and extent. After reading Module 7, you should be able to

- Distinguish the views of a universalistic utilitarian from views that focus upon a more limited range of consequences.
- Given a possible state of affairs, list considerations of intensity, duration, propinquity, and extent of the consequences of actions or practices relative to that state of affairs.
- Describe the manner in which utilitarians seek to achieve agreement about normative concerns.
- Contrast limited and universalistic utilitarianism.

THE CASE OF GHETTO CRIME

Two college friends are discussing whether blacks who live in the ghetto should cooperate with a city police investigation of ghetto crime if they know that the criminal is a fellow black.

"As much as I like you, Borroughs, there is no way I can agree that blacks should rat on a brother, especially when it involves cooperation with honky cops."

"Look, Jackson, we've talked about your general hatred of the white establishment before. You know I understand where you're coming from. But this is one area where I've got to draw the line. A law is a law is a law. Cooperating with the police is just something you have got to do, no matter how strong your hatred for cops or your love for your brothers."

Angrily Jackson replies, "I just don't see why the law is so important here."

"There must be some way we can come to agreement on this," says Borroughs.

"I doubt it," snaps Jackson.

At this point Carlos Wright, who has overheard the discussion from the next room, comes in. "I know how far you guys have come in getting to know one another, and I'd like to help smooth things out here so you can continue to get along. Let's see if there are some things you both can agree on."

After both Jackson and Burroughs accept Wright's suggestion, he says, "I think you should look at the results of cooperating or not cooperating. If the criminal goes free, he may well commit more crimes, and it is sure that for now at least his victims will not recover any damages. Sure he'll be happier running free, but what about the other brothers and sisters he has been into or might still rip off? If people don't cooperate in such investigations, the crime rate in the ghetto will continue at its high level and it will be other black brothers and sisters who are hurt most by it. The white cops are not the one's who suffer if these criminals aren't caught. You're not doing the cops any big favor by turning in the criminal. And it's not simply that a law is a law is a law but rather that cooperation with the law leads to what you should both agree are good consequences, at least in this case."

Jackson and Borroughs look at each other and then back to Wright. They do agree.

7:1.1 The Quest for Common Ground. Utilitarian theory begins by seeking a common ground for agreement, through which it hopes to arrive at a kind of objectivity in normative matters. It looks for this common ground by focusing on the evaluation of the consequences of actions and practices in an attempt to find characteristics of good and bad things that are at least roughly quantifiable. Utilitarian theory plausibly assumes that intersubjective agreement will be rather easy to achieve.

In the case study Jackson is caught up in his subjective feelings about turning in a brother to people he generally despises. Utilitarian theorists argue that this kind of feeling cannot serve as the basis of agreement in normative matters: feelings simply are not always shared. Borroughs, on the other hand, is caught up in an inarticulate respect for authority. He believes it is right to cooperate with the law, but he is unable to say just why. Wright shifts the focus of the discussion to something he hopes all can agree upon. As a good utilitarian, he asks Jackson and Borroughs to consider the consequences of the action or practice in question. He suggests that Jackson's sentiments may, at least in this instance, be misplaced, owing to the bad consequences of non-cooperation. He suggests that no immediate good will result for the white police and, more importantly, less harm will result for all involved if people cooperate rather than not. Wright provides a substantial base for Borrough's beliefs about the law by citing precisely the same consequences and suggesting that they count as good reasons for cooperation with the law. It is because both Jackson and Borroughs readily accept the evaluation of the consequences that their dispute is settled and intersubjective agreement attained.

7:1.2 At least two important questions arise concerning the utilitarian focus upon evaluation of the consequences of actions and practices: (1) good or bad consequences for whom? and (2) how are we to calculate the value of these consequences? Let us turn to the first of these questions.

7:2.1 Classical Utilitarianism as Universalistic. Classical utilitarians hold that one must consider the consequences for all who might be affected by the act or practice in question. This is the meaning of their being called *universalistic utilitarians*. They are committed to egalitarianism—the view that each person counts equally in one's normative deliberations. Each person counts for one: the person making the decision counts for one if he is affected by the decision, as does each other affected person. Therefore, a person making a decision on universalistic utilitarian grounds is called upon to assume an attitude of personal disinterest. This means that he or she is not to judge the situation on the basis of feelings or emotions that arise because of his or her own involvement or because of the involvement of persons dear to him or her in the situation affected by the decision. Rather, he or she is to assume an attitude of generalized benevolence, which means that the interests of all human beings, and perhaps of all sentient creatures, are dear to him or her and count equally for him or her simply because they are the interests of those creatures.

In the case study Wright asks the others to consider the consequences of cooperation or noncooperation for all who might possibly be affected by the decision. The white police are thought to be affected little by it. Although the consequences for the criminal are thought to be bad, since he will be deprived of his freedom, this is thought to be outweighed by the good consequences for the victims of his crimes as well as the others in the ghetto who might be affected by such crime in the future. Universalistic utilitarian theory requires that one not exclude consideration of the consequences for anyone who might be affected by a decision.

7:2.2   Universalistic utilitarianism may be contrasted with other, more limited views about who is to be considered in evaluating the consequences of actions and practices. It contrasts with the views that only consequences for identifiable groups should be considered—for example, that (a) the agent and no one else, (b) everyone else excluding the agent, or (c) a select group of persons (including or excluding the agent) should be considered. These contrasting views may be called (a) egoism, (b) altruism, and (c) limited utilitarianism. Egoistic utilitarianism is the view that in making normative judgments one should evaluate only those consequences that apply to oneself; no other consequences are relevant. The sole difference between altruistic and universalistic utilitarianism is the latter's insistence that the agent is to be considered equal in importance with each of the others who might be affected by an action or practice. Limited utilitarianism is appealing to those who believe it important to be impartially concerned for others, but not *all* others. Limited utilitarianism is clearly a species of relativism, since its judgments about what is right or wrong are not universal, but relative to the membership of the group to which the speaker belongs or with whom the speaker identifies.

7:2.3   Anyone who believes one should be exclusively concerned about the well-being of one's race, nation, family, or the members of some particular group or organization may be a limited utilitarian. If, for example, one were to be concerned exclusively about the effects of crime upon black ghetto residents or upon whites outside of the ghetto, then one would be a limited utilitarian. One would be a limited utilitarian if he or she held that the United States government should concern itself solely with what is good for America and never consider seriously the effects of American policy on the citizens of other nations.

Classical utilitarians have preferred their universalistic position because of their belief that the well-being of each person is of equal moral concern. They believe that being moral requires one to take into account the effect of one's actions or practices upon those who happen not to be members of the select group one favors. Moreover, they find great practical difficulty in (a) selecting which group of the several to which one might belong is to be the preferred group and (b) deciding what one ought to do when alternative courses would benefit different groups of which one is a member.

Universalistic utilitarianism, then, is like limited utilitarianism in that both seek the greatest good—that is, the best balance of good compared to bad consequences. But whereas limited utilitarianism seeks the greatest good of a limited group of people, universalistic utilitarianism seeks the greatest good of the greatest number of all those who are affected, with each counting equally.

7:3.1 Determining the Value of Consequences. Let us return now
to classical universalistic utilitarianism and our second question in 7:1.2:
how do you determine the value of the states of affairs that are the consequences of actions or practices? Utilitarians propose consideration of
four objective characteristics of states of affairs that, taken together, count
toward making a situation more or less desirable. These characteristics
are the intensity, duration, propinquity, and extent of the good or bad
involved.

7:3.2   In seeking to determine the *intensity* of the good or bad in a
state of affairs resulting from an action or practice, one is seeking to
estimate how much good or bad exists for every affected person. Are
some people affected more than others? In the case study, Wright brings
to bear considerations of intensity in estimating the consequences of
cooperation or noncooperation. He argues that the white police will be
affected little either way. He suggests that the criminal will be affected
greatly in either being allowed to go free or being apprehended and
imprisoned. The criminal's victims have already been affected greatly by
his actions, and they may well be affected greatly again by cooperation,
for they may be able to recover what they lost. Future victims may
or may not be spared intense suffering as a function of the decision.
Others who may never be the actual victims of such crime may nevertheless enjoy the less intense benefit of living more securely in the neighborhood. And, while the one who cooperates with the police may, as a result,
be subjected to some undesirable peer pressure for having done so, such
suffering is probably less intense than that of the criminal's victims.

We hope you found the judgments of intensity just presented
intuitively clear. Critics of utilitarianism have objected, however, that
such judgments, even if intuitive, are not obviously quantifiable. Their
objectivity, therefore, has seemed to some critics to rest on such "subjective" judgments as that physical suffering and property loss are worse
evils than mental anxiety. We shall see in Module 9 how utilitarians
attempt to respond to such criticism.

7:3.3   Utilitarian theory also looks to the *duration* of the good or
bad involved as an important consideration in evaluating the desirability
of states of affairs. The concern here is whether the good or bad in
question is short-lived or long-lasting. While Wright does not explicitly
mention such considerations in the case study, he might well have done
so. For the white police there is but a momentary inconvenience in noncooperation. For the criminal the decision can obviously have far-
reaching long-range consequences. For the victims and potential victims
of future crimes the consequences may also be enduring ones. The
damage done, loss incurred, or injury sustained may well affect their
lives for some time to come. The neighborhood security to which

cooperation might contribute could be long-lasting as well. Any social harassment of the person who cooperated would not likely continue as long as these other effects.

7:3.4   The third consideration involved in evaluating consequences, on the classical utilitarian view, is the *propinquity* of the results of the action or practice. The question here is how near to the present are the various good or bad results. How long is the interval between the present and the good or bad that comes about? In the case study, noncooperation would result in *immediate* frustration to the police. The victim of the unsolved crime would continue to suffer the impact of the crime. Cooperation might lead to apprehension of the criminal and restoration of some of the damages done by the crime *in the not-too-distant future*. Noncooperation would result *immediately* in the criminal's continued enjoyment of his freedom. Cooperation could result in his loss of freedom *in the relatively near future*. Other potential victims of his future crimes could be spared into the *indefinite future*. A pattern of cooperaton could well result in greater security *in the relatively distant future* for those who were not the victims of crime. The peer pressure upon those who cooperated would likely be felt *immediately*.

There has been much debate about whether nearness makes a good better or an evil worse. Many philosophers have felt that propinquity is irrelevant, but in Module 9 you will see why others deem it not only relevant but important.

7:3.5   The fourth consideration used in classical utilitarian theory is the *extent* of the good or bad consequences. *How many persons* are involved in the state of affairs brought about by the decision? In the case study the extent of the effects of the decision is great. Not only are the police, and those who do or do not cooperate with them, involved and affected, but at least the criminal and likely the victims of his past crime are too. Potential victims of his future crimes are affected also, though it may be impossible to specify the particular individuals. Wright is careful to mention, however, that it is not simply these principals who are involved. Rather, it is reasonable to suggest that all who live in the neighborhood are affected by the crimes committed by people against their neighbors. Thus, the decision to cooperate or not may well implicate a large number of people.

In the remaining modules of this cluster you will be introduced to additional aspects of the utilitarian evaluation of actions and practices in terms of their consequences. You will encounter some of the implications and objections to utilitarian views.

Exercises for Module 7: The Evaluation of Consequences

1. Write true statements, one each, about the intensity, duration, propinquity, and extent of each of the following. (7:3.2–7:3.5)

   a. A population's being immunized against a disease.

   b. A city's collecting garbage once a month.

   c. A tornado's hitting a town without warning.

   d. A tornado's hitting a town after two hours of well-publicized warning.

2. a. Given Jackson's hatred of whites, what rewriting of the case study would present Jackson as a limited, rather than a universalistic, utilitarian?

   b. Define in general terms the difference between a limited and a universalistic utilitarian. (7:2.1, 7:2.3)

   c. Suppose Jackson knows who the criminal is. Explain how his deliberations would be different if he were a limited utilitarian rather than a person who considered only the consequences affecting him.

   d. What grounds can you think of to argue in favor of universalistic, rather than limited, utilitarianism?

3. In each of the following sets of comments, only one expresses a universalistic utilitarian stance. Identify it. Then explain how each of the others fails to qualify. (7:2.2, 7:2.3)

   a. (1) "Do whatever you want. If you feel like it now, do it."

      (2) "The fair is likely to be more exciting than the mismatched game. You ought not go to the game."

      (3) "You can't go to the game; that would involve breaking your promise."

   b. (1) "Not returning money when you know who lost it is really stealing; that's wrong."

      (2) "If you don't return the money, someone will probably find out and punish you."

      (3) "Even if someone finds out, you can't worry about some old man's losing his money."

   c. (1) "Since traffic is heavier on Main than on Claremont, the light should be green longer for Main to promote traffic flow."

      (2) "Everyone should have an equal chance to go, so the lights should be green equally long each way."

(3) "Mostly college kids drive up and down Claremont, while the townspeople use Main. So Main should be green longer."

4. Explain the involvement of each of the following in utilitarian theory:

   a. State of affairs.

   b. The future in contrast to the past.

   c. The quantifiable.

Selected Answers to Exercises for Module 7

1. *a*. Here are some possible answers: *Intensity:* The pain of the immunization is much less than the pain of the disease. *Duration:* Immunization will typically last 14 months. *Propinquity:* The population's being immunized within six months will save more lives than if the immunization is further delayed. *Extent:* Twenty million people are likely to require immunization.

2. *a*. One way for Jackson to be a limited utilitarian would be by ignoring any consequences for police or for white people. In such cases he would *limit* his concern about consequences to those persons who were not police or not white.

   c. In Jackson's limited utilitarianism it would not be only the consequences of the action for one person (Jackson) that would count. Rather, consequences of the action for *anyone within the group* (blacks) would be regarded as equally significant.

   d. "All people ought to be respected," or, "Everyone has equal rights to live and to do as he wants," you might plausibly say. *Note:* The point of this question is to show that the obvious ways in which to defend universalistic, rather than limited, utilitarianism are not themselves utilitarian ways. The arguments seem to say that respecting persons and their rights is intrinsically right. This is not to say that utilitarianism is proved indefensible at this point; it is only to present a difficulty to which utilitarians must respond. For instance, a utilitarian might say that everyone will be happier if secure in the assurance that his rights will be respected.

3. *a*. (1) Not utilitarian because it urges lack of *concern with consequences* of an action.

   (2) Universalistic utilitarian.

   (3) This response seems to say that breaking promises is wrong regardless of consequences—nonutilitarian view.

   b. (1) This statement suggests that stealing is intrinsically wrong; there is no concern here to evaluate consequences.

   (2) Universalistic utilitarian.

(3) Apparently a limited utilitarian view ignoring consequences for old people.
  c. (1) Universalistic utilitarian.
  (2) No concern for consequences shown.
  (3) Perhaps a limited utilitarian view excluding college students from the considered group.
4. Your explanation should indicate at least that to evaluate the morality of a given action utilitarians look to its future consequences. (They do not look to past precedents, intentions, motives, or other elements of past behavior.) The consequences are states of affairs the action will bring about. Certain aspects of these state of affairs are thought to be quantifiable and, so, measurable and open to objective evaluation.

MODULE 8
UTILITARIANISM—THE RIGHT AND THE GOOD

The fundamental utilitarian thesis is that an action or practice is right or wrong precisely because of the consequent state of affairs, good or bad, that it brings about. In this module we complete the account of the way utilitarian theory would require that actions and practices be evaluated. We shall introduce three additional factors to be considered: purity, fecundity, and certainty. We shall then look at the diversity of views held by utilitarians concerning what kinds of things are the intrinsically good (or bad) things that we should strive to maximize (or minimize) as we decide what to do. After reading Module 8, you should be able to

- Distinguish and present examples of the factors of purity, fecundity, and certainty as these apply to evaluating actions and practices.
- Define "right" and "wrong" in terms of "good" and "bad" as utilitarians would.
- Present a unified statement, with examples, of how utilitarian theory requires that actions or practices be evaluated.
- Distinguish hedonistic utilitarianism from other utilitarian views designed to identify the desirable ends of action and practice.

THE CASE OF THE BAN ON TUNA FISHING

The usual way of catching tuna for commercial use is to search for a school of porpoises and to lay nets for the tuna where the porpoises are heading, since in fact tuna tend to swim with the porpoises. In recent years it has been determined that enough porpoises have become ensnarled in tuna nets and have died of suffocation to warrant the United States government's banning this method of catching tuna.

Tuna fishermen, asked to evaluate the rightness or wrongness of the government's ruling, tend to point out the following considerations: every other method of catching tuna is less efficient and more expensive. It would take some time and a lot of capital investment to buy equipment that would make any other method feasible. Whatever methods United States fishermen use, foreign fishermen, not bound by United States law, will continue to use the banned methods and will, therefore, gain an economic advantage over United States fishermen. United States tuna fishermen conclude from this that the regulation should be revoked.

8:1.1 Consequences as Fundamental.   The case study exemplifies many of the characteristics of utilitarian thought. Notice that the tuna fishermen judge the ban entirely on the basis of its consequences. No method of tuna fishing is viewed as right or wrong in itself. The possible methods are judged right or wrong solely on the bases of the desirability or undesirability of the *states of affairs* they lead to. Fundamental to the utilitarian tradition is the assumption that *no action whatever is intrinsically good or bad*. Actions are only instrumentally good or bad because of the desirable or undesirable consequences (states of affairs) they bring about. For instance, a utilitarian tuna fisherman might feel justified in violating the government ban. He or she might reason that if he or she violates the ban, he or she will catch more tuna than otherwise. The chances of getting caught may appear slight and the consequences of being caught—the fine paid as penalty—insignificant compared to the profit to be made on the extra tuna. Such reasoning denies that defying the ban is wrong simply because it is the law of the land. The only "wrongness" the tuna fisherman accepts is the undesirability of the consequences.

8:1.2   In contrast to actions, utilitarianism readily admits that *some states of affairs are intrinsically good and others intrinsically bad*. Pain, disease, and the loss of liberty might be examples of intrinsically undesirable states of affairs. Similarly, happiness, pleasure, health, and increased freedom might be seen as intrinsically desirable. Accordingly, because the utilitarian denies that actions are intrinsically right or wrong, the entire utilitarian focus of moral evaluation is on the states of affairs that result from a given action or practice. Thus the most fundamental normative concepts for the utilitarians are the goodness and badness of states of affairs. The rightness and wrongness of actions and practices are derivative concepts to be defined in terms of the more fundamental ones.

8:2.1 Evaluating Actions and Practices.   Utilitarianism is insistent that one must look toward the consequences of actions and practices; it is forward-looking in its evaluation. In Module 7 we saw how utilitarian theory requires that *four determinants of states of affairs*—the intensity, duration, propinquity, and extent of the goodness involved—be taken into account as one evaluates potential consequences. Beyond these matters intrinsic to the states of affairs themselves, three additional factors are involved in completing the evaluation of actions and practices. These factors have to do with the tendency of the actions and practices to actually result in such consequences—that is, the relation between the actions or practices and their outcomes. The basic question is: What consequences are most likely to ensue from the actions and practices in question? The factors to be considered are the *purity, the fecundity, and the certainty of the actions and practices* as their consequences unfold.

8:2.2   In seeking to determine the *purity* of an action or practice, one is asking whether the consequences that it will actually tend to produce will be *purely* those (desirable) consequences that are intended, unmixed with undesirable, unintended consequences.

In the case study the earlier decision to catch tuna with the aid of porpoises was found by the United States government to have both the desired consequences of yielding large tuna catches and the additional undesirable and unintended consequence of killing unacceptably high numbers of porpoises. This impurity of consequences was used as the justification for the ban on the fishing method. Moreover, it is plausible to read the ban as providing the incentive necessary for fishermen to seek an alternative fishing method with less impure consequences. In turn, as suggested in 8:1.1, a fisherman might well consider violating the ban in terms of the possible consequences of doing so. He, or she too, contemplates likely impure consequences. To defy the ban is to continue to be competitive with foreign fishermen and to catch large numbers of tuna, but also perhaps to incur a fine.

Utilitarianism requires more than an evaluation of proposed actions or practices. Rather, it demands evaluation of a *range of alternative possible actions and practices* in an effort to determine which among them will produce the intended end with the least amount of undesirable side effects. Thus, utilitarians would not have us settle for just any procedure that results in a desired end. The concern for purity is the concern that the undesirable, though foreseeable, bad consequences be put in the balance with the good they accompany. The utilitarian is, thus, concerned that we select the procedure that results not in the greatest total good but rather the greatest net good when the bad is also taken into account. Indeed, it may turn out that in some particularly trying circumstances one confronts only undesirable alternatives, in which case one must endeavor to minimize the bad. For instance, could a selective or a partial ban save most of the porpoises while retaining high tuna yields? We are to strive to determine the purest of actions from among the several alternatives available.

8:2.3   The second factor in evaluating the tendency of actions and practices to produce good consequences is their *fecundity*. By this is meant the tendency of nearer consequences to cause, or help to cause, desirable consequences later on. Does what we do now make it easier or harder to handle a problem later? The utilitarian suggestion is that besides considering what an action or practice will immediately contribute toward the solution of a problem, we must also consider whether the immediate solution will make future circumstances easier or harder to handle. Piano practice, for instance, has good fecundity, because if you practice now, the problem of learning new pieces in the future is reduced because of the abilities that practice develops. By contrast, having a heroin habit has bad fecundity, because the body becomes used to heroin, and greater doses are required to attain the same effect later. Indeed, if it is judged that heroin addiction is itself a problem requiring a solution—that is, withdrawal—then it is also clear that that problem becomes more difficult to solve the longer the habit of using the drug continues. What we do now can make it easier to bring about the good later, or it can aggravate the difficulty of relieving the bad later. Actions and practices need to be evaluated not only for the good and bad they bring about for persons but also for the extent of the difficulty of the problems they create for persons.

In the case study one can contemplate the possible consequences of fishermen uniting and defying the government ban. This would ensure a continued high yield of tuna. It might also, however, make future relations with the government far more difficult. Thus, the solution to the immediate problem might aggravate future problems. On the other hand, compliance with the ban and a crash program of development of technology enabling them to catch comparable numbers of fish, without comparable loss of porpoises, might in the long run give the fisherman a competitive advantage over foreign fishermen, who might at some future time become subject to a similar ban by their own governments or by international agreement.

8:2.4   The last factor to be considered in evaluating actions and practices is the *certainty* of their tendency to produce good consequences. Utilitarians argue that each of the possible consequences of an action can be predicted to occur with differing degrees of probability. Typically, immediate consequences are predicted with the greatest certainty, while remote consequences, where intervening factors, foreseen and unforeseen, multiply, are predicted with the least certainty. All other things being equal, utilitarian theory requires that in making decisions you assign greater weight to the consequences that are more certain, more likely to occur. As an example, if it is certain that the price of electricity produced from coal will double in ten years, then it would be wise to invest now in solar heating for one's home. On the other hand, if it is more probable that the price of electricity will increase by only 30 percent in that time, then investment in solar heating at present may be unwise.

In the case study, some of the consequences of complying with or defying the ban are more certain than others. It is quite certain that continued use of the banned method will continue to yield large numbers of tuna and continue to involve the deaths of significant numbers of porpoises. It is relatively certain that much time and money would be required to develop new methods. It is quite certain that compliance will put United States fishermen at a competitive disadvantage. Prediction of possible future relations with the government after defiance is less certain. It is also less certain that fishermen of other nations will eventually be subjected to a similar ban. Thus, it is less certain that compliance and development of new methods will in the long run lead to a competitive advantage for United States fishermen.

8:2.5   We are now in a position to present a unified account of how utilitarian theory would require that people evaluate the rightness and wrongness of actions and practices. The fundamental thesis is that rightness and wrongness are a function of the actions' or practices' tendency to produce good consequences. The goodness of the consequent states of affairs is to be measured in terms of the intensity, duration, propinquity, and extent of the goodness involved in these states of affairs. The tendency of the actions and practices to conduce to good consequences is to be determined in terms of the purity, fecundity, and certainty of those actions or practices relative to their range of possible consequences.

8:3.1 Utilitarians on "The Good." So far we have developed utilitarianism as a theory about objective characteristics that make states of affairs good or bad, and about the rightness or wrongness of actions and practices as a function of their bringing about such states of affairs. The as yet unanswered question is: What makes a state of affairs good or bad?

In its reply utilitarian theory contrasts with ancient theories of what is desirable. The ancient theories assumed that human beings have an essence or basic nature and, in turn, that there is something that is essentially or naturally good for humans to pursue because it entails the development or fulfillment of the potential in that nature. Utilitarianism does not make these kinds of assumptions. Rather, it focuses on the right of the individual to decide for himself or herself what is desirable. In the utilitarian view, the individual knows himself or herself best and is therefore best able to determine his or her own good. So, utilitarians argue, what the individual desires (provided that it does not harm others) is what he or she ought to be encouraged to pursue. A valuing of liberty and personal autonomy is detectable here, underlying the utilitarian view that what is good is the happiness of persons, which they are best able to choose for themselves. Indeed, utilitarians may suggest that knowing oneself and choosing for oneself are themselves conditions of personal happiness.

8:3.2   Utilitarian theory has developed along different lines as a function of different theoretical suppositions about what human beings will choose for themselves. The two classical positions are (a) that pleasure is the only thing of intrinsic value to people and thus worthy of pursuit (advocated by Jeremy Bentham, 1748–1832), and (b) that happiness is the singular intrinsic value worthy of pursuit (advocated by John Stuart Mill, 1806–1873). In Bentham's view, called *hedonistic utilitarianism,* actions and practices are right if they lead to pleasure (or prevent pain) and wrong if they lead to pain (or prevent pleasure). The method of determining the rightness or wrongness of actions in terms of the variables of intensity, duration, and so on, thus became known as the "hedonic calculus," a method of calculating pleasure and pain and the likelihood of their occurrence. Bentham himself seems to have been somewhat confused about the relationship of pleasure to pain. Although he spoke of them as opposites, he generally thought of pleasure as a generalized feeling state, while he thought of pain as a physically locatable phenomenon. Hedonic utilitarianism becomes more plausible if sensual pleasures, the avoidance of physical pain, pleasures such as the anticipation and satisfaction at completing a task, and pains such as frustration and anguish are all considered in calculating the best course of action.

Some have held, Mill among them, that happiness is the only thing of intrinsic value and, moreover, that happiness is not merely the sum total of pleasures of whatever variety. Utilitarianism here assumes the view that actions and practices are right if they lead to happiness (or prevent unhappiness). The good, interpreted as happiness, is not merely the sum total of pleasures because there are important qualitative as well as quantitative differences among pleasures. Thus, two lives of equal pleasure, quantitatively, may be of different value because the one includes pleasures of higher quality. Such "higher" pleasures would include those of the intellect, the appreciation of culture, and the general refinement of sensibilities. In this view these more intellectual or spiritual pleasures are preferable to more sensual pleasures, such as eating and sex. In turn, actions and practices that contribute to the living of a life filled with such pleasures are deemed preferable in this version of utilitarianism.

8:3.3 Utilitarianism is seriously challenged by the variety of answers utilitarians have given to the question, "In virtue of what are states of affairs good? Is it the pleasure involved, the happiness, or some-

---

JOHN STUART MILL (1806–1873)

John Stuart Mill was one of the most influential British philosophers of the nineteenth century. His thoughts had impacts on liberal political philosophy, economic theory, scientific research methodology, and ethical theory.

Mill was an unusual man. He never went to school. His father and Jeremy Bentham designed his education, which started at age three and focused on classic authors, mathematics, and political theory. He worked for the East India Company and rose from clerk to department administrator. His early intellectual development was balanced with great emotional sensitivity in adulthood. He won a seat in Parliament, although he refused to campaign. He waited twenty-three years to marry the woman he loved (Harriet Taylor). He discussed all his philosophy in detail with her and praised her genius as the greatest influence on his writings.

Mill reformulated Bentham's utilitarianism, arguing that certain pleasures were superior to others. He showed that it could incorporate the human wisdom embodied in traditional moral guidelines by justifying them on utilitarian grounds. Mill's noninterventionist theories of government freed utilitarianism from its prior belief that only government action produced social reform. Mill believed that the pursuit of intellectual and moral self-perfection was the best way for a person to contribute to the common good.

thing else?" This variety is embarrassing because it is not obvious that intersubjective agreement can be secured by rational means, although such agreement is one of the greatest attractions of utilitarianism.

A second embarrassment is also implicit. The utilitarians must say that the measured quantities—the intensity, duration, and so on—are quantities of *pleasure* or of *happiness*. A hedonistic utilitarian, for example, is committed to saying that the good is the pleasurable and that the pleasurable can be objectively measured. Each of these types of claims has proved controversial.

Exercises for Module 8: Utilitarianism—The Right and the Good

1. *a.* The assertion, "Petroleum will be periodically scarce between 1975 and 2000," was much more certain in 1975 than in 1970. What knowledge (data) gained between 1970 and 1975 changed this degree of certainty?
    b. Provide an original example of increased and of decreased certainty. (8:2.4)
2. Describe a problem situation. Then define two responses to it, such that one should have much greater purity than the other. (8:2.2)
3. *a.* Explain the (positive) fecundity of developing in children the habit of walking on the right side of halls and sidewalks.
    b. Provide original examples of positive and of negative fecundity. (8:2.3)
4. *a.* The Robins have promised their children a chance to work at the county fair. The only other commitment they made for the summer was to let Grandma Robin have the children come for a visit. Now Grandma has written that the children should come the same week the fair is on, because of the special activities in her town that week. As utilitarians, describe the sequence of steps the Robins should take to resolve this conflict.
    b. How does this sequence bring out the utilitarian idea that actions are intrinsically neither right nor wrong? (8:1.2, 8:2.5)
    c. Provide a utilitarian definition of what it means to say an act or practice is right or wrong. "An action (or practice) is right if and only if. . . ." (8:2.5)
5. *a.* List the steps of utilitarian conflict resolution.
    b. Provide an example of your own that states a conflict and follow the steps.

6. Describe a case where a hedonistic utilitarian would disagree with another utilitarian who believed in the greatest happiness of the greatest number.

Selected Answers to Exercises for Module 8

1. *a*. (1) An actual scarcity occurred.
   (2) Natural cause of scarcity became better known.
   (3) Environmental laws registered an impact on alternating scarcity.
   (4) The Organization of Petroleum Exporting Countries was formed. Each of (1)–(4) in some way renders petroleum scarcity more probable.
2. Remember that impurities tend to enter a situation to the extent that either unpredictable or uncontrollable elements are involved. Thus, for example, an alternative requiring good weather or reliance on an untrustworthy person might well lead to impurities.
3. *a*. Once a person has such a habit, he can do things automatically, without thinking about them. Others can rely on those habits, increasing liberty. This training is easily transferred to later activities, such as bicycle riding and driving motorized vehicles, thereby improving personal and public safety.
4. *a*. Here is an outline of the answer (incomplete except for its first step, where the alternatives are filled in):
   (1) Define alternative courses of action.
       (i) Let the children work at the fair, go to Grandma's another week.
       (ii) Send them to Grandma's during fair week, let them work at the fair another year.
       (iii) Work part of the week at the fair, visit Grandma's part of the week.
       (iv) Allow them neither to visit Grandma nor to work at the fair.
   (2) Detail the foreseeable consequences of each alternative, including collecting further available data.
   (3) Decide whether pleasure or happiness will determine the good (and bad).
   (4) Specify the intensity, duration, and so on of each good or bad consequence.
   b. The only elements to calculate in choosing an alternative are the quantities of the pleasure or happiness involved in each alternative's consequence. Thus, actions are viewed as right only instrumentally as they conduce to desirable states of affairs. (See 8:1.2 and 8:2.5.)
5. The four steps are described in the answer to 4*a* above. Answer 4*a* shows how you might answer 5*b*.
6. Your case should involve more sensual pleasures as one alternative and more intellectual, cultural, or spiritual pleasures as a conflicting alternative.

MODULE 9
COMPLICATIONS OF UTILITARIANISM

In the first two modules of this cluster we have outlined the basic concepts and recommendations of utilitarian normative theory. It remains for us to consider problems and complications in the interpretation and practical application of that theory. In this module we will consider whether utilitarianism is most plausibly understood as recommending that actions be evaluated in terms of their utility or in terms of their conformity to rules that have utility. This is the issue between *act utilitarianism* and *rule utilitarianism*. We shall discuss whether utilitarianism requires that agents be held responsible for the actual or merely the foreseeable consequences of their actions. We shall focus upon contemporary uses of utilitarian theory in economics, especially in cost-benefit analysis, as a response to the practical problem of finding goods that are readily quantifiable as the objects of utilitarian calculation. After reading Module 9, you should be able to

- Distinguish the act and the rule interpretations of utilitarian theory.
- Provide both act and rule utilitarian justifications of actions.
- State some of the difficulties with both the act and the rule interpretations of utilitarianism.
- Describe a case in which you distinguish actual and foreseeable consequences of actions and practices.
- State the importance of the difference between actual and foreseeable consequences in estimating the responsibility of agents according to utilitarianism.
- Characterize economic cost-benefit analysis as a contemporary species of utilitarian theory.
- Provide examples of cost-benefit analysis employing utilitarian categories.

THE CASE OF THE FUGITIVE SLAVES

The scene is Fostoria, Ohio, along the famous Underground Railroad, which successfully smuggled many fugitive slaves to freedom in mid-nineteenth-century America. A father is explaining to his son why he may have to lie to slave hunters if they should make direct inquiries as to the whereabouts of the fugitives.

"My son, if ever anyone asks you about the slaves we're hiding out in the old shed, you must simply tell them you don't know what they're talking about."

"But, Dad, does that mean I should lie straight out, even though you've told me never to do that?"

"That's right. Otherwise they'll capture those slaves and take them back to nothing but suffering. And your daddy might get into a lot of trouble, too."

"But what about those times when you told me that people shouldn't lie to each other so as they can get along better and be able to trust each other?"

"That's generally true, son, but this is one of those few times when that kind of rule has to be broken or something even worse will happen."

9:1.1 Act and Rule Utilitarianism. The case study illustrates a concern about the place of moral rules in governing conduct. Two different views come into play as the father tries to explain to his son why lying about the escaped slaves, which is an exception to a general rule that one should not deliberately deceive someone in response to a direct question, is the best response to the slave hunters' inquiries. The two views are those held by what have come to be called act and rule utilitarian theorists. Fundamentally, both the act and rule theorists are utilitarians in sharing the view that the ultimate measure of the rightness or wrongness of human conduct is the tendency of that conduct to result in good consequences. But the crucial question is this: Do we apply this ultimate measure to individual actions, or to general practices described by the rules that govern them? *Act utilitarianism is the view that an action is right or wrong as a function of the specific consequences of that particular action. Rule utilitarianism is the view that the evaluation of the rightness or wrongness of an action is a three-step process.* First, one must *state the alternative actions* that could have been taken in a given situation. Second, one must *define the rules* under which one would be acting in taking each of the possible actions. Third, and ultimately, one must *determine the comparative acceptability of the rules* in question by evaluating the utility of the practices implied by each of the rules. In the act view, the utility of the act is primary. In the rule view, the utility of the rule is primary.

In the case study the son is puzzled about the status of the general rule that one should not lie. Apparently in the past his father has given him a rule-utilitarian justification of the practice of never lying. The justification points to the good consequences of everyone's following the rule—namely, harmony and trust among people. In this view, the right thing is always to tell the truth, owing to the general utility of the rule that requires it. Yet the father is now suggesting that the general utility of such a practice should be subordinated to consideration of the consequences of a particular lie, which he recommends his son tell to the slave hunters. He provides an act-utilitarian justification of the lie by pointing out the likely bad consequences for the fugitives and himself if the truth is told. It turns out, then, that the boy misinterpreted his father's intended meaning in originally justifying the rule against lying. It was only apparently, but not actually, a rule-utilitarian defense of the practice of telling the truth. A true rule utilitarian would hold that there can be no exceptions to the rules once they have been shown to be useful.

An act utilitarian need not dismiss talk of moral rules as altogether pointless. Rather, in the act-utilitarian view, moral rules can be understood as having a place in morality as handy guides. They are viewed as rules of thumb—aids to decision making when one is in circumstances that greatly resemble earlier ones where similar decisions were made. However, all such rules are subject to suspension, especially when circumstances arise unlike those to which the rule ordinarily has been applied. In the case study the ordinarily reliable and useful rule against lying is suspended, and the focus is upon the utility of the particular act of lying in the unique circumstances that the son might confront— namely, talking to slave hunters.

9:1.2 In summary, then, the usefulness of performing *particular* actions is quite distinct from the usefulness of functioning with a set of moral rules that require or prohibit specified *kinds* of action. It is on this point that the distinction between act and rule utilitarianism turns. It is quite possible that they could require different actions, as illustrated in the case study, where rule utilitarianism requires telling the truth but act utilitarianism dictates the lie.

9:1.3 Critics who have looked closely at both the act and rule interpretations of utilitarian theory have detected what they take to be difficulties in determining which view is most plausible. The difficulty with act utilitarianism is that the wrongness of breaking promises, killing, and the like turns out to be nothing more than a matter of statistical generalization, which is false in given cases. That is, act utilitarians view moral rules as not really binding upon human conduct. Rather, they regard rules as usually reliable guides to behavior that have grown out of past calculations of the consequences of particular actions. Rules, so conceived, are at best a practical shorthand in decision making but in no way morally authoritative. This strikes many as an implausible interpretation of the place of rules in normative theory and practice.

On the other hand, in the rule-utilitarian view it turns out that at times it is actually right to do things that can be known in advance not to have the best possible consequences. It is puzzling how a view that

would judge human conduct in terms of its conducing to good consequences could ever sanction doing things that are known not to maximize the good.

The case study illustrates both of these difficulties. The son experiences difficulty in understanding the place of rules in morality when
his father suggests that a moral rule can readily be set aside in particular
circumstances, where following the rule would not maximize the good.
On the other hand, there is genuine implausibility in supposing that
the rule against lying, however useful the general practice of telling the
truth might be, should be observed. A violation of the rule would, in
the case at hand, prevent significantly bad consequences. How could a
utilitarian require that one tell the truth to a slave hunter, when lying
to the slave hunter was known to result in better consequences?

9:2.1 Foreseeable and Unforeseeable Consequences. A second
complication in the interpretation of utilitarian theory is whether utilitarians would hold people responsible for the actual or merely the foreseeable consequences of their conduct. On one view, what has been
called one's *objective duty* is to perform those actions or adopt those
practices that actually turn out to produce the best possible balance of
good compared to bad. In this view, all the foreseeable and unforeseeable consequences of actions and practices are to be taken into account
in the ultimate retrospective evaluation of their rightness and wrongness. The point made by the concept of objective duty is that, at least in
the utilitarian view, what makes an action right is its actual consequences, regardless of whether they are foreseen and regardless of
whether they are intended.

Since, however, many future circumstances cannot be foreseen, one
may clearly fail to do one's objective duty—yet it would not seem reasonable to count such a failure as one warranting blame. How could the
agent be blamed, the argument goes, for what could not be foreseen?
Out of the acceptance of this argument has grown the concept of one's
subjective duty. By definition, one's subjective duty is to perform those
actions, or adopt those practices, that are likely to produce the best
balance of good compared to bad foreseeable future consequences. In
this view, people are to be praised or blamed on the basis of the rational
quality of their planning and their decisions, not on the basis of unforeseeable but actual results. If it turns out that, owing to unforeseeable
turns of events, one's best calculations are mistaken, one is not to blame
for any undesirable unforeseen consequences, even if one fails to live up
to one's objective duty. To fail at the time of deliberation to take into
account foreseeable consequences would probably result in a failure to
perform one's objective duty. It would also be a failure to do one's sub-

jective duty, and such failure would warrant censure on utilitarian grounds.

In the case study the consequences discussed are foreseeable. It is possible to predict that the fugitives will get away and the family will be spared future trouble if the lie is told. It is also possible to predict that the fugitives will be captured and the family endangered if the truth is told. The father, then, is doing his subjective duty in taking into account the important and foreseeable consequences of the alternatives involved. It may turn out, however, that each of the fugitives on reaching freedom will become a murderous criminal who commits a series of heinous crimes. If so, then aiding them in their escape will turn out to have consequences far worse than those of turning them over to the slave hunters, so that protecting the slaves turns out to be contrary to objective duty. However, such consequences are unforeseeable and not of the sort for which the father or the son should reasonably be held responsible. In failing to take into account unlikely and unforeseeable consequences there is no failure of subjective duty.

This distinction between objective and subjective duty is important to utilitarians. Utilitarians aim at evaluating every action by appeal to actual consequences; they are forced to say that a person does wrong whenever he or she fails to do his or her objective duty. But if the bad consequences are unforeseeable, utilitarians can agree with many others that a person should not be held responsible, praised or blamed, for what he or she could not foresee and, thus, could not rationally intend or avoid.

9:3.1 Contemporary Economic Utilitarianism. One of the problems most frequently posed in reflection upon classical utilitarianism centers upon the proposed calculation of either pleasure (pain) or happiness (unhappiness). In our everyday talk it is plausible to speak of greater or lesser pleasures and pains. Likewise, it is plausible to speak of our lives, or periods of our lives, as being extremely happy, very happy, relatively happy, relatively unhappy, very unhappy, or extremely unhappy. This talk reflects a basis in our everyday experience for a rough concept of pleasure (pain) and happiness (unhappiness) as varying in quantity. Yet the introduction of precise calculation, involving the assignment of units of value to pleasure and pain, happiness and unhappiness, strikes many as simply a practical impossibility. Thus, the usefulness of utilitarian theory itself is called into question. We might concede to utilitarians that pleasure (pain) and happiness (unhappiness) are normatively important considerations in ethics and social philosophy; that is, utilitarians are theoretically right about the kinds of things that make actions and practices right or wrong. Yet there remains a large stumbling block in the path toward practical application of the theory unless these problems of quantification and measure are solved.

9:3.2 The practice in contemporary economics of cost-benefit analysis can be understood as a partial response to this difficulty of classical utilitarianism. Whereas it is difficult to calculate over pleasure (pain) or happiness (unhappiness), it is easy to calculate over monetary gain and loss. Cost-benefit analysis is precisely such a calculating procedure, through which it seems possible to generate clearly objective characterizations of the consequences of actions and policies. Although economists would not pretend that economic profit and loss are the whole story of the goodness and badness of consequences, they are convinced that monetary quantification is at least part of the story. They believe it unlikely that we can develop a single calculation procedure for evaluating all the factors contributing to the goodness or badness of consequences. They believe, however, that we should proceed to use and refine procedures, such as cost-benefit analysis, that yield objective results pertaining to at least some of those contributing factors.

Cost-benefit analysis may be briefly outlined as follows. First, the probable costs and benefits of an action or policy are listed—not only such things as developmental costs, the expenses of developing and marketing a product, but also the social costs, such as the cost of air pollution in terms of bad health and doctor bills. Second, a dollar price tag is assigned to each of these costs and benefits. Third, the propinquity of the consequences—how soon the costs or benefits are going to accrue—is brought into play. Propinquity is taken to be very important in economics. Because the costs and benefits are monetary, we can say that if the benefit comes sooner than the costs, then one can increase the value of that benefit by the interest one can gain on it before the costs must be paid. The fourth and final step of cost-benefit analysis is to subtract the costs from the benefits in order to define the margin of either profit or loss. This procedure can be followed with a number of alternative actions or policies, and the preferable one, according to economic utilitarianism, is the one that brings the greatest profit, or at least the smallest loss.

Exercises for Module 9: Complications of Utilitarianism

1. To say that a person owns some property is not merely to say that it is his or her possession, but that he or she is entitled to it. The owner of property is generally entitled to use his or her property as he or she sees fit. In our society people own houses, cars, boats, pets, and clothes. They buy food and fuel.

    a. What usefulness does our society's practice of allowing private ownership of property have?

    b. Can you define stealing in relation to a person's right to own?

    c. How would a rule utilitarian explain the wrongness of stealing? (9:1.2)

    d. Describe a case in which stealing might seem right despite the rule utilitarian's argument.

    e. How would an act utilitarian explain the wrongness of stealing?

    f. Why is the act-utilitarian view of the wrongness of stealing implausible? (9:1.3)

2. *a*. Why would a utilitarian probably say that a person scarcely ever does the right thing?

    b. In light of this, how does the concept of subjective duty allow the utilitarian to avoid blaming people for continually acting wrongly? (9:2.1)

    c. Describe a case in which a person's objective and subjective duty diverge.

3. *a*. The following is a cost-benefit exercise. Your instructions are (1) to pick out the costing items and the benefits to the homebuyer, (2) to associate the correct dollar figures with each costing or benefiting item, and (3) to identify the quantities in the exercise which measure the factor of propinquity. You need not calculate the costs and benefits.

Cost-Benefit Exercise

Homebuilders, Inc., has designed two houses that you are considering buying next summer. The houses are identical except for their heating systems. The first has a conventional furnace and electric heat; the second house is designed to use solar power as its main heat source, backed up by a small, conventional furnace with electric heat. The houses, exclusive of heating systems, are designed to sell for $39,000. The furnace for the first house will cost an additional $1,000. The smaller furnace for the second house will cost only $500, but the solar collection system will cost $5,500. Electricity to heat the first home will cost $750 for the first winter. The electric cost to heat the second home will be 10 percent of the cost to heat the first home in any given year. You will put 20 percent down on either home, and the mortgage will cost you 9 percent interest for 25 years. If you were opening a certificate-of-deposit savings account, the bank would be willing to pay you 7 percent on your savings. The cost of electricity will rise 20 percent at the end of every third year.

    b. Any process that requires a balanced input and output can be subject to cost-benefit analysis if the inputs and outputs can be quantified. For instance, if the digestive system used more energy digesting food (cost) than the energy released (benefit), then the organism would die. This idea applied to business yields the idea of profit and loss. What is the application of this idea to (1) an electric energy-producing plant? (2) an educational system?

Selected Answers to Exercises for Module 9

1. *a.* Property provides *security* by assuring persons that they will have what they have expected to have and have legitimately acquired.
    b. Stealing is violating a property right by exercising control over something that another person has the right to control.
    c. Stealing is wrong, the rule utilitarian would say, because it disrupts the security maintained in *a*. This security is important in society, for example, so that Person X can rely on Person Y when Y wants to use his property as collateral in obtaining a loan or securing a contract. Without security, trust is difficult; without trust, cooperation is difficult; without cooperation, life is difficult or impossible.
    e. The act utilitarian would say stealing is wrong because the penalty for the thief, if caught, and the owner's loss of the property, together are usually worse than the good the thief gains from the stolen item.
2. *a.* Almost all actions have unforeseeable consequences, some of which are bad. Usually, the utilitarian would argue, some adjustment in any act you actually did would have produced a better balance of good over bad consequences.
    c. Such a case is, essentially, one in which the act with the best balance of foreseeable consequences differs from the one with the best balance of actual consequences.
3. *a.* (1) The costs of the house without heat and of the alternative heating systems—that is, the costs of the down payments and the costs of the mortgages (principal plus interest), the costs of heating. If you have the money for the down payment on the more expensive, solar house, you can reap the benefit of interest on a savings account by buying the cheaper house.
    (2) Cost of the houses – $39,000
    Heating systems – $1,000 or $6,000
    *Down payments – 20 percent of $40,000 or $45,000
    Mortgages – $32,000 or $36,000, plus 9 percent interest in either case
    *Heating – $750 or $75 per year for three years
    – $980 or $90 per year for years 4–6, and so on
    *Savings – $1,000 plus 7 percent interest, compounded indefinitely
    (3) Propinquity is involved in all starred lines.

b. (1) Net energy *equals* energy produced by generating plant *minus* energy used to produce energy.

(2) Net knowledge and abilities *equals* knowledge and abilities gained by students *minus* knowledge and abilities of teachers used to teach students. (But given some theories of education the teachers may expend energy, but they gain knowledge and ability through practicing their art. Thus the gross could also be knowledge and abilities gained by students *plus* knowledge and abilities gained by teachers. If these could be reduced to dollars, we might then get the "net" by subtracting the dollar costs of physical resources, salaries for teachers and staff people, and lost hours of wages for students who are studying rather than working for pay.)

FREEDOM

Freedom is a central concept of normative philosophy. In this cluster you will explore freedom in its relationship both to responsibility and to the question, "Exactly what characteristics make freedom valuable?"

Freedom relates to questions of responsibility. How can people be held responsible for what they do if they are not free to act otherwise? Questions of responsibility depend on how freedom is understood and indeed on whether or not agents can be said to be free. Module 10 responds to these issues by outlining the "Dilemma of Determinism." Module 11 presents the concept of autonomy and discusses the conditions under which people might rightly be said to be autonomous and, so, presumably responsible for what they do. The relationship between personal autonomy and the freedom-vs.-determinism controversy is spelled out in Module 12.

A second important normative concern related to freedom involves the precise nature and limits of freedom within society. Although freedom is almost universally valued, there are vast differences in what is meant by "being free" and in what justifications are given for limiting a person's freedom. Module 11 introduces the distinction between positive and negative freedom. Module 12 explains several of the more prominent theories of punishment. Module 13 details five alternative proposed justifications for limiting a person's freedom. The educational goal of this cluster is to explain the role of the concept of freedom in such normative questions as the nature and limits of personal responsibility and social autonomy.

MODULE 10
THE DILEMMA OF DETERMINISM

Almost everyone will agree that it is senseless to hold people morally responsible for what they do if they cannot do otherwise. If they are not free to actually select what they will or will not do, how can they be praised or blamed for what happens? We do frequently hold people responsible for their actions, praise and blame them. Yet are people free? Given all that we know about hereditary, environmental, and psychological influences on behavior, is any person ever really free? The "hard determinists" say no, the "libertarians" say yes, and some try to argue a middle position. This module examines the tension between freedom and determinism. It presents the issue, stakes out the basic positions and lists the standard objections to each. After reading Module 10, you should be able to

- Define and contrast the positions of hard determinism, soft determinism, and libertarianism.
- Distinguish the claims that would be made by hard determinists, soft determinists, and libertarians in provided examples.
- Explain why determinism constitutes a dilemma for freedom and responsibility.
- State the major objections raised against hard determinism, soft determinism, and libertarianism.
- Given a human action, describe it as it would be seen by a hard determinist, a soft determinist, and a libertarian.

THE CASE OF AMY HOLDEN

The defense attorney rose and approached the jury. Her face was composed, almost stoic. She spoke without emotion. "We all agree that the defendant, Amy Holden, went boating with the deceased, Thomas Shaw. They had gone out on Lake Erie many times, but this time Shaw was killed. The autopsy shows that he was shot to death and then was pushed, or fell, into the lake. Amy admits she shot him. But she did not commit premeditated murder because she was not free. I'm not sure that I, nor anyone else, can detail all the causes that led Amy to shoot

Shaw. But here are some. Her act was caused in part by her guilt and depression over the accidental death of her two children, which she feels was her fault. Also, she was always prone to respond violently to crisis situations and she claims that on this particular trip Shaw made sexual advances. Her emotional instability was further increased by the fact that she had been fighting a heroin problem more or less unsuccessfully for five years. She comes from a broken home. She never graduated from high school and has never been able to hold a job more than six months. For a brief time her life seemed to be making sense. But then, along came Shaw and his free-spending ways. In a month he was dead, her children were dead, and she was back on heroin. She shot him, yes, but she could not have avoided pulling that trigger. Her whole biology, her whole history, these caused Shaw's death. She could only have acted as she did. Her act was as unavoidable and inevitable as the falling of rain to earth. She could not help herself at that moment."

With equal calm and force of personality the prosecuting attorney, in his turn, addressed the jury. "Amy Holden killed Thomas Shaw. It's as simple as that. She did not use heroin that day; no, she did not resume her habit till one week after the killing. She went out with Shaw intending to force him into a hasty marriage. She was already pregnant by him. He was rich and she wanted his money. He refused, he laughed at her. She pulled her gun from her purse and threatened suicide. When he laughed that off, she turned the gun on Shaw and shot him. She was not forced by history or biology, she acted freely and she is guilty of murder."

10:1.1 The Dilemma. The problem of whether or not people are free, in some morally relevant sense of "free," has traditionally been posed as a dilemma.

PREMISE (a)   Either every event is caused or some human choices are not caused.

PREMISE (b)   If every event has causes, then human choices, being events, are caused.

PREMISE (c)   If all human choices are caused, they cannot be other than they are.

PREMISE (d)   If no human choices can, or could, be altered, then people are not free.

PREMISE (e)   If human choices are not caused, then they are random.

PREMISE (f)   If human choices are random, then people do not have control over their choices.

PREMISE (g)   If either people are not free, or people cannot control their own choices, then they are not morally responsible for what they do.

CONCLUSION: So, people are not morally responsible for what they do.

This typical statement of the dilemma shows the traditionally expressed connections between believing that events are all caused and believing that people are not free. Similarly, it shows how believing that choices are uncaused leads to the view that they are random and, so, people cannot be held morally accountable for them.

10:1.2   If you wished to avoid the conclusion of this dilemma you would be forced to argue either that the argument is logically faulty or that one or more of its premises are false. Many have challenged various of its premises. For example, some philosophers have argued that premise (b) is false. They distinguish human actions from physical events. In so doing they can maintain the scientific belief that all events are caused but maintain that human actions are not caused. A variation on that theme is the view that human actions are self-caused in the sense that humans are self-determining beings, whereas all other beings or events in nature are more or less interconnected causally. Another challenge might be mounted against premise (e) by arguing that human choices are not random, even if they are uncaused.

Although few have attacked the dilemma as illogical, it may be possible to show that crucial ambiguities in the concepts of "causality," "event," "choice," "custom," and, most centrally, "free" actually mislead us into accepting this argument when we should not. If these terms are ambiguous or vague in ways that affect the logic of the argument, then pointing out these conceptual problems could lead to the dissolution of the dilemma. For example, some people maintain that by training and education we are taught to make rational choices, and so, in a sense, we are conditioned or caused to act freely.

If you accept the argument, you may find some difficulty trying to decide what the causal conditions of human choices are. Do you look to heredity, psychology, character, physical environment, social environment, divine intervention, human desires, or what as the causes of human actions? If you do not accept the argument, on what do you base your rejection? Most of the historical debate focuses on these three statements:

(1) Every event has a cause.
(2) At least some human choices are free.
(3) If every event has a cause, then no human choices are free.

10:2.1 Determinism.   Determinism is the philosophical thesis that for every event there is some set of causal conditions such that, given these conditions, no other event could occur. This thesis is one of the oldest and most forceful in human intellectual history. It led to the growth of science, because it was the bedrock upon which the scientific hope of predicting nature was built. It is not the kind of thesis that can be confirmed or disconfirmed by a single set of experiences. Rather, it is one of the most central beliefs of human experience.

To grasp how central this belief is, contrast the following two arguments:

(A) People have looked for unicorns for years and have never found any. Therefore, probably there are no unicorns.

(B) People have looked for causes of cancer for years and have never found them. Therefore, probably cancer does not have causes.

Notice that although these arguments are structurally similar, Argument (A) appears quite sensible while (B) does not. The reason may well be the strength of belief in universal causality. Some philosophers suggest that the contrast between (A) and (B) shows that "Every event has a cause" is not an assertion capable of being shown false. It is the kind of thesis that may be denied in one form only to be reexpressed and embraced in another. In ancient philosophical traditions the thesis of determinism was manifest in divine power to know the truth or falsity of all statements, even those about future events. In the scholastic tradition it reappeared in the conflict between predestination and free choice. Physical determination dominated scientific thinking at least until the twentieth century and the advent of the physics of subatomic particles. Developments in contemporary psychology and biochemistry lend strong support to some version of the deterministic hypothesis as it applies to human behavior.

10:2.2   A determinist is, by definition, one who accepts statement (1) in 10:1.2: "Every event has a cause." In so doing, some determinists will deny (2) and accept (3), while others will accept (2) and deny (3). *Hard determinists* accept (1) and believe it entails that people cannot help but be as they are. Being physical objects involved in the space-time causal nexus, humans, like any other animals, act as they do on the basis of those conditions that determine their lives. Whatever those conditions are—physical, social, psychological, or what have you, known or unknown—they totally determine what each human being will do. The hard determinists argue that there is no such thing as a free choice. Like all determinists they point to science's successes in explaining and predicting human behavior as increasing the weight of evidence in support of their position. We are, they argue, beyond talk of freedom and talk of dignity; we should talk the language of behavior modification. Our concern should not be so much with praise or blame, but with modification and control. We should positively reinforce desired behaviors and negatively reinforce undesirable ones, attaching no moral stigma to either.

10:2.3   *Soft determinists* accept statement (1) but reject statement (3) and, in so doing, accept (2). That is, they try to develop a middle position that acknowledges the scientific determinism of (1) and also the moral freedom of (2). To accomplish this they must find some reason to reject the statement that expresses their incompatibility: statement (3). Soft determinists argue that when people are able to choose rationally and/or without being compelled or coerced into a given choice, then they are free, even though their choices are caused. In other words, the soft determinists argue that choices are caused, perhaps by our desires or character traits or even our habitual tendencies, but that these factors are compatible with calling choices free. Some soft determinists would insist that to be called free our choices must be made rationally with full consciousness of what we are doing, with deliberate consideration of the pros and cons of the issue at hand. Other soft determinists emphasize that to be free, people must not be coerced, that there be no constraining factors, such as overwhelming fear or hallucinatory drugs, that mitigate freedom. In favor of their position soft determinists argue that the scientific evidence in favor of determinism in general also supports soft determinism but that soft determinism is also compatible with our moral practices and our intuitions about deliberative choice. The appeal to intuitions forms the major argument for the third major position on this issue.

10:2.4   *Libertarianism* is the view that human choices are uncaused, free actions (or events). Thus, libertarians affirm statement (2) of 10:1.2. They accept (3) and deny (1). The major support for the libertarian position is drawn from our intuitions about our experiences of free choice. We all experience times of deliberation as we consider alternative courses of action or weigh our options. We weigh our options without knowing exactly what we should do in all cases and without fully knowing all the consequences of our choices. Most importantly, we experience the moment of decision. We are aware of choosing an alternative, of selecting an option. We, libertarians argue, describe ourselves as free.

Rather distinct from this line of reasoning, libertarians advance the second argument that we have the experience of being tempted and we have the ability to resist temptation, regardless of whether a given person usually does resist or usually gives in to temptation. As the libertarian sees it, the ability to resist temptations shows that human actions are not caused. The libertarian argues that if determinism were right, then the events that are the causes of human actions would be like desirable impulses that tempt us in a certain direction. Therefore, our ability to resist temptation seems, to the libertarian, to be evidence of our ability not to act on what, if anything, could be described by the determinists as the causes of human action.

Both of these arguments invoke the idea of the will. As the libertarian sees it, we experience ourselves, in the moment of decision, as freely willing one course of action. We do not experience our wills as compelled or caused. Similarly, in the resistance of temptation, we experience our own, uncaused willpower exerting itself against the causal tendencies of habit and impulse we also experience. The similarity between these two libertarian arguments is that, as the libertarian sees it, both point to the freedom of the will, which the libertarian sees as basic to human freedom.

A third argument sometimes advanced by libertarians is related to the concept of punishment. They maintain that at times people act in the knowledge that what they are doing deserves punishment, but they would not deserve punishment unless they acted freely, hence they must be acting freely.

Go back to the case study now and review the two positions presented by the two lawyers. It should be easy to identify the hard determinist and the libertarian. You should spend a moment closely reviewing the prosecution and the defense, listing the libertarian and the determinist considerations advanced in their speeches.

10:3.1 Objections to Each View. The standard objection to both the hard determinist and the libertarian positions is that each fails to critically examine the connection between caused events and human choices alleged in statement (3) of 10:1.2. This objection is the spawning ground of the soft-determinist position. Against the libertarians the hard determinists point to the successes of science. Against the hard determinists the libertarians point to our intuitive experiences of free choice. Both seem to leave the soft-determinist position unchallenged. In a sense the hard determinist and the libertarian in attacking each other simply assume that soft determinism is false; neither shows that it is.

However, strong objections have been voiced against soft determinism. It would seem that in the soft-determinist view a person is both free and yet unable to avoid his or her choice. The notion of freedom advanced by the soft determinist appears to be either inconsistent or irrelevant to the moral issue at hand. The notion of freedom thought to be relevant to the moral question is the idea that a person is free to act differently than he or she does. For example, suppose you choose to go to a movie rather than watch television. The morally relevant sense of freedom is that you could have chosen the other option—to watch television and not go to the movie. In the soft-determinist view we are, apparently, denied this concept of freedom. Although free, we could not have acted in any way other than we did. The objection is that this is not the notion of free choice we find morally relevant.

Exercises for Module 10: The Dilemma of Determinism

1. Below are three assertions. Hard determinism, soft determinism, and libertarianism are distinguished as positions by their acceptance and rejection of different ones of these assertions. In the column marked *HD* put a T next to each assertion accepted by the hard determinist as true. Put T's similarly in the columns marked *SD* and *L* for the soft determinists and libertarians, respectively. (10:1.2, 10:2.1–10:2.4) 10:2.4)

$$\underline{HD} \quad \underline{SD} \quad \underline{L}$$

   Every event has a cause.
   Some human actions are free.
   If every event has a cause, then no human actions
      are free.

2. Define hard determinism, soft determinism, and libertarianism as positions simply by reference to which of the above assertions each accepts as true and which each rejects as false. (10:2.1–10:2.4)

3. Below is the statement of a typical human decision, followed by a series of claims that hard determinists, soft determinists, or libertarians might want to make in support or in defense of their respective positions. After you read the case, mark each of the claims true or false for each position: *HD, SD,* and *L*. (10:2.2)

Terri Terahan struggled with herself. She knew time was short and she would soon need to decide and act. She greatly wanted to go to the Whosits concert. They were her favorite group and she had a keen appreciation of their music. She had promised, however, to help in the final preparations for homecoming. Now the Whosits concert had been scheduled, unexpectedly, for the night before homecoming. Terri could not possibly help finish the homecoming preparations and also attend the concert. She knew her friends were counting on her and she knew she'd deserve their censure if she disappointed them. Finally Terri decided. Going to the concert was a great temptation, she would certainly enjoy it more than the alternative.

But Terri had made a promise, so she summoned up her willpower, resisted the temptation, and, true to her word, she helped prepare for the home-coming.

$$HD \quad SD \quad L$$

a. Terri had apparently been strongly conditioned to do her duty.

b. Terri freely decided because she carefully and calmly thought her way through to her conclusion.

c. The ability to resist temptation to do what would please her most marks Terri's will as free.

d. The experiences of temptation and resisting temptation are also simply experiences of tension between two choices that are close to being equally attractive to a person of a given conditioning.

e. Even if Terri were conditioned to be rational implies her being free.

f. The assertion Terri knew she would be blameworthy if she did not help with homecoming preparations makes sense; it would not unless Terri were free. So indeed she must be free.

4. Given the answers to Exercise 3 and your knowledge of hard determinism, soft determinism, and libertarianism, rewrite the Terri Terahan narrative three times, using the perspectives of each of the three positions and emphasizing what each would view as central and crucial.

5. a. What are the apparent, unhappy consequences with respect to freedom and with respect to responsibility, if determinism is true? (10:1.1)

b. What are the apparent, unhappy consequences with respect to freedom and with respect to responsibility, if determinism is false?

c. Use the definition of a dilemma and your answers to a and b to explain why determinism constitutes a dilemma for free will and responsibility.

6. State the major objections raised against hard determinism, soft determinism, and libertarianism. (10:3.1)

Selected Answers to Exercises for Module 10

	HD	*SD*	*L*
1. Every event has a cause.	T	T	—
Some human actions are free.	—	T	T
If every event has a cause, then no human actions are free.	T	—	T

2. Hard determinism is the view that every event has a cause and that if every event has a cause then no human actions are free.

Soft determinism is the view that every event has a cause and that some human actions are free.

Libertarianism is the view that some human actions are free and that if every event has a cause then no human actions are free.

(All three of these definitions could be expanded by adding that each position denies the third statement not listed in the above definitions.)

3. Statements *a* and *d* would be made by hard determinists and might be made by soft determinists.

Statements *b* and *e* would be made by soft determinists.

Statements *c* and *f* would be made by libertarians. A soft determinist might also agree with *f*, but it does not help to establish the compatibility of freedom and causality.

5. If determinism is true, it would seem that no action is free, since, it would seem, no one could ever do other than what he or she did.

If determinism is false, it would seem that no action is free, since, it would seem, all human behavior would be random, none self-determined.

If it is true either that no one could ever do other than what he or she did or that all human behavior is random, then, it would seem, no one is ever responsible for what he or she does.

Module 11
AUTONOMY

A person can be said to be autonomous if he or she acts rationally and acts without constraint. This idea was first presented in the discussion of soft determinism in 10:2.3. In Module 11 we will more carefully define the notion of autonomy by analyzing the ideas of acting rationally and without constraint. This leads to the distinction between positive freedom and negative freedom later in the module. After reading Module 11, you should be able to

- Describe cases of acting rationally and irrationally.
- Describe cases of acting under various kinds of constraints.

- Define being autonomous.
- Distinguish examples of positive and negative freedom.
- Define positive and negative freedom.
- Give examples of autonomous actions and of positive and negative freedom.

THE CASE OF CINDY SMOKER

"Look," Cindy began, "I'm eighteen now and there is no law against my buying or smoking cigarettes."

"You're right, Cindy, but tell me, why do you want to smoke?" replied her father. "I don't plan to forbid you to smoke. I want you to consider your health and to decide for yourself."

"My health is fine and I don't believe all that business about cancer and heart attacks. Anyway, it's my choice isn't it? If I want to decide to risk those dangers I can. You cannot legislate what people do with their own health."

"I'm not sure about that. We require all kinds of safety devices on cars, we require young people to go to school and we teach them personal hygiene, we prohibit the sale of many dangerous drugs, we even outlaw suicide!"

"Well, that's different. Here I'm talking about rationally deciding that I want to smoke—it's my own choice."

"Maybe it is, but did you ever stop to consider how you might be influenced by advertising or even by a desire to assert your own will now that you are nearly an adult?"

"Nearly an adult! I am an adult and I'm gonna smoke if I want to. And that's it!"

"Well, Cindy, I think I understand. Go ahead and smoke if you want to."

11:1.1 The Concept of Autonomy. There are two aspects to being an autonomous individual: exercising one's rationality in making decisions, and being free from coercion and constraint both in making decisions and in acting on them. Indeed, we can define being autonomous in terms of being rational and being unconstrained. If a person chooses rationally and without constraint and then acts without constraint, then he or she is acting autonomously. Cindy, in the case study, seems to be capable of acting autonomously. She is old enough to deliberate about her choices and rationally decide between them. She is free from the obvious forms of external constraint such as legal or parental prohibition and the influence of drugs or medications. But assessing autonomy, even autonomy relative to certain questions at certain times, is a complex business. Let us look briefly at the two conditions for autonomous choice.

11:1.2 *Being rational* about one's choices involves a number of factors: (a) one must express one's goals at least to oneself and (b) prioritize those goals for oneself, (c) one must identify the means available to achieving these goals, (d) one must anticipate the possible and probable consequences, both intended and unintended, of employing these means, and (e) if the available means are either too inadequate or too likely to cause very undesirable consequences, one must assess the possibilities both of developing further means and of abandoning or revising the goal. All these factors must receive their due place in any rational decision. Is Cindy in the case study being rational? She seems to know her options, which are to smoke or not; however, she does not make the distinctions one could make concerning how much to smoke, whether to smoke filter tips or not, or whether to smoke only for a short time as an experiment. She seems unwilling to acknowledge the possible adverse consequences of smoking. There is some question about what her goals really are. Does she want to smoke because she thinks she'll like it or because she wants to assert her adulthood and individuality? Since her goals are not clear, she seems not to have explored other ways to achieve them; nor has she, in what we read, examined the small financial commitment necessary to take up and continue smoking. We have to say that, as presented, she is not acting rationally.

There are many ways that one can diminish or undermine one's own rationality. To act on the basis of bias or emotion, to be stubborn or noncommittal, to be unable to infer the consequences of options, to be unable to maintain attention on the issue at hand, to fail to become informed of available data affecting the probable outcomes of one's action, all of these make one's decisions less rational. Sometimes these threats to rationality come from the person's own shortcomings, such as possessing underdeveloped logical abilities or allowing oneself to act on biases and unquestioned prejudice. Other threats are external. Too many distractions or too little time can both prevent one from fully examining the consequences of all available options.

Not being informed of all relevant information can lead even a rational person to unreasonable decisions. Being ignorant can be a function of one's own inability or unwillingness to learn. It can be a result of some form of denial of the truth, as was the case with Cindy's refusal to believe the facts about smoking and health. Ignorance can also result from being deceived or from being cut off from information. False or misleading advertising can yield crucial misinformation and lead people to irrational choices, even if at the time of decision the people act rationally, given the information, however misleading, that was available to them. Propaganda, government secrecy, and censored news reports also have generally negative effects on decision making. Democracy is predicated upon people's ability to make rational choices. Governmental or institutional or corporate practices that deceive, misinform, or withhold vital information undermine the possibility of rational choices. The instrumental value of a free press in a democratic society derives from its ability to provide the information people need to make rational choices without itself being gagged by legal sanctions or prohibitions. Similarly, adequate education to ensure a logical and literate public is necessary if the information is to be used to full advantage by voters. For democracy to work, the press should be largely free from constraints so it can provide information. Also, the public should be constrained or forced to be educated so that it can rationally use that information. These normative positions raise questions about whether, indeed, one should ever be forced to be more rational. More detailed treatment of this basic issue is provided in Module 13.

11:1.3   *Being unconstrained* in one's choices, both in one's deliberating and in one's acting, is the other aspect of being autonomous. The concept of rationality sketched in 11:1.2 carries a requirement that the person have a more or less full and accurate understanding of the situation and its limitations. This sense of not being constrained from a realistic appraisal of the circumstances of one's decision is built into the deliberative process. The concept of *constraint,* then, includes both (a) conditions that prevent persons from finding certain courses of action to be rational, though they might otherwise find them so, and (b) conditions that come into play after the decision that prevent persons from doing what they have rationally decided to do. Type (a) constraints are the limitations that one must take into account as one decides rationally what to do. Constraints of type (b) are unforeseeable limitations, which cannot, therefore, be taken into account in the deliberative process.

At least three kinds of constraint can come into play *either before or after decisions* are made. First, there are absences or insufficiencies of the means to carry out the actions, which thereby prevent our action. You may wish to travel, yet realize you have no money or vehicle to transport you. Or you may decide to travel and, before you can go, encounter unusual additional expenses or lose your car through an accident. A second type of obstacle is the imposition of coercive force by others. Such coercive force itself comes in many varieties. One may be *physically* constrained, or one may be coerced by a *threat* of harm or injury. Such constraints or coercions, to be effective, will involve some sort of power, which may be that of a legitimate authority or may be completely illegitimate and unscrupulous. You may wish to do something but decide not to, either because you have found a law against it or you are threatened with injury by a bully. Or you may decide to do something and then either discover that a new law is passed prohibiting it or discover a threatening note from a suspicious source warning against doing it. Third, our physical, biological, or psychological state may constrain us. Such states, or changes in them, can make certain courses of action unreasonable for us or prevent our carrying out rational decisions. A broken leg may prevent your deciding to run a mile to keep in shape. Or, after you have decided to go on a picnic, a recurrence of an old allergy may prevent your going.

Go back over the case study. Was Cindy constrained by factors that fall into any of these categories? She does not seem to lack the financial resources necessary to begin smoking. Parental prohibition and legal constraints are explicitly removed. She does not seem to be compelled by a nicotine addiction or by a psychological need to smoke. Her father does not seem to be trying to manipulate her emotionally to prevent her from implementing her decision. She seems, then, to be free from constraint and coercion as she considers her decision. Perhaps, however, there are deeper psychological forces operative in her relationship to her father and in her self-image as a late adolescent or young adult that influence her in ways that are not in the forefront of her consciousness.

11:2.1 Forms of Freedom. To gain additional perspective on the nature and significance of autonomy, we shall discuss what philosophers have sought to distinguish as "positive" and "negative" freedom. Some say that positive freedom is "freedom to" behave in certain ways, while negative freedom is "freedom from" certain constraints. Their distinction turns on the use of the key words "to" and "from." So, freedom to worship as one wishes would be a positive freedom, freedom from fear a negative freedom. Others find this way of making the distinction to be of little use, because by rewriting various expressions you can change a positive freedom, such as the "freedom *to* worship" into a negative freedom, "the freedom *from* constraints upon one's religious practice."

A second way of distinguishing positive and negative freedom is to associate negative freedom with freedom from constraint or coercion and positive freedom with specific spheres of activity and individual liberty. This approach grew out of the same British traditions of liberal political philosophy that influenced the Declaration of Independence and the Bill of Rights. These traditions express the desirability of personal liberty in the areas of worship, assembly, and speech. One of their chief concerns is to secure personal freedoms by restricting the areas within which civil authority can legitimately function. In our century the spheres of personal liberty or positive freedom can be extended to include the freedom of state employees to form labor unions, and individual freedom to control one's own body in matters concerning its health, safety, and even its life. Some find this way of distinguishing positive and negative freedom problematic. The identification of a sphere of positive freedom is reducible to the identification of a limit to legitimate constraints. In other words, an area of positive freedom is a sphere free from constraint—and so the distinction between positive and negative freedom collapses.

The problem seems to be one of providing for the idea of positive freedom a genuine content that does not ultimately reduce to negative freedom. Let us accept the view that negative freedom is freedom from constraint or coercion. We can define a separate concept of positive freedom by equating it with rational choice or action. This means that one has positive freedom if one is able to engage in the activities listed in 11:1.2: (a) set one's own goals, (b) establish one's priorities, (c) identify the means to achieve one's goals, (d) predict the probable consequences of choices, (e) reassess goals as necessary, and (f) deliberate and choose in the light of the earlier activities. So defined, positive freedom is not always guaranteed by negative freedom (freedom from the kinds of constraint listed in 11:1.3). Cindy in our case study illustrates this point, in that she has negative freedom but seems to lack positive freedom. In our review in 11:1.3 we argued that Cindy was probably free from each of the kinds of constraints. In 11:1.2 we argued that she was, nonetheless, acting at least somewhat irrationally. Her decision, while deliberate and conscious, was not rational for the reasons we gave in 11:1.2.

11:2.2   Let us accept this last way of distinguishing positive and negative freedom. To have positive freedom is to act rationally or be rational. To have negative freedom is to act without constraint or coercion. Thus characterized, to have both positive and negative freedom is, by definition, to be an autonomous individual.

Let us consider an example situation to see how a variety of factors can be introduced that limit either negative or positive freedom. Consider the case of Saul Rosen. Saul, age 25, lives in Denver. Raised as an Orthodox Jew, Saul now wishes to reconsider certain of his religious practices. He wants to decide, for example, whether or not he should eat pork. What factors may limit his negative freedom to do that? He may not be able to acquire pork because it costs too much, it is unavailable, or the food stores are closed when he is free to go to them. Thus the means to implement his goal may not exist. Or, Saul may feel constrained by religious strictures, family traditions, or communal norms not to eat pork; thus an authoritative prohibition may limit his negative freedom. He may not be able to eat pork because he utterly dislikes its taste, because he has allergic reactions to it, or because he has some psychosis about eating pork; thus biological or psychological factors can also limit his negative freedom. Saul may be operating under posthypnotic suggestion not to eat pork, he may have been deliberately misinformed about pork, he may be threatened with loss of his job if he is discovered to have eaten pork. Any of these can operate to manipulate Saul and limit his negative freedom.

Suppose that there are no limits to his negative freedom; does this mean that Saul has the positive freedom to eat pork? No, other factors can limit his positive freedom. Saul may not be able to identify his options; he may, for example, not realize that he can buy pork in any of a variety of convenient quantities and forms ranging from ham, bacon, hot dogs, and sausage to chops, ribs, and roasts. He may not see that one option is to eat a hot dog at the ball park and another is to buy a six-pound roast for a family dinner. He may not be able to predict the possible or probable outcomes of his choice to eat pork. If he brings home a big roast, will that upset his family, considering their religious practices? If he eats a hot dog at the park, will that upset his family? He may not have considered what his goals are. Why does he want to reconsider whether or not to eat pork? What does he hope to gain by such a decision? Is it a matter of trying something new for the experience of it? Does he want to reconsider in order to reevaluate his whole religious life style? What are his more important goals? He may not have given adequate thought to his priorities. Another limit to his positive freedom may be his failure to discover where pork can be conveniently purchased in his neighborhood. He may not have located a store that sells pork and is open when he is able to buy. A final possible limit on his positive freedom may be his inability to deliberate about this question in the light of all the information he has gathered. He may simply not be able to organize his thinking well enough to rationally decide what to do. He may find there are too many variables or too many unknowns for him.

11:2.3 Society can seek to provide the conditions for positive freedom, as discussed in 11:1.2. It can also set limits on freedom, especially on negative freedom. A government can prohibit behavior; it can withdraw the means to achieve certain goals; it can alter living conditions so that doing certain things becomes psychologically or biologically impossible; it can control information flow and use propaganda and economic and political pressure to manipulate choices. Liberal political philosophers have traditionally been concerned to identify areas of personal liberty that should be free from such governmental interventions. They raise the interesting question of how much, if at all, government can rightfully limit a person's negative freedom. Other philosophers ask the question from the other point of view. How much autonomy can be tolerated before the legitimate goals of society can no longer be achieved? (A more thorough discussion of these issues is found in Modules 22 and 23.) Depending upon how far-reachingly you construe these goals, you might find severe limitations on negative freedom acceptable. For example, if one goal is to maintain a well-informed adult electorate, might a government not set severe limits on who can vote, requiring certain minimum levels of intelligence, knowledge, and experience?

Exercises for Module 11: Autonomy

1. Rational decision making involves (1) knowing one's own goals, (2) prioritizing those goals, (3) identifying means to the goals, (4) anticipating consequences of those means, and (5) reassessing one's goals when necessary. (See 11:1.2 for a fuller statement.) Describe five cases of persons making decisions such that each clearly exemplifies a failure to make a rational decision in one of the above five ways.

2. Autonomy involves freedom from constraint both in decision making and in implementing one's decision. (A fuller account of the varieties of constraint is to be found in 11:1.3.) Describe three cases of persons making decisions and three cases of persons implementing decisions such that each of the three kinds of constraints is illustrated twice, once in decision making and once in decision implementation.

3. Define autonomous action. (11:1.1)

4. In each of the following descriptions a person's freedom—positive or negative—is limited or lacking. State which kind of freedom is at issue in each case. Explain your answer by associating limited positive freedom with less than fully rational behavior and limited negative freedom with constraints upon one's decision making. (11:2.1, 11:2.2)

    a. By the time we fought our way through the traffic for three hours, we would have had no time to enjoy ourselves there before we had to head back home.

    b. I wanted a Hoopla-Do hula hoop so much that when I heard the Mart had them I went right down and bought one, even though the Mart is more expensive than the Supermart, which usually has the same items on sale.

    c. After we got registered at the ski lodge, we found we couldn't ski after all, because somebody had stolen our skis while we were registering.

d. I kept trying to think through what I ought to do, but the neighbor's party was so loud I could not concentrate on my problem, and I never really did get to think it through.

e. We started out in the morning with the idea that launching a model rocket might be a pleasant way to spend a spare afternoon. When none of the shops in town had models we liked, we headed for a shop some 25 miles distant. By then it was noon, and they didn't have any either. I guess we knew it would take a couple of hours to build the rocket before we could fly it, but we kept searching. Eventually we went over 125 miles, driving around looking. We found some rockets, but none really struck our fancy. Eventually we got home late, without supper, exhausted, and without even buying a rocket.

f. We spent the whole day building a little decorative fence for Mrs. Taylor, only to find out when we finished that she wanted the fence to keep her big dog in the yard.

g. As I crossed the parking lot toward my car, a man emerged from the shadows, pointed a gun at me, and demanded my money.

h. When I cleaned out my garage, I wanted to set the trash out onto the street immediately, but it wasn't my pickup day, and the city has an ordinance against putting trash on the street before the pickup day.

5. State the definitions of positive and negative freedom.

6. Construct a thorough example of a person acting autonomously. (11:1.2, 11:1.3, 11:2.2)

Answers to Exercises for Module 11

1. Check your descriptions against the account of rational decision making in 11:1.2. Be sure both that each of your examples clearly illustrates one and only one of the failures. Also be sure that each failure is illustrated by one of your cases.

2. Check your descriptions against the account and examples of constraints in 11:1.3. Again, be sure that all six of your examples are clear and that each illustrates only one failure.

3. An action is autonomous when it is implemented unconstrained as the product of deliberation that is itself both rational and unconstrained.

4. a. Negative freedom; traffic constrains their freedom.
   b. Positive freedom; did not seek the means most appropriate to the goal.
   c. Negative freedom; lack of skis prevents implementing decision.
   d. Negative freedom; noise constrains me from concentration and decision making.

e. Positive freedom; did not reassess goal in light of unavailable means. Negative freedom; lack of means compounded by eventual lack of time and energy to continue search. [*Note:* Limits on our negative freedom often lead to extra occasions for the exercise of positive freedom, because they place extra demands on our rationality.]

f. Positive freedom; did not define the goal of action in advance.

g. Negative freedom; coerced by a threat of physical violence.

h. Negative freedom; constrained by the city's authority.

5. See 11:1.2 for the appropriate definitions. You should have these concepts clearly in mind; they are central to Modules 12 and 13.

6. To check the adequacy of your example, go back to the various aspects of the definitions of positive and negative freedom—the various aspects of acting rationally and without constraint—and check to see that each has been incorporated into your example.

Module 12
RESPONSIBILITY AND PUNISHMENT

In Module 11 we developed the concept of a person's being autonomous. Our question for Module 12 is: Under what conditions is an individual to be held responsible for his or her actions? Specifically, are people who are acting autonomously to be held responsible? We shall show how hard determinists, soft determinists, and libertarians would answer that question. We will then relate the concepts of responsibility to the dominant justifications of punishment: the retributive, deterrent, preventive, and rehabilitative theories. After reading Module 12, you should be able to

- State and explain the hard determinist's, soft determinist's, and libertarian's answer to the question, "Are persons acting autonomously to be held morally responsible for what they do?"
- State and explain two possible exceptions to the assertion, "Only persons who act autonomously are responsible for their action."
- Identify examples of retributive, deterrent, preventive, and rehabilitative justifications of punishment.
- Compare and contrast the retributive, deterrent, preventive, and rehabilitative theories of punishment.

THE CASE OF ROMAN FULTON

Roman Fulton was 15 years old when he and Roberta Ackron, age 18, were arrested and charged with first-degree murder. They were found guilty of the ax killing of a family of seven in rural Wayne County,

Michigan. At that time Michigan punished heinous capital offenses by death. Roberta was executed in the electric chair. Roman, who was a minor, was given a life sentence. After six years he earned a high school diploma. He then spent ten years working in the prison laundry and 19 years working in the kitchen. Thirty-four years after his arrest, at age 50, Roman was paroled. At his parole hearing he said that he never fully understood the wrongness of his crime at the time he committed it. The prison officials testified that he had been a model prisoner and was, in their view, fully rehabilitated. Roman Fulton left prison as a middle-aged man who had no family nor any friends outside of prison. He has not been arrested or convicted of any crimes in the four years since his release.

12:1.1 Responsibility and Autonomy. Consider the following statements:

(1) If a person acts autonomously, then he or she is morally responsible for what he or she does.

(2) Only persons who act autonomously are responsible for what they do.

It is possible to maintain that these are both true, both false, or that one is true while the other is false. Each of the four choices has implications for how we should treat practical cases of desirable and undesirable behavior.

Before we explore the truth or falsity of (1) and (2), let us distinguish between being a responsible person and being morally responsible for some specific action. A responsible person is someone who, generally speaking, lives up to or fulfills his or her obligations or responsibilities. Responsibility in a person is thought of, in most cases, as a personality trait like reliability, loyalty, or honesty. On the other hand, to say that a person is morally responsible for something is to say that he or she is worthy or deserving of praise or blame for that event or action. To fix moral responsibility is to assert where praise or blame should appropriately be set. It is thus possible that a responsible or trustworthy person might have no responsibility for some situation. Similarly, an irresponsible person might be responsible for a specific situation. Our question is the relationship of moral responsibility to autonomy.

12:1.2   Soft determinists would say that statement (1) is true. For them the concept of freedom (as developed in 10:2.3) is identified with, or very close to, the concept of autonomy (developed in 11:1.1). Soft determinists would say that if a person chooses rationally and without constraint, then he or she is autonomous and, so, morally responsible. On the other hand, both hard determinists and libertarians would regard (1) as false. Hard determinists would argue that no one can be morally responsible for something unless he or she was free when it was done. But, according to the hard determinist, we are never free in the sense that we could have chosen to act otherwise than we did. (See 10:2.2.) The autonomous person is not free in that sense, so he or she is not morally responsible for what he or she did, acting autonomously. Libertarians argue that acting autonomously does not guarantee being capable of having acted otherwise and, thus, of being responsible. (See 10:2.4.) Libertarians would add one further point. They would argue that at times people do act freely in the morally relevant sense of "free to have done otherwise." They would say that if, when acting autonomously, a person was also acting freely, then in that case he or she would be morally responsible. Any unfree autonomous acts would be acts for which, the libertarians would say, the person is not morally responsible.

12:1.3   Now let us consider statement (2). It asserts that only persons who act autonomously are responsible for what they do. Another way to put that is in terms of its equivalent:

> (2′) A person who does not act autonomously is not morally responsible for what he does.

Our question, then, is whether (2′) is true or false. Most people would be inclined to say that it is true. They would point out that it seems unreasonable to hold someone morally responsible for an act he or she performs either under constraint or irrationally. But others would distinguish these conditions. Some would say that being under a constraint or coercion relieves one of moral responsibility, but they would not allow people who act irrationally to be so easily relieved of moral responsibility. Rather, they would claim that a failure to deliberate rationally, especially where no constraint is operative, is a fault for which people can and should be held morally accountable. One can argue that they can be held morally responsible because they have squandered the opportunity to deliberate rationally. Philosophers have offered two arguments for holding such people responsible: first, because they were responsible for not acting autonomously; second, because not holding them responsible has the bad social consequence of encouraging others not to take seriously the importance of rational deliberation.

Another argument against the truth of (2′) can be mounted by examining the common social (and legal) practice of holding someone liable for accidents that occur through negligence. In many states it is, or was, the practice that people who "cause" accidents be held legally and financially liable for the damages that may result. If a child falls and gets hurt on your property, if you miss a traffic sign or exceed the speed limit and become involved in an accident, then you are obligated to pay. This notion of liability does not presuppose autonomy. Actually it is predicated on the falsity of (2'), for it does not raise the question of autonomy, only of liability and responsibility. If the issue of autonomy were raised, then simple accidents would have to be treated as malicious and deliberate attempts to hurt others before persons were held responsible. Similarly, parents are held liable or responsible for damage done by their mischievous children. But the law does not regard the parents as having acted autonomously in either doing the damage themselves or in having ordered their children to do it. The operative presumptions are rather that damaged property should be restored and that the person who caused the damage, or those responsible for that person, should make the restoration. Why? Because that person is thought to be less innocent than either the victim whose property was damaged or any other member of the community, who had no part in the mischief or accident at all. The person who is more guilty should be held liable or responsible, even if that person was not acting autonomously, or, as with the parent, not even acting at all.

An objection to this appeal to common legal practice is that the concept of legal liability is not exactly the same as the concept of moral responsibility. Therefore, appeal to these practices does not bear on the truth or falsity of (2'). According to this position we might be able to say that Fulton and Ackron were legally responsible for their crimes, although one or both of them may not have been morally responsible. Even if these facts about liability reflect more on legal responsibility than on moral responsibility, it is important to be clear about the values reflected in our practices of defining liability. When a person is held liable, even though he or she has not acted autonomously, it is in effect being judged that it is more important to ensure safety and protect property than to limit a person's liability to autonomous actions.

12:2.1 Punishment.   To be morally responsible is to be in a position where praise or blame is appropriate and, some would say, deserved. Not many people ask for justifications for offering praise, and most of us willingly accept it whenever it comes our way. There are, however, essentially two theories or justifications for praise. The first is basically that people should get what they deserve, so if they deserve praise they should be given it. The second is that praise operates so as to reinforce certain behaviors. Praising leads to desirable consequences of various kinds, and so to promote those consequences we should give people praise. The desirable consequences might be that the person whom we praise will tend to repeat the desirable act that earned him or her that praise, or that others who desire praise will tend to imitate the behavior that earned the first person praise.

12:2.2 Theories of punishment, like theories of praise, can be divided into two basic groups. One group looks at punishment in terms of giving people what they deserve, the other in terms of the desirable consequences of punishing. The *retributive theory* of punishment is that we should punish guilty people because they deserve it. This theory is held by some who view punishment as a form of *revenge,* which exacts the deserved pain or suffering from the guilty party. The revenge is sometimes measured by the amount of pain or harm the criminal is thought to have caused. At other times the revenge is measured by the degree of the statutory penalties, fines, or imprisonments associated with the violation of specific statutes or laws.

In contemporary thinking the argument for the retributive theory is based, not on revenge but on a notion of *respect* for persons, involving fair treatment for all. Thus, it is argued that everyone ought to accept and live under the same limitations of freedom. Criminal actions are seen as the criminal's taking unfair advantage of other members of society. The criminal has disrupted the balance of equal limitations, and punishment is seen as an attempt to restore the balance that the criminal has disrupted. In summary, then, this argument says that respect for noncriminals, who accept the limitations of life in society, demands punishment of criminals, who have taken an unfair advantage over others.

The supporters of punishment as retribution also argue that failure to punish is failure to give a person what he or she deserves, which amounts to failure to respect the person. To treat people as responsible is to give them what they deserve, be it praise, blame, or punishment. In this view mercy is not a virtue; it is a vice, for it shows disrespect. To be merciful is to treat a responsible agent as a child; it denies his or her autonomy and responsibility. On this theory Fulton, in the case study, was treated as if he were not fully responsible; Ackron, by being executed, was treated with respect, and her responsibility and the blame she deserved were acknowledged. This reading of the case study raises several questions, among them are whether execution does show respect for a person and, more generally, whether one who does wrong really deserves to be punished at all.

12:2.3 Consequentialist theories focus on the desirable outcomes of punishment in order to justify it. The consequences usually examined are those for other potential criminals, for society in general, and for the criminal himself or herself. Whereas the retributive theory merely assumes that those who do wrong deserve punishment, these consequentialist theories look at blame and punishment in terms of their utility. The *preventive* theory maintains that imprisonment serves the socially useful goal of preventing criminals from repeating their crimes and so further harming society. On this theory prisons need be little more than storage houses for criminals. A careful social analysis would measure the cost of housing a criminal in prison against the cost of that person's being free to commit further crimes. Whenever it became economically or politically disadvantageous to allow the criminal his or her freedom, then he or she would be put in prison. But, if the cost of prisons, in terms of taxes, were too high, then a certain number of less dangerous criminals would have to be allowed to go free. Economy is not the only factor, however, that influences actual practice. If it were, all dangerous criminals would surely be executed, for the crude dollar cost of extermination is lower than that of maintaining them in prisons. Both of the punishments cited in the case study served to protect society by preventing Fulton and Ackron from repeating their crime.

The *deterrent theory* is, like the preventive theory, aimed at holding down the rate of crime. The deterrent theory aims at using punishment as a threat to deter *other* potential criminals from crime. Once they see, for example, that murder is punished by death, they will think twice about murder and be deterred from committing it. In order to function as deterrents, punishments need not be as severe as capital punishment; rather, they must be just severe enough to be undesirable. More importantly, punishment must be sure and known. That is, the potential criminal must be aware of the type and severity of punishment he or she risks and must know that he or she will probably receive it. If the criminal does not expect to be caught, or if caught does not expect to be punished, then punishment cannot deter. Likewise, if we do not publicize the type and severity of the punishments associated with specific crimes, then we cannot expect that potential criminals, unaware of their likely fate, will be deterred. It is an empirical question whether or not capital punishment is more or less effective than other severe punishments in deterring specific heinous crimes such as kidnapping, treason, first-degree murder, and the like. Some would rather die than spend a lifetime in prison.

The *rehabilitative theory* of punishment seeks to serve society and the criminal by restoring the criminal to society as a contributing member. The question of responsibility does not really enter the picture. Society is served if the criminal is rehabilitated, even if the criminal was not fully responsible or autonomous when he or she committed the crime. Whether or not our prison system, or our criminal justice system, actually serves the goals of rehabilitation is an open empirical question.

Much evidence suggests that our prisons do not return better citizens to society; instead they return better criminals. On the other hand, it can be argued that there are several successful rehabilitation programs and that, given adequate support financially and socially, there could be more. It is impossible to justify capital punishment on the rehabilitation theory. Whether or not a person such as Fulton was rehabilitated by his prison experience is an open question. Do his routine jobs in the kitchen and laundry count as genuine efforts at rehabilitation? If he commits no more crimes, most will say he was rehabilitated. If he commits another crime, some will say his rehabilitation failed; others will say society failed to accept his return. Perhaps he was rehabilitated in the sense that he has now seen the light, knows the error of his former ways, and will never kill again. Perhaps he has just grown too old and lost interest in committing another such crime.

12:2.4 Hard determinists, who are not fond of the concepts of moral responsibility and just deserts anyway, to be consistent must take a consequentialist view of punishment. Many soft determinists in fact tend to look at punishment in terms of the utility of its consequences also. The historical motivation for reconciling determinism and human freedom has been to show that a scientific view of the world is compatible with holding persons responsible for their actions. Accordingly, there is nothing in the soft determinist's position to prevent him or her from adopting a retributive view of punishment.

Libertarians usually emphasize respect for persons as free agents, so they tend to take a retributive view of punishment. Libertarians feel they are showing the criminal respect by holding him or her responsible and punishing him or her as he deserves.

Exercises for Module 12: Responsibility and Punishment

1. *a.* Here are three assertions. Each would be accepted by only one of the following theorists: a hard determinist, a soft determinist, and a libertarian. Associate each assertion with the proper position. (12:1.2)

   Every autonomous action is free.
   No autonomous action is free.
   An autonomous action may be, but need not be, free.

   b. After you have checked your answers, use your knowledge of the three positions to construct arguments. The premises of each argument should be drawn from the appropriate position, and together they should entail each of the three above assertions.

2. *a.* Explain how a person's behavior could plausibly be used to argue for the falsity of the assertion, "Only persons who act autonomously are responsible for their action."

    b. State, in general terms, what is typically true of a drunken driver in virtue of which it is plausible to assert that he is responsible for his behavior.

    c. Provide another concrete example where these general terms would also apply. (12:1.3)

3. *a.* Of the following four assertions, one each is involved in the retributive, the preventive, the deterrent, and the rehabilitative theories of punishment. Associate each assertion with the proper theory.

"At least those criminals can't commit more crimes while they're locked up in jail." (12:2.3)

"The only way to keep some people from committing crimes is to show them very clearly that criminals are regularly severely punished." (12:2.3)

"Criminal action is blameworthy. A criminal deserves to be held responsible for his action and be punished because it is blameworthy."

"If the criminal doesn't learn to do something better than commit crimes, then the criminal is going to keep on being a criminal."

    b. Which of these views is consequentialist? Which not? Explain.

    c. Provide the argument that shows why a hard determinist must take a consequentialist view of punishment.

Answers to Exercises for Module 12

1. *a.* SD, HD, L.

    b. A person lacks freedom to the extent that he or she is constrained.
No autonomous action is constrained.
Any action that is not constrained is free.
Hence, every autonomous action is free. *(SD)*

Every event has a cause.
Whatever is caused to be as it is, is not free.
Thus, no action is free.
Hence, no autonomous action is free. *(HD)*

In acting autonomously it is possible, and sometimes true, that the agent could have done other than what he did.

In acting autonomously it is possible, and sometimes true, that the agent could not have done other than what he did.

An action is free if, and only if, its agent could have acted otherwise.

Hence, an autonomous action may be, but need not be, free. *(L)*

(For a review of each position check Module 11.)

2. *a.* A person knows he or she is causing a state of affairs in which either he or she or others will be unable to control undesirable but foreseeable consequences. This knowledge and choice make the person responsible for those consequences.

b. Typically a drunk driver knew before beginning to drink that he or she would become drunk, and typically he or she knew that he or she would, perhaps of necessity, drive after becoming drunk. Thus, typically the drunk driver knew in advance that he or she was making it more difficult or impossible for himself or herself to act responsibly. Therefore, the driver is responsible both for having caused his or her drunkenness and for the foreseeable, although not necessarily predictable, results of his or her diminished capacity to drive.

c. A known epileptic who neglected to take his or her medicine before driving.

3. *a.* Preventive, deterrent, retributive, and rehabilitative.

b. Only the retributive view is not consequentialist. You should be able to identify the consequence suggested in each of the other three statements.

c. No human action is free.

So, no one is ever responsible for what he or she does.

Thus, no one is deserving of punishment.

Hence, punishment should be administered only for its useful consequences.

Module 13
LIMITS OF FREEDOM

In Modules 11 and 12 we have raised the question of placing limits on negative freedom. Punishment by fines or imprisonment certainly limits negative freedom. Taxes, compulsory education, military obligations, zoning laws, traffic laws, and other legal prohibitions are just a few of the other limits imposed on the negative freedom of individuals in various societies. This module looks at the goals or reasons that have been offered to justify limitations of this kind. Five basic purposes or aims have been proposed: (a) treating people equally under the law, (b) giving all people a fair chance in society, (c) preventing anyone's doing bodily harm to others, to their property, or to himself or herself, (d) promoting further development of each person's positive freedom, and (e) restricting socially offensive or morally distasteful behavior. After reading Module 13, you should be able to

- Distinguish legal restrictions aimed at each of the five purposes listed above.
- Explain how each of the five purposes seems to limit negative freedom.
- Give examples of limitations on negative freedom designed to serve each of the five purposes.
- Explain how sample laws would be justified under various of the five limitations.

THE CASE OF REDFORD SMITH

Redford Smith graduated from high school in fairly typical fashion. He came from a white middle-class background and entered the college where his father was president, hoping to major in finance and go into business after graduation. As the president's son he was given first choice at registration, so Redford Smith always got the courses he requested. He joined a fraternity that kept a secret file of exams, so Smith was able to maintain an advantage over other students in most of his courses. Upon graduation he went into business selling real estate. The brokers he worked for had a policy of blockbusting. They would sell a home to a minority family in an all-white neighborhood, then use scare tactics to play on white bigotry and economic fears and so seek to list a large number of white homes significantly below their market value. They sold a few to minority families quickly and bought most themselves to sell later to other minority families at greatly increased prices. Smith went along with this policy and became adept at getting whites to list low and minorities to buy high. He was especially good at distracting prospective buyers from noticing substandard electrical work, inadequate heating or ventilating, and potential fire hazards. After many years, however, he came to feel that his financial success was an empty victory. He took up drinking and in time became an alcoholic. He lost his job, his home, and his savings. His wife divorced him. His health deteriorated, and he was subject to hallucinations and exaggerated emotional states of jubilation and depression. He slept in all-night porno theaters and took to begging for money from passersby. He was arrested often for drunkenness, vagrancy, disturbing the peace, and public nudity. He eventually died in a prison hospital of malnutrition and pneumonia.

13:1.1 Formal Freedom. We have already defined negative freedom as freedom from constraints. It is easy to imagine that the ideal would be a freedom involving absolutely no constraints. By implication, however, such freedom would have to be very rare indeed. For suppose that there were just one person who was absolutely free from constraints. If he or she wished to drive down the left side of the road, he or she would be free to do so. If she or he wished to harm someone else, she or he would be free to do so. Such freedom would necessarily be scarce, because everyone else would be constrained by that one person's exercise of freedom. No one could safely drive on either side of the street if one person were continually free to drive on both.

The traditional response to this problem has been that negative freedom cannot be absolute for everyone and, therefore, in fairness to all, no one should have absolute freedom. Rather, everyone should be subject to some set of restraints.

But how restrained should we make people? The traditional answer has had two parts, the first being egalitarianism. According to egalitarian thought, everyone ought to count equally and so everyone ought to be restrained equally. That is, if anyone ought to be restrained in a given way in a given circumstance, then everyone else ought to be restrained similarly in that similar circumstance. This egalitarian statement is thought of as following from the principle of universalizability.

The second half of the traditional answer has been that the justification of any restraint should be that, universally applied, it tends to maximize, rather than minimize, freedom. Consider, for instance, the traffic-safety policy of having signal lights at busy intersections red in both directions for two or three seconds. In this situation everyone is similarly restricted. But obviously everyone would be similarly restricted if there were no double red, or if the double red lasted for 60 seconds. How long, then, should the double red be? Here we can use the conception of maximizing freedom. Without any double red, several more accidents would occur. Cars would be damaged and people would be injured and killed. This harm to property and persons is itself a restriction of freedom. The justification of the double red, then, is that it reduces the number of accidents and thus increases freedom. If the double red lasted ten seconds, however, rather than three seconds, freedom would probaby not be increased. Rather it would tend to decrease. On the one hand there would probably be no fewer accidents at the intersection, and on the other hand every motorist and pedestrian would be restricted from moving for seven additional seconds at each red signal light. The net effect on persons' freedom, therefore, with a 10-second double red would be a decline, for not only would traffic accidents fail to decrease further, but persons' time restricted at red lights would increase.

It is very important to understand the concept of maximizing freedom abstractly. Any restriction, even if placed equally on everybody, does limit people's freedom. The argument in favor of restrictions of freedom is not simply that it is fair because it is done in an egalitarian fashion but also that *more freedom is gained* (fewer traffic accidents) than has been lost (waiting at the double red signal light). The idea of maximizing freedom, then, is the idea of the greatest positive balance of freedom over restrictions.

The justification of formal freedom is that restrictions of persons' negative freedom are justified as long as they are *egalitarian and result in a net gain or maximization of freedom.*

13:1.2   Equal freedom under the law is called *formal freedom.* This freedom is achieved by passing laws that apply the same restrictions to each person. Laws that restrict some people but not others do not serve to create formal freedom for all but rather to create (or preserve) privileged classes of people. These privileges allow some people to take advantage of others while remaining immune from legal prosecution by the exploited. Considerations of race, wealth, religion, sex, national origin, age, maturity, expertise, aristocratic heritage, and occupation have been used from time to time in order to justify, or attempt to justify, nonegalitarian legal systems. At times it is argued that the overall good of society warrants treating people differently in terms of their legal rights or formal freedom. For example, few countries apply their laws against murder to their own secret service agents, who may kill in the pursuit of their duty as defined by their government. In the case study Redford Smith, the president's son, was given a privileged status by the college. This special status gave him an advantage at registration time. Perhaps the registration people did it without telling the president, or perhaps it was a college tradition to treat the president's family in a special way. Whatever the reason, this privilege puts unequal constraints on the negative freedom of those who attend that college. Egalitarian considerations lead not only to the imposition of restrictions but also to the abolition of special privileges. This justification for limiting negative freedom, thus, aims both at restrictions and at equal restrictions for all.

13:2.1 Effective Freedom.   Applying equal restrictions to everyone under the law by no means guarantees everyone an equal chance in life. Some have superior abilities, some are born into wealthier families, some are hindered by accidents or by illness. A free and open marketplace does not mean that all the goods are free for the taking, nor does it mean that everyone is able to purchase as much as he or she wishes. Just as there can be limits to one's own financial resources, there may be limits on what is available to be sold. Formal freedom is compatible with poverty, ignorance, and other forms of unequal opportunity.

Two possible societal goals are to increase and/or equalize *effective freedom*. Effective freedom is the possession of the means necessary to accomplish one's aim, whatever it may be. There are many policies a society can use to try to increase effective freedom. Legislation requiring equal opportunity in employment, welfare legislation, affirmative action legislation such as racial or sexual quota systems, school desegregation and bussing to achieve equal educational opportunity, graduated income tax rates, and special tax exemptions and/or deductions for handicapped, unemployed, or poor people are among the ways used in the United States to achieve and equalize effective freedom. The replacement of private enterprise by government ownership and planning is a means used more frequently in socialist countries.

KARL MARX (1818–1883)

Karl Marx was one of the strongest advocates of equalizing effective freedom. In his earliest writings, the *Economic and Philosophical Manuscripts* (1844), he described the alienation and human misery that characterize the capitalist economic system. Under capitalism, he claimed workers are deprived of all but a subsistence wage. Their labor is exploited to support the capitalists, who own the means of production. This exploitation leads to a class system in which owners experience effective freedom but workers are deprived, by economic necessity, of similar opportunities.

As a student Marx was a political radical and a militant atheist. This background prevented him from teaching in his native Prussia. He exiled himself to Paris in 1843, where he met his lifelong collaborator, friend, and benefactor, Frederick Engels. Expelled from France in 1845, he moved to Brussels, where he and Engels wrote the *Communist Manifesto* in 1848. The *Manifesto* proposes ten reforms that would increase effective freedom—for example, compulsory education for the young, an end to child labor, and a graduated income tax system. Marx was expelled from Brussels in 1849 and moved to London. There he lived in poverty and worked on his major economic study, *Das Kapital,* until his death. His political philosophy continues to influence the course of world history.

13:2.2   One argument in favor of differential tax systems and the other policies and legislation mentioned above is that governments should limit some of the freedom of their more advantaged citizens in order to guarantee some minimum floor of opportunity to all their citizens. This argument does not claim that everyone should be made equal in wealth, skill, health, or the like. Rather, limits are imposed on the negative freedom of the more advantaged people only to the extent necessary to achieve a basic minimum level of effective freedom for everyone in society.

Some who advance this justification for limiting negative freedom maintain that the advantaged people should never be made to fall below the minimum level in the government's zeal to achieve effective freedom for some other group. Others urge that at times a government is justified in giving special advantages beyond formal equality to people who previously have been unfairly disadvantaged. Thus, practices of reverse discrimination in hiring may be used to hire a less qualified minority person over a more qualified white. This discrimination reverses the old pattern of favoring whites. It is a conscious effort to rectify a past wrong, and the argument to justify it may rest on the grounds that it will tend to improve the effective freedom of minority persons in society.

Sometimes effective freedom is not governed by specific civil legislation. Such is the case with the students in Redford Smith's college, relative to their chances of success on exams. Redford's access to old exams gave him an advantage over his classmates, which to some extent may even have caused some of them to flunk out. School regulations against cheating, while not necessarily laws of a civil government, are designed to guarantee equal effective freedom to do well on exams and papers. Traditionally in the United States the most prominently emphasized means of securing effective freedom has been by securing equal opportunity, especially equal educational opportunity, for all citizens.

13:2.3   A moment's reflection will show you a potentially strong conflict between negative freedom and effective freedom. Whenever goods, resources, or opportunities are scarce, these means of effective freedom can be supplied to less advantaged persons only by imposing restrictions upon more advantaged persons. Clearly the pursuit of effective freedom clashes with the simple ideal that everyone ought to have the maximum amount of negative freedom compatible with the equal amount of negative freedom for everyone else. Yet, as Karl Marx insisted, and as the poor of any nation intuitively know, talk of freedom has a hollow sound to persons who lack the funds for a minimal nutritious diet, much less for the luxuries the rich pursue with their freedom.

13:3.1 Harm.   We have seen that limits on negative freedom may be used to try to achieve equal treatment before the law or effective freedom within a society or both. A third goal is to prevent harm. Valuables susceptible of being harmed have classically been categorized as life, liberty, and property. The harm can be directed against particular individuals or against society as a collective group of people. Laws against treason, bribery, sedition, conflict of interest, and tax evasion, as well as governmental regulation of commerce, and, to some extent, the food and drug industries and land use, all are designed to protect the general public or society as a whole from various kinds of harm.

Laws against battery, murder, and rape are designed to protect people from physical harm. Laws against kidnapping, detention against one's will, and depriving someone of his or her legal opportunities are designed to prevent harm to individual liberty. Laws against theft, fraud, and industrial espionage, as well as laws regulating financial and real estate transactions, all are aimed at preventing harm to individuals through loss of property.

13:3.2   The justification for limiting actions that cause harm is that people, either individually or collectively, should not be harmed if they do not give prior consent. Often people are harmed with their consent. The blockbusting described in the case study is an example of harm with consent. The whites were not forced to sell low and the minorities were not forced to buy high (although patterns of discrimination in the sale of real estate may have placed greater constraints on the minorities than on the whites). Both entered into legally binding contracts; both groups were harmed.

13:3.3   Laws preventing people from harming themselves cannot rely on the concept of nonconsent. People can always claim that they wish to harm themselves. Rather, such laws are based on the idea that people do not really understand in all cases where their own best interest lies. We are familiar with laws allowing parents or guardians to decide for children or for the legally insane what is in their best interests. These laws are designed to prevent the child or the insane person from harming himself or herself. With sane adults examples are less common. Prohibitions against the use of alcohol or against smoking would not be tolerated. Yet some laws, such as those against suicide or requiring safety helmets for motorcyclists, may be argued for on this basis.

There are two kinds of objections to such laws. One is the libertarian view that negative freedom should be maximized in general and specifically when no harm to others is involved. The second is that the government is not able to perceive the best interests of individuals as well as they themselves are. So, governmental efforts to protect people may well work out to harm them after all.

13:4.1 Positive Freedom.   The fourth reason offered for limiting negative freedom is that certain limitations can work to increase a person's positive freedom. In the previous module we used the example of compulsory education to illustrate this goal of increasing a person's positive freedom. Laws designed to help people decide and act more rationally can be directed against the person's own negative freedom or against the negative freedom of other people. For example, laws concerning informed consent, truth-in-lending, and unit pricing can be seen as designed to increase at least the opportunity for positive freedom. They also can be seen as laws protecting people from harming themselves and others. The goal of increasing positive freedom is closely related to the goal of preventing people from harming themselves and others. The operative assumption is that, given more information usefully and clearly presented, people can make more rational decisions and better avoid harming themselves. Laws against the use or possession of drugs can be viewed as aiming in part at helping people avoid any potentially harmful situations that might arise when their rationality is impaired by drugs.

13:4.2   The laws cited above support the ideal of positive freedom only to the extent that they ensure a person the opportunity to make a decision based on fuller information. A more direct approach would go beyond laws attempting to ensure people the opportunity to be rational and would prohibit them from being irrational in various ways. Laws warning people about the danger of smoking, for example, do no more than present information for grounding a rational decision. They do not attempt to enforce rationality by prohibiting persons who profess to value their life from smoking. The one set of laws we do have that tends to enforce positive freedom in the strong sense is that concerning mental health. Under some laws it is possible to have a person committed to a mental institution against his or her will, even though he or she has not harmed anyone and there is no clear present danger that he or she will do so. Such laws attempt to enforce positive freedom by permitting the incarceration of a person judged of unsound mind, punishing him or her by deprivation of liberty, and thereby constraining him or her from engaging in his or her esoteric practices.[1]

The case study illustrates the harm that a person can suffer and cause to himself or herself when his or her rationality and positive freedom are impaired. Although the causes of Smith's alcoholism are not made clear, the effects are.

13:5.1 Offensive Behavior.   A final reason offered for limiting negative freedom is to prevent behavior that, while not essentially harmful, offends the norms and values of society. Socially distasteful or offensive behavior is prohibited in order to prevent anxiety, frustration, mental anguish, and social disturbance. Laws regarding sexual propriety

[1] Thomas Szasz has been a leader in arguing that such practices of involuntary commitment are unjustified.

and prostitution, the sale of goods on Sundays, and pornography are examples of attempts to prevent behavior that some, or many, find offensive. These laws often arouse strong feelings, because many view them as unfair attempts to legislate morality and encroach on personal liberties, while others view them as necessary to maintain the moral fiber of society and prevent some people from antagonizing and annoying others by their distasteful or offensive behavior. In the case study Redford Smith runs up against these laws toward the end of his life.

13:5.2   A pluralistic society with its confluence of ethnic groups, different cultural traditions, and diverse religious and sexual codes of behavior can expect the problem of offensiveness to be great and feelings on the subject to be high. The behaviors and mores of any group can be viewed with outrage by some other group, which in turn may practice something thought utterly distasteful or offensive by some other group. The experiencing of cultural differences can also lead in the other direction, away from prejudice and ethnocentrism toward increased tolerance and even personal enrichment. The experience of diversity can be a liberating and rewarding one; it need not be threatening or upsetting.

13:5.3   Laws based on the offensiveness of a behavior certainly conflict with the ideal of negative freedom, since a majority may readily find a behavior offensive even though it does not harm others. Most persons, realizing that everybody has such harmless quirks and manners, may agree that it would be better if persons could enjoy the wider negative freedom conferred by greater tolerance of individual idiosyncrasies. It is at least fair to note, however, the extremely strong feelings people have about some behaviors they find offensive. Imagine, for example, two white parents who have adopted black children. They take these preschool children into a restaurant in the South, where fears about the "mingling of the races" run deep. The children are not sure they like the food or want to eat it, so the parents encourage them. Daddy picks up his son's fork, puts a morsel of his son's food in his own mouth, and expresses his pleasure with it. Then he picks up more food with the fork and gets his son to taste it. You do not yourself have to be at all racially prejudiced in order to imagine the outrage and disgust that some persons in the restaurant might feel upon seeing that behavior. Or consider a contrasting example. Grave-robbing and mutilation of corpses is simply disgusting to most people. The mutilation, however, harms neither the corpse nor the bereaved.

Exercises for Module 13: Limits of Freedom

1.   *a.* Below you will find descriptions of five purposes served by 16 real and possible laws. You are asked to distinguish the general

ways in which each imposes a limit upon negative freedom of the individual. Laws marked with an asterisk (*) serve more than one purpose. The five general purposes for which laws limit negative freedom are to treat persons equally under the law (*E*); to give persons equal opportunity or a fair chance, beyond the realm of legal proceedings, in society (*EO*); to prevent harm to persons and property (*H*); to promote further development of persons' positive freedom (*PF*); and to restrict offensive behavior (*OB*). Beside each description mark the purpose or purposes served by such a law.

(1) _____ No person should be required to witness against himself.

(2) _____ Extortion should be illegal.

(3) _____ Broadcasters should be required to present some public service advertising free of charge.

(4) _____ A person's national origin or ethnic background should not prevent or hinder him from securing housing.

(5) _____ Sexual intercourse with dead persons should not be legal.

(6) _____ *Garage mechanics should have to be certified as proficient in their work.

(7) _____ *Any person convicted of armed robbery should serve a seven-year prison term.

(8) _____ *Grass on a person's property should not be allowed to grow over six inches long.

(9) _____ *All cigarette advertisements should be accompanied by warnings of the dangers of cigarette smoking.

(10) _____ A person's sex should not influence the person's eligibility for employment.

(11) _____ Beating persons should be prohibited.

(12) _____ *Pornographic materials ought to be banned from sale.

(13) _____ *Public education should be required for all children.

(14) _____ Arson should be illegal.

(15) _____ People ought to be able to question their accusers when legal actions are taken against them.

(16) _____ Places of business should remain closed on Sunday when people are worshipping.

b. Whenever regulations achieve any of these purposes, the negative freedom of some persons is limited. Take the first five regulations listed above. Identify some person whose negative freedom would be limited by each regulation.

   c. When you are sure you have made a correct identification, state how that person's negative freedom would be limited by the regulation.

2. *a*. Either by reference to a real regulation or by making them up yourself, provide four examples of regulations, each designed to serve one of the five aims listed above.

   b. Identify in each case the person or persons whose negative freedom would be limited.

   c. State how that person's negative freedom would be limited by the regulations.

Answers to Exercises for Module 13

1.   *a*. (1) *E:* provides every accused person with equal treatment.
         (2) *H*.
         (3) *PF:* increases information upon which to base decisions.
         (4) *EO:* prohibits various forms of discrimination to provide equal opportunity.
         (5) *OB*.
         (6) *H, PF:* gives people assurance that they can trust the mechanics to do a competent job.
         (7) *H, E:* provides equal treatment for all who are convicted.
         (8) *OB:* prevents offense where tall, weedy grass is viewed as offensive and unaesthetic. *H:* controls rodents and insects and maintains property values.
         (9) *H, PF*.
        (10) *EO*.
        (11) *H*.
        (12) *OB, H:* prevents the entry or spread of organized crime in a community.
        (13) *PF, EO*.
        (14) *H*.
        (15) *E*.
        (16) *OB*.
   b. (1) Prosecutors and those allegedly harmed by the person required to witness.
         (2) The would-be extortionist.
         (3) The broadcasters.
         (4) The realtor and the seller or landlord of the house.
         (5) Persons desiring sexual intercourse with corpses.

c. (1) The prosecutor would be prevented from forcing the person to testify and the person harmed might be prevented from gaining a desired restoration or revenge through the law.

   (2) The extortionist is threatened with punishment for the extortion.

   (3) The broadcasters are prevented from accepting only profitable, commercial advertising.

   (4) The realtor and seller or landlord are all prevented from making national origin a criterion for selecting a buyer or renter for the house.

   (5) Persons desiring sexual intercourse with corpses are threatened with punishment for such behavior.

RIGHTS AND DUTIES

Normative statements about what people or societies ought, or ought not, to do often refer to the supposed rights or duties of the parties involved. In order to evaluate these statements, you need a firm conceptual grasp of the nature of the rights and duties under discussion. You must also understand the justifications that may be offered in support of the views that such rights or duties are important normative considerations. The educational goal of this cluster is for you to acquire these understandings. Module 14 displays the wide variety of claims about rights, both legal and moral, that have been recognized and distinguished by normative theorists. Conceptual analysis clarifies the relations of the concepts of rights to other normative concepts, especially that of duty. In Module 15 we clarify the concepts of "indefeasible" and "inalienable" moral rights and the categorical duties to honor them. We introduce as an example Kant's ethical theory, which holds that some actions are intrinsically right or intrinsically wrong. In Module 16 we present a possible justification of claims that indefeasible and inalienable rights and categorical duties exist. The justification is developed in terms of the concepts of respect and integrity.

MODULE 14
CONCEPTS OF RIGHTS

To claim that a person has a right is to claim that he or she is entitled to behave in certain ways in certain circumstances. Typically, it also is to define expectations concerning the behavior of other people relative to the possessor of the right. This module conceptually analyzes major types of rights. We achieve this by relying on distinctions among (a) the circumstances within which assertions about rights arise, (b) the behaviors to which possessors of the right are entitled, and (c) the behaviors expected of others toward the possessors of the rights. The concept of a right will be related to the concepts of duty, liberty, scarcity and abundance of resources and opportunities, legality and morality, liability and immunity. We will contrast the eighteenth- and twentieth-century concepts of moral rights primarily by noting the expectations of others that their possession would entail. After reading Module 14, you should be able to

- Distinguish and explain the distinction between nonconventional moral rights and conventional rights.
- Distinguish and explain the distinction between rights that imply correlative duties of noninterference and those that do not.
- Distinguish moral rights from legal powers.
- Compare and contrast legal powers, liabilities, and immunities.
- Distinguish and explain the distinction between eighteenth- and twentieth-century concepts of rights.

THE CASE OF CHUCK GRUNDSLEY VS. BOBBY-JO PRINCE

Chuck Grundsley, owner of the Sidney Athletes professional tennis team in the Australian National League, had the million-pound sale of his star player, Ms. Bobby-Jo Prince, to the Outback Koalas overturned by the league commissioner. Grundsley arranged the deal in the light of Ms. Prince's expressed intention to allow her current contract to expire. She wanted to become a free agent at the end of the season and, thus, be free to negotiate with other teams. The commissioner squelched the deal, however, on the grounds the practice of selling outstanding players could undermine competition within the league and lead to the rich owners' buying the contracts of all of the best players. The case was submitted to arbitration. Here is an excerpt of the discussion:

"I think it all boils down to this, Commissioner. She's my girl. I've got her contract. As long as she's mine, I've got a right to sell her contract when a reasonable offer is made. She can help the Koalas, and I can use the money to hire new young talent. If her contract expires, I wind up with nothing. The contract is a legal one, and it gives me the power to trade her when I see fit. She wasn't coerced into signing with me. In fact, I've paid her well and she should have no reason to beef."

"I'm not disputing the fact that Bobby-Jo has been under a valid contract with you, Chuck. I'm just exercising a power that is mine as commissioner and that is specified within the contracts of all players in the league. That clause clearly states that all provisions of the contract can be overridden if, in the judgment of the commissioner, it would be in the best interests of the league. Sure, commissioners rarely exercise this prerogative, but it is clearly mine, and that you can't deny."

"Hold it," said Bobby-Jo. "Before you fellas go on, I'd like to lay a little number of my own on you. I've got a right to say what I feel about all of this. First, it sounds to me as if you both consider me nothing more than a rather valuable piece of property to be bought and sold. As a person I resent this. I've got my dignity, you know, and I don't think anyone can really own anyone else. Just where do you come off with this 'She's my girl . . . she's mine' routine, Chuck? When I signed with you and the Athletes I didn't think I was selling myself into slavery. I thought we were behaving as civilized adults, free to make agreements which would do us both some good. I've enjoyed playing for and living in Sidney, and you've paid me well. You ought to remember who has been bringing the paying customers into the stands, Chuck. You should have a little more respect for your players. It's because you don't that I plan to become a free agent at the end of the season. I want to sign with someone who will respect me more than you do. And, by the way, I didn't really care for your selling me to the Koalas. You know I'd hate living out there hundreds of miles from nowhere. I just couldn't live my kind of life out there. Shipping me off to the Outback would deprive me of a meaningful life. I feel everyone is entitled to that. As for you, Commissioner, all you seem interested in is the precious competition in a league you seem to think is your own. You are as bad as Chuck here when it comes to the players in the league. For several years now I and the Agitated Athletes Association have been pushing for no-trade clauses in player contracts. If American baseball players cannot be traded without their consent after they have been with the same team for seven years, I think we should get the same break. We're gonna keep fighting that battle until we win. And, furthermore. . . . "

The Commissioner interrupted, "You are perfectly free to agitate for whatever cause you wish. But as long as you are bound by the contracts now in force, you can be traded at the owner's discretion. The rules can't go both ways. Either the owners have their way, as they do now, or you and the AAA will win the day. Whatever else you might have against me, surely you aren't objecting to my stopping Chuck here from trading you to the Outback Koalas."

"No. But I'm greatly distressed by your reasons for doing it and your standing in the way of players' rights."

14:1.1 Rights and Doing the Right Thing. The question, "Are anyone's rights involved?" is not to be confused with the question, "What is the right thing to do?" The questions are not unrelated, however, since it is often true that persons' rights are cited as part of the basis for deciding what is right to do. In the case study there is dispute about several questions concerning what Grundsley, the Commissioner, and Prince ought or ought not to do. Much of the argument, as we shall see below, may be understood in terms of the claims of each that he or she has rights at stake in the matter. Each claims that the rights either *entitle* him or her *to do something* (Grundsley's ownership rights allow him to sell his players) or serve as a *ground for censure of others who violate* the rights (Prince's right as a person not to be treated like property grounds her claim that Grundsley and the Commissioner are behaving objectionably, compromising her dignity for their business concerns).

In general, statements such as "The right thing for Bill to do is X" do not mean the same thing as statements such as "Bill has a right to do X." The second claims that Bill has the prerogative to do X if he so desires. It is a statement about what Bill is permitted to do, or entitled to do, though he would not ordinarily be remiss in not doing it. The first statement makes the much stronger claim that Bill ought to do whatever X amounts to. For example, the right thing to do may be to do one's duty, or to exercise one's right, or to add flour only after beating the eggs.

Statements such as "It would be right for Bill to do X" may be supported by claims about Bill's rights or the rights of others, but other support also may be offered. Other factors that may be considered include self-interest or the happiness of others. Thus, it may well be right for a person to act out of benevolence toward another, although it is implausible to suggest that anyone is entitled to (or has a right to expect) such benevolence.

14:2.1 Varieties of Rights Claims. The case study illustrates a wide variety of rights claims, reflecting the variety of entitlements persons may enjoy either by virtue of their being persons or by virtue of their circumstances. Let us focus first upon a typical and important connection that joins several rights with what we shall call *correlative duties.* Consider some examples. If you have a right to raise your children as you please, then we have a duty not to interfere with your raising of your children. Indeed, if two parents have that right, then *everybody* else has the duty not to interfere with the way those parents raise their children. Similarly, if you have the right to sell your house, then everyone else has the duty not to prevent you from selling your house. Likewise, if you have the right to a public education, then everyone else has the duty not to prevent you from obtaining that education. Notice the general relationship between rights and duties in these statements. There are a large group of rights such that part of what it means to say that *one* person has a certain *right* is that *every other* person has the *correlative duty not to interfere with* that person's proper exercise of that right. In the case study, when Bobby-Jo Prince asserts her right to be heard on the matter in dispute, this implies that the others have a duty to hear her out.

It is important to note how the framers of the Bill of Rights conceived the rights they listed in the Constitution. They thought of rights such as those of free speech and a free press as being possessed by persons independent of governmental structure. They regarded any form of government that failed to acknowledge these entitlements as violating the rights of persons as human beings. Thus, they did not think that the Constitution itself created the rights or that people were justified in claiming the rights because they were granted in the Bill of Rights. Rather, they thought of the Bill of Rights as providing a guarantee that in the United States those preexisting human rights would be acknowledged and supported, and not violated, by the power of the government. In their view the duty not to interfere in the exercise of the rights exists independently of the Constitution and is simply acknowledged in the Bill of Rights as a duty of government.

14:2.2   Other rights that are correlated with duties include what might be called *conventional rights,* such as the right to enter into contracts, the right to make a will, the right to buy and sell property, the rights to operate a car or borrow money, and the like. Corresponding to these rights are duties of noninterference in their exercise. In a society such as ours, the actions that count as official acts of exercising these rights are specified by convention. For example, to make a will you must be of sound mind, write down your wishes, and have the document witnessed. Once this is accomplished, it becomes everyone's duty to honor that will. In the case study, Grundsley and Prince had both exercised their rights, or legal powers, to enter into a contract. Given that they both met the specifications of the convention for contract making— for example, they were both competent adults, and they were not contracting to violate the law—it would have been wrong for anyone to try to prevent their making the original contract.

14:2.3   *Conventional rights* may be contrasted with what might be called the *moral rights* discussed earlier. Conventional rights are entitlements that come into existence within conventional structures such as the law, whereas moral rights are entitlements that exist regardless of such structures. In the case study Prince raises a question that illustrates this contrast. She acknowledges the legality of the contractual arrangements between her and Grundsley. She is well aware of the legal powers that all of the players and owners have exercised. She asks, however, whether the convention is not operating in such a way that the moral rights of the players are violated. Specifically, she wonders whether anyone should have a right to own another person, whether the practice under examination doesn't amount to a kind of slavery. Indirectly she refers here to what some believe to be a moral right of persons not to be exploited and treated as property.

14:2.4   Here you need to distinguish two sets of rights and duties. Beyond the right to act in ways that conventions allow you to act, there are rights, and corresponding duties, that may be specified within or arise because of arrangements brought about by the exercising of the original conventional rights. That is, contracts, deeds, wills, and the like may themselves spell out new rights and duties for the parties involved. Thus, a person may have a right to have another do something for him or her because the other has contracted (under the contracting conventions operative within the particular social or legal context) to do that thing. Grundsley's contract with Prince gave him the right to her playing services and required of her that she play. In return he had to pay her. Grundsley claims the right to sell Prince's services to the Koalas. He further claims that the Commissioner has a duty not to interfere with the sale. In turn, the Commissioner claims that under a special clause in all league contracts he has the right, as Commissioner, to halt the deal. He further claims that if he does halt the deal, Grundsley has the duty to comply with his order. In a nonlegal context, our practice of making promises has similar aspects. The person to whom the promise is made has the right to (is entitled to) expect that the person who made the promise will do the promised thing. The person who makes the promise has a corresponding duty to do it.

14:3.1 Liabilities and Immunities.   Within the framework defined by specifically *legal* conventions, there are legal entitlements, or rights, that may be understood in terms of *liabilities* of persons. Let us suppose that the legal powers discussed above are exercised. In some cases the rights of some persons imply liabilities of others. If a person has a right to make a will, then another person (a despicable relative, say) is liable to be excluded from that will. If a person has a right to bring suit for damages sustained on another's property, then the other is liable to be sued for the damages. In the case study, if Prince is under league contract to Grundsley, then she is liable to be traded under the provisions of the contract. If the Commissioner has the legal power to overturn deals in the interests of the league as a whole, then Grundsley is liable to have his sale of Prince squelched.

14:3.2 In other cases, the having of legal rights amounts to the having of *immunities* against legal action. Persons who work for the diplomatic service of a foreign nation are immune from having to obey traffic summons and having to pay traffic fines; that is, they have the right to ignore those items. This is an example of an immunity enjoyed by a specific group of people. To say that persons have such a right is to say that they are *immune* from prosecution for such action. In the case study, Prince expresses her concern about the fact that veteran players such as herself are not immune from being traded after having served a team for a number of years. She and the players' organization have been agitating to acquire this legal right (immunity), which they do not presently enjoy. There are also cases where everyone enjoys an immunity from prosecution for actions that are normally subject to legal challenge. For instance, people can be sued for slander. People who make false accusations about others in such a way as to damage them emotionally or financially are liable to having a suit brought against them. But if the person talked about is a public figure and if the talk was not intended maliciously, then the speaker is immune from being sued, even if what he or she said was false. All of us enjoy this immunity by virtue of our current laws and court rulings.

14:4.1 Licenses to Compete. There is a type of right that all may not be able to exercise successfully, owing to a scarcity of resources. In such circumstances it is reasonable to say that persons have a right to compete for a share of the resources. The rights we considered earlier included the corresponding duties not to interfere with the exercise of these rights. But now we are dealing with a different type of right—one that, because of scarcity, involves competition. The nature of this competition itself includes limited interference, which may eventually allow some competitors to win out. For example, it may be that people have a right to drive a car. It may also be that so many people have such a right that there are too many cars; there are simply not enough highways to accommodate all driving at once. At this point some regulation of traffic and access to roads, some interference in the exercise of the right to drive, becomes necessary.

14:4.2 To see how the type of right that we have called a *license to compete* contrasts with the variety that entails a corresponding duty of noninterference, consider two of the rights guaranteed by the Bill of Rights, the right to free worship and the right to operate a free press. If people worship in ordinary ways, including singing, praying, and meeting together, it remains possible for everybody to sing, pray, and meet together in different places without having to interfere with each other. It is not that interference is impossible, but rather that noninterference can be carried off pretty well. So far there is no scarcity of meeting places. In contrast, if there were ever to be a sufficient shortage of paper, freedom of the press might well become a competitive thing. In fact, in the United States today the scarcity of low-salaried transportation workers in the postal system is making freedom of the press more competitive, as presses compete for the scarce dollar of the reading public. In any event, it is when competition for scarce resources is justified, and the resources are indeed scarce, that rights claims of this new variety (rights to compete) arise.

Other examples of such rights are the rights to open a business and compete with other businesses in the free enterprise system, or to agitate and lobby for legislative changes. Given that the supply of consumer money is limited, only some who exercise their right to compete for business will be successful. It is also fair, within limits, for business people to compete for customers, even though this may limit the financial success of the other competing businesses. Given that only some laws can be enacted, and especially given that contradictory proposals for legislation cannot both be adopted, it is clear that agitating for a particular piece of legislation does not entail a corresponding duty of others not to compete with those efforts. In the case study the Commissioner points this out as a truth that Prince and her players' organization must recognize. He acknowledges that her group has a right to compete in the market of ideas to try to get new league rules adopted. But he also reminds her that the right to compete is not identical with the right to succeed in the competition and have one's proposals adopted.

14:5.1 Eighteenth- and Twentieth-Century Concepts of Rights. There is an important difference between the concept of moral rights commonly espoused in the eighteenth century (and out of which our Bill of Rights emerged) and a concept of moral rights that has developed in twentieth-century normative thought. The eighteenth century conceived of moral rights as entitlements that hold independently of any governmental structure. Freedom of speech, freedom of worship, freedom of assembly, and freedom of the press were thought of as things to which human beings were entitled by virtue of their being human. The correlative duties attending them, if there were any, were at most *duties of noninterference.* The duty of the other agent, in other words, was not conceived as a duty to act in a certain way, but at most as a duty to refrain from doing anything that would interfere with the exercise of the right. As we have seen in 14:4.1 and 14:4.2, in some cases even saying that there is a duty of noninterference would be too much.

The twentieth-century concept that departs from this notion is reflected in the 1948 United Nations "Declaration of Human Rights." That document proclaimed that persons have rights to education, a decent standard of living, medical treatment, dignified employment, leisure, and the like. It is important to notice two contrasts between this and the eighteenth-century concept of rights. First, the existence of these rights implies a lot more than noninterference as a correlative duty. If you have a right to education, then all of the noninterference in the world will not guarantee you that education. A right to work will do no good if there is no job to be done. If there are correlative duties corresponding to such rights, they are duties to take positive steps so that people receive that to which they are entitled. Second, problems of scarcity arise with regard to rights so conceived. Considerable expenditure of resources would be necessary to the exercise of such rights, and

---

JOHN LOCKE (1632–1704)

One of the foremost champions of individual rights was John Locke. At twenty, Locke became a student at Oxford, where he later taught classics. Although deeply religious, his ideas about religious toleration led him away from the ministry. He became the personal physician and advisor to the Earl of Shaftsbury, a powerful party politician. In this position Locke helped write the constitution of the Carolina colony.

Shaftsbury was accused of treason by the Stuart monarch. After the Earl's death, Locke fled England. He returned as an advisor to Queen Mary in 1689. In 1690 he published the *Essay Concerning Human Understanding* and *Two Treatises on Government*. These were followed by the *Reasonableness of Christianity* (1695). Locke argued that moral law can be demonstrated by appeal to human experience if one focuses on the long-range consequences of moral decisions and on the evidence of Christianity. In 1704 Locke died, a man with many friends, well respected for his simple way of life, wisdom, and practicality.

Locke believed in each individual's basic and inalienable rights to life, liberty, and property. The government's role is to ensure these rights. Locke advocated the political equality of all men and held that ultimate political authority should reside with the people.

these resources are very often scarce; they are not abundant or limitless as are resources such as places to exercise the rights of free speech or freedom of worship.

The contrast between eighteenth- and twentieth-century rights can be illustrated with respect to the right to life. On an eighteenth-century interpretation this amounts to the right not to be killed; your right to life is honored so long as no one interferes with your living. On a twentieth-century interpretation, however, mere noninterference does not honor your right; you have a right to be kept alive, which may require that food or medical services be provided for you.

14:5.2   There are conflicting interpretations of moral rights as conceived in the twentieth century. One school of thought suggests that indeed there are correlative duties, and that a person's having a right to education, for example, implies that someone has a duty to provide the

---

THE DECLARATION OF HUMAN RIGHTS

The United Nations was organized for several purposes in addition to maintaining world peace. One of these, the reaffirmation of faith in fundamental human rights, is the responsibility of the U.N. Economic and Social Council (UNESCO). It moved to abolish slavery, human debt bondage, and selling women as marriage partners. It worked for the equal political status of women, economic aid for refugees, health care and social services for children, and world literacy. Toward these ends it drafted an international bill of human rights in 1947. On December 10, 1948, this document was approved by the General Assembly as the "Declaration of Human Rights."

The Declaration's 30 articles reaffirm several eighteenth-century rights such as the rights to life, liberty, personal security, privacy, a fair trial, and a presumption of innocence. It proclaims rights of nationality and political asylum. It adds rights concerning one's economic and social condition, such as the right to work, rest, leisure time, social security, well-being, health, community participation, and education.

These rights are not thought of as arising out of human nature as much as they are described as goals. They are to be a "common standard of achievement for all peoples and nations." As such, their ever fuller realization becomes the responsibility of government at all levels.

education. Most plausibly it has been suggested that the state through the agency of the government has the obligation to provide the conditions that will allow persons to fulfill such rights. Some object to this analysis as follows: If the state has such duties, then surely the state ought to do whatever its duty requires. Yet it seems quite unreasonable to say that any agency, individual or collective, ought to do something that it cannot do. It may well be beyond the power of the state, or anybody, to do what it is said ought to be done here. Thus, it is unclear whether any sort of duty can be said to be correlated with rights as conceived in the present century. Of course, this objection is quite compatible with maintaining the less stringent view that the state has the duty to see that these rights are fulfilled insofar as possible.

An alternative analysis of twentieth-century rights claims translates them as descriptions about the ideal conditions under which human life would be lived. In this view it ought to be a universal goal that conditions conducing to the fulfillment of such rights be brought about. Thus, ideally people would have meaningful work and leisure, ample opportunities for education, quality nutrition and medical care, and so on. But on this analysis it is clear that there is no duty to try to fulfill these rights for persons in circumstances where scarcity of resources renders it impossible. Indeed, on this "rights-as-ideals" analysis these statements assert only what the best state of affairs would be without assigning any particular duties to any party at all, including the state.

In the case study Prince at various points makes rights claims illustrating the contrast between eighteenth- and twentieth-century concepts. She claims the right to speak her mind on the issue in dispute, and this is clearly a claim to a freedom where, at most, the others have the duty not to interfere. At another point she seems to maintain a right to meaningful employment. Moreover, she apparently associates such employment with her location. Cosmopolitan Sidney allows her to live her kind of life, and she thinks a move to the Outback would deprive her of the meaningful life to which she is entitled. It should also be noted that if every player were to insist that meaningful life could only be lived in cosmopolitan Sidney, either the league would fold or some players would have to live unfulfilled lives, scarcity again becoming problematic.

Exercises for Module 14: Concepts of Rights

1. Below is a list of rights. Some are conventional moral rights (*CMR*); some are moral rights not based on conventions (*NCMR*). Dis-

tinguish each right as one or the other. Where you identify rights as based upon conventions, specify what kind of convention must be operating in societies where people can be meaningfully said to have the rights. (14:2.1–14:2.4)

_____ a. The right to assembly with other persons.

_____ b. The right to make a will.

_____ c. The right to have a job.

_____ d. The right to run for political office.

_____ e. The right to sell one's property.

_____ f. The right to worship as one chooses.

_____ g. The right to refuse medical aid.

_____ h. The right to donate one's body to science.

_____ i. The right not to have others conceal information from one.

_____ j. The right to have a clean environment.

2. Below is a list of rights. Some of these rights involve correlative duties of noninterference (CD); some do not (NCD). Distinguish each right as one or the other. If there is a correlative duty, specify what is not to be interfered with. If there is no correlative duty, state what rights others have that imply they have no duty of noninterference.

_____ a. The right to speak as one chooses.

_____ b. The right to open a business.

_____ c. The right to run a successful business.

_____ d. The right to offer one's property for rent.

_____ e. The right to have someone buy one's property.

_____ f. The right to become the renter of any property offered for rent.

_____ g. The right of a person who is the only one who applies to rent property legally offered for rent.

_____ h. The right of a landlord not to rent his or her property to any applicant.

3. Below is a list including some moral rights and some legal powers. Mark the moral rights MR and the legal powers LP. (14:2.3)
A person has a right

_____ a. to favor and back a particular candidate for office.

_____ b. to initiate the recall of an elected official.

_____ c. to have as many children as he or she chooses.

_____ d. to make a contract.

_____ e. to write a will.

_____ f. to choose the town in whch he or she wishes to live.

_____ g. to have a friend visit in one's home.

_____ *h.* to have one's lawyer move for dismissal of the charges against one.

4. The following narrative contains many statements that assert or are based on legal powers, state liabilities, or state immunities. Mark appropriately: *LP, L,* or *I.* (14:3.1, 14:3.2)

_____ *a.* Lyn Lovelacer signed a contract with the Shady Shoelace company.

_____ *b.* She agreed to appear in five television commercials for them.

_____ *c.* They agreed to pay her $2,000.

_____ *d.* She agreed to make the commercials at any time during the month following the signing of the contract.

_____ *e.* She gave her lawyer the authority to negotiate a second contract for commercials with Shady.

_____ *f.* Lyn, in the second contract, would not be bound to refuse to work for any other advertising agencies.

_____ *g.* Shady would pay her a greater amount in the second contract.

_____ *h.* Her lawyer would not have to guarantee Lyn's willingness to sign a second contract. (14:5.1, 14:5.2)

5. Below is a list of rights. Some of these would have been recognized as human rights in accordance with eighteenth-century criteria, others only in accordance with twentieth-century criteria. Mark each right listed below *E* or *T* and explain for each *T* what characteristics disqualify it to be an *E.*

_____ *a.* The right to move oneself from one town to another.

_____ *b.* The right to receive an education.

_____ *c.* The right to worship whatever deity one chooses.

_____ *d.* The right to adequate health care.

_____ *e.* The right to do meaningful work.

_____ *f.* The right to offer what one produces for sale.

_____ *g.* The right to hold meetings with other people who want to attend them.

_____ *h.* The right to have leisure time.

Answers to Exercises for Module 14

1. *a.* NCMR.
   b. *CMR:* in order for people to make wills, a procedure for making a legal will has to be set up; for example, the will must be witnessed or notarized.

      c. NCMR.

      d. CMR: a person must go through the conventional procedure of filing for office in order to be an official candidate for the office. There are often other legal requirements as well, such as age.

      e. CMR: selling one's property involves the conventional action of making a contract.

      f. NCMR.

      g. NCMR.

      h. CMR: donating one's body requires a legal convention parallel to the one that allows a person to will his property.

      i. NCMR.

      j. NCMR.

2.   *a. CD:* not to interfere with or prevent another person from speaking.

      b. CD: not to interfere with or prevent another person from opening the business.

      c. NCD: others have the right to open businesses of their own, which may successfully compete with the first party's business, even making it fail.

      d. CD: not to interfere with or prevent another person from offering his property for rent.

      e. NCD: others have the right to offer their own property for sale, and scarcity of customers may mean that some who want to sell can find no buyers. It is also true that this alleged right is very suspect, because if anybody had the right to have someone buy his property, then someone else would have the corresponding duty to buy the property, which would seem to be an infringement of that person's right to spend money as he chooses.

      f. NCD: if all persons have an equal right to rent the property, then there must be legal ways for persons to compete with each other concerning who shall rent a piece of property. Such competition is a form of interference.

      g. CD: for no one, including the prospective landlord, to interfere with or prevent the applicant from renting the property.

      h. CD: for no one to interfere with or prevent the landlord from deciding that he does not want to rent the property to any applicant. (If it is true that only applicants have the right listed above, then landlords do not have this right. Also, landlords may be prohibited from using race as a criterion in deciding not to rent, yet they may retain this right if it is exercised on the basis of some other criterion; for example, all people who apply have pets, and the landlord refuses to allow pet owners to rent.)

3.   *a. MR.*   *b. LP.*   *c. MR.*   *d. LP.*   *e. LP.*   *f. MR.*   *g. MR.*

    h. LP

In some countries there are legal powers to permit acting on the basis of certain moral rights. In some countries there are laws that abridge some moral rights.

4.   *a. LP*—to enter into a contract.

      b. L—to go on television.

    c. *L*—to become liable for payment.

    d. *L*—to become liable to be called to work at a specific time.

    e. *LP*—to authorize her lawyer to act on her behalf.

    f. *I*—she would be immune from having to restrict herself to only one ad agency.

    g. *L*—to pay her more.

    h. *I*—from being bound by what her lawyer negotiated.

5.   *a*. *E*.

    b. *T:* the right to receive an education cannot be satisfied simply by other persons' performing a duty of noninterference. An opportunity, and perhaps teachers, must be provided if the person is to receive the education.

    c. *E*.

    d. *T:* the right to adequate health care cannot be satisfied simply by other persons' performing a duty of noninterference. Persons will receive adequate health care only if medicines, medical equipment, and medical personnel are available or made available to them.

    e. *T:* the right to do meaningful work will not necessarily be satisfied simply by other persons' performing a duty of noninterference. Others may have to cooperate in order to create opportunities for meaningful work.

    f. *E*.

    g. *E*.

    h. *T:* the right to have leisure time will not necessarily be satisfied simply by other persons' performing a duty of noninterference. An elaborate social and technological base may be necessary in order to ensure that persons can survive without working all of their waking hours.

Module 15
CONCEPTS OF DUTY

    Some hold that there is a type of right to which persons are entitled without qualification and which they may not, under any conditions, renounce. This is to say that there are moral rights that are indefeasible and inalienable. In this module, after initial conceptual analysis, we shall examine Kant's view that there are corresponding duties to respect such rights without exception. The view that there is such a duty (called a *Categorical Imperative*) will be contrasted with the view that all duties are hypothetical. Three formulations of the Categorical Imperative will be presented and interpreted. The views that there are indefeasible and inalienable rights and a Categorical Imperative will be shown to be instances of what is called a deontological ethical theory. Such a theory maintains that some actions are intrinsically right. After reading Module 15, you should be able to

- Characterize indefeasible rights.
- Characterize inalienable rights.
- Distinguish and apply instrumental, conventional, and deontological justifications for doing one's duty.
- State three formulations of Kant's categorical imperative.
- Explain why various actions violate the categorical imperative.

THE CASE OF ELROD CLAYMORE

Elrod Claymore was an energetic, vibrant, athletic young man of 25. He thrived on physical activity and was especially satisfied when working with his hands. He had always hoped to work for the National Park Service, enjoying the sensations that nature and hard labor had to offer. Tragically, Elrod was caught in a forest fire in Bluestone National Park, where he had just begun working as a ranger. A rescue squad was able to pull him from the flames and save his life, but not before he suffered severe burns over two-thirds of his body. His limbs and face were burnt worst of all. He would henceforth be blind and unable to walk or use his hands. Moreover, to survive at all, he must undergo years of painful treatment.

Because the wounds and the treatment combined to make Elrod's first few months after the fire hellishly painful, he was treated without his consent, for there was no time when the effects of the pain and medication left him lucid enough to express his own desires. The medical staff worked dedicatedly to bring him back from the brink of death, hoping that he would someday find new reason to live.

During several months of severe agony, fluctuating between wakefulness and nightmare, Elrod gradually recovered his lucidity. After a period when it was hard to tell whether he was rational or was still under the influence of the trauma he was suffering, the time finally arrived when all concerned, including psychiatrists and lawyers, acknowledged that Elrod was able to express his rational wish.

Throughout the early stages of his agony Elrod, on occasion, had managed to cry out that he wished he were dead. Now, obviously self-possessed, he clearly articulated his wish to have treatment discontinued and to be allowed to die.

His reasons were these: He was well aware that the painful treatment was by no means over, and he did not believe future prospects were bright enough to make his continued suffering worthwhile. He saw no good reason for him to wish to live, since he could no longer enjoy any of those things that he had found most meaningful and satisfying. He hinted that he suspected the medical staff were interested in his case more because of what they were learning about burn-treatment techniques than because of a concern for his future well-being. He asserted that he had an absolute right to choose to die. He believed there would not possibly be any overriding concerns of others, or of the state, that could cancel that right or justify his continued suffering. He requested that he be released from the treatment center and be returned to his home to die.

The treatment center staff did not grant Elrod's wish. They were well aware that discontinuing treatment and releasing Elrod at that time would inevitably lead to his contracting a fatal infection. His mother had spoken with Elrod and the staff and begged that he not be released, even if that meant not honoring his wishes. She prayed for a meaningful future for him and for his eventual forgiveness.

15:1.1 Indefeasible Rights. To say that a person has a right is to say he or she has an entitlement—your right to worship as you please entitles you to worship as you please. To say that a right is *indefeasible* is to say that there can be no circumstances where others can justifiably override that right. If you have indefeasible rights, others cannot undo, annul, or cancel them for any reason whatever: they may be ignored or violated, but never justifiably. By contrast, to say that a right is defeasible is to allow that (a) while having the right contributes to the justification of action in accord with it and to the justification of the claim that the right should be honored, still (b) in some circumstances a contrary stronger justification may be offered, leading to the conclusion that the right should not be honored. Thus, to talk about whether a right is indefeasible or defeasible is to talk about whether someone else's right or someone else's circumstances might override it. There has been much dispute over whether there are, indeed, any indefeasible rights. Some that have at times been characterized as indefeasible are the right to life, the right to liberty, the right to free speech, and the right to develop one's talents to the extent that one does not violate the rights of others.

15:1.2 In the case study Elrod maintained that he had a right to die. In claiming that no circumstances were imaginable to him under which he could justifiably be denied the exercise of that right, he was claiming that his right to die was indefeasible. Whether or not his mother and the medical staff believed that he or anyone else had a right to die is unclear. What is clear is that, if they did believe people had such a right, they did not believe the right to be indefeasible. They were acting in accord with a belief that overriding considerations in Elrod's circumstances justified their not honoring his right.

15:2.1 Inalienable Rights.   To say that a right is *inalienable* is to say that a person cannot give it up or in any way properly renounce it. Contrarily, to say that a right is alienable is to say that a person can justifiably renounce his or her claim to it or transfer it to another. As an illustration, consider two cases of supposed ownership of property. In one case a person who owns things (say, a car or furniture) enjoys an alienable right of property with regard to them. What makes it alienable is the fact that ownership of the property can be transferred or renounced. If the owner sells the furniture or car, she or he loses all title to it and is no longer entitled to treat it as she or he sees fit. By contrast, many believe that no person has a right to sell himself or herself into slavery. In other words, the right not to be a slave is inalienable. If so, then ownership of one person by another can never be justified. A person might submit to the bondage of another as if he or she were a piece of property, but his or her right not to be enslaved would not thereby be renounced; rather, it simply would not be asserted. Thus, the entiitlement to affirm one's personhood would remain throughout the bondage relationship. The fact of the original submission could never count as a cancellation of the inalienable right not to be enslaved.

15:2.2   The Declaration of Independence refers to the rights to life, liberty, and the pursuit of happiness as inalienable. It is possible to think also of many of the rights in the Bill of Rights as inalienable. In the case study, Elrod hints that his case may be of interest to the medical staff primarily because of the knowledge they are gaining about burn therapy; he may thereby be voicing a concern that what he takes to be an inalienable right not to be exploited is being violated. He might also claim that his right to die is inalienable. The nonexercise of the right to die by people who choose to continue living would be quite compatible with continuance of the entitlement on their part. Similarly, a person does not lose the right to sell his or her property simply because he or she chooses to keep it for some time.

15:3.1 Contrasting Indefeasible and Inalienable Rights.   If a right is indefeasible, is it also inalienable? If it is inalienable, is it always indefeasible? The concepts of indefeasibility and inalienability are distinct, and you will understand them better if you can see how some rights might be one without being the other.

Consider the right to use one's own property as one chooses. The idea of inalienability is that a person cannot renounce a certain right. One does, however, give up rights to one's property when one rents or sells it. If you had an inalienable right to use your property as you chose, then you would not be able to relinquish that right by renting your property and transferring those rights to the renter. Indefeasibility, on the other hand, does not have to do with a person's renouncing or relinquishing his or her own rights. Rather it involves other persons' conflicting and overriding rights. Some people would say that as long as the property in question is legally yours, no one, under any circumstances, has rights overriding yours. That is, no one can make you use, or himself or herself use, your property as he or she sees fit. This is the claim that the right to use your own property as you see fit *is indefeasible,* although we have just seen that it *is not inalienable.*

Now consider the right to life. Unlike the right to the use of your property, the right to life has been considered by many as defeasible but inalienable. To say that your right to life is inalienable is to say that you cannot renounce it. It is to claim, for example, that whatever Elrod says, the right to life remains inalienably his for the medical staff to honor. On the other hand, some people who view the right to life as inalienable also support capital punishment. That is, they hold that certain circumstances, namely those of having been convicted of a capital offense, such as murder, give society the overriding right, and perhaps even a duty, to take the life of the criminal. This is the view that the right to life *is defeasible*—capable of being justifiably overridden by a conflicting right or duty.

15:4.1 Deontological Ethics. If any indefeasible and inalienable rights exist, then it would be morally right under all conditions to honor them. That is, the corresponding duties to honor such rights would be unconditional. It is a small step from this to the view that performing such duties is intrinsically right. This view, that some actions are intrinsically right, is the defining characteristic of what has come to be called *deontological ethical theory,* or *deontology.* Deontological theory contrasts with all ethical theory that would define actions as right in terms of their consequences, either for the agent or for others. Such contrasting theories may be called *consequentialist,* since they maintain that actions can only be considered as *instrumentally* (as opposed to intrinsically) right or wrong, to the extent that they conduce to good or bad consequences.

15:4.2 The ethical theory of Immanuel Kant (1724–1804) may readily be interpreted as an instance of *deontological theory.* Kant argues that some rights indeed are both indefeasible and inalienable, and that other people have obligations to honor such rights. These obligations are not merely *hypothetical* but rather are universal and *categorical*. Categorical duties exist under all possible circumstances, whereas hypothetical duties exist merely under certain specifiable conditions, when a certain "hypothesis" is true. In Kant's view morality is not a function of any hypothesis that other goals besides duty are to be served. Thus, it is not the case that persons have duties only on the condition that they are interested in pursuit of particular ends, consequences, or benefits. Categorical duties are unconditioned duties. It is intrinsically right to do one's categorical duties.

To be more concrete, according to Kant, morality is not a matter of rationally pursuing one's own self-interest (enlightened egoism). Neither is it a matter of rationally coordinating the interests of the majority of the people (universal utilitarianism). Nor is morality merely a matter of conforming to convention and performing one's duties as they arise within, and are conditioned by, social or legal conventions. Thus, morality is not a matter of pursuing any hypothetical or conditional ends. It makes no difference in terms of one's moral duty whether those ends be the production of good consequences or the preservation of arbitrarily constructed conventions. According to Kant morality is fundamentally a matter of doing one's categorical duties—that is, doing those duties that correspond to the indefeasible and inalienable rights people enjoy regardless of circumstance.

Of course, particular conventions may well be designed to capture or reflect our categorical duties. For example, the Hippocratic Oath is our society's conventional way for a new doctor to undertake a commitment to human health. But what makes such conformity moral is not the existence of the conventions, but rather the existence of the indefeasible and inalienable rights that inspired and served as justification for the conventions. What justifies the doctors' taking oaths committing themselves to human health and life is the rights of persons to health and life and to having commitments to them honored.

We can read the case study as illustrating the contrast between hypothetical and categorical duties. Elrod claims he has an indefeasible and inalienable right to be allowed to die. He believes that for this reason the staff and his mother have a categorical duty to allow him to exercise that right. The duty is not hypothetical, because it is not conditioned by any considerations of any future benefits for Elrod or the others involved, nor by any particular conventions that may govern hospital practice. If Elrod has the right he claims, then he has it even if no official body, be it a hospital governance board or a state legislature, acknowledges its existence. It is his simply by virtue of his being a person.

15:5.1 The Categorical Imperative.   We have explained what Kant meant by claiming that moral duty is categorical as opposed to hypothetical. Now let us see what our categorical duty is according to Kant. In an attempt to make himself clear on this point, he offered three distinct formulations of the Categorical Imperative. Kant did not see these three formulations as implying three distinct categorical duties. Rather, at bottom, each formulation amounts to an alternate way of specifying the same duty. Thus, each formulation provides but one possible perspective, or insight, into the single categorical duty that for Kant defines morality.

15:5.2   The first formulation of the Categorical Imperative is, "So act that the maxim of your will could always hold at the same time as a principle establishing universal law." In this formulation Kant expresses the concept of the universalizability of moral principles discussed in Module 3. One should act in such a way that the principles governing one's actions are universalizable; no arbitrary distinctions between persons are to be captured in those principles. Of course roles, abilities, and circumstances are relevant to the specification of precisely what actions are being performed. Kant's point is that despite these disclaimers, an action can be morally permissible for one person only if that same action is permissible for anyone in the same situation.

Let us briefly consider examples reflecting Kant's concern for universalizability—his concern that inequitable or unfair exceptions for particular persons be counted as immoral. Consider first whether breaking a promise for personal convenience could become a universal practice. Kant believes not, for not everyone could indulge in the practice. Although a few could do so, if everyone were to attempt it, then no promises would be taken seriously. Ironically the very act of promising with the end in view of breaking the promise when convenient would become impossible. Or, put another way, suppose everyone made promise-like declarations with the mental qualification, "That is, unless I just don't feel like it." In such a society, no one would accept any of these declarations as ways of unconditionally giving one's word. Similarly, if everybody indiscriminately used resources no matter to whom they belonged, the institution of private property, like the institution of promising, would be impossible.

In the case study, Elrod seems willing to maintain that the maxim (general principle) of the action he requests of his mother and of the medical staff is a universalizable moral principle. His request is that they release him from the hospital in the light of his admittedly rational request to be allowed to die. The action could be universalized to the practice of honoring such requests made by patients who are in similar circumstances.

15:5.3   Kant's second formulation of the Categorical Imperative is, "Act so as to treat humanity, whether in your own person or in that of another, always as an end and never as a means only." If the moral law is to apply to all persons, as the first formulation of the Categorical Imperative indicates, then all persons are to count as equally valuable. It cannot be, then, that any person's goals can come to have such value that another person's goals may be subordinated to them to such a degree that the other person is used simply to accomplish those goals. In this view, there is a categorical duty to treat other persons like human beings with indefeasible and inalienable rights, rather than like tools or machines. It is the having of such rights that distinguishes persons as having intrinsic value from things, the value of which is merely instrumental. This is a claim that to each person is due, minimally, a higher kind of respect, an inviolable dignity, that is incompatible with his or her being brainwashed, made into a docile instrument for the purposes of others, enslaved, manipulated, or converted into a domesticated animal. To fail to accord persons this minimal respect is to blur the distinction between persons and things; it is disrespectful of human moral autonomy.

In the case study Elrod is suspicious that the medical staff are interested in gaining knowledge about burn therapy through keeping him alive against his wishes. He is suspicious, then, that he is being exploited, or treated simply as a means rather than as an end. Treating him as an end could well require that his decision to be allowed to die rather than suffer continued agony be honored. Not to do so would be to subordinate the value of his moral autonomy to a supposedly higher value, improved burn therapy.

It is important for you to notice Kant's exact wording in this second formulation of the Categorical Imperative. He states the imperative as that of treating humanity always as an end and never as a means *only*. Imagine Elrod when he first arrived at the hospital. At that point it was reasonable to presume that Elrod would want to live if it were at all possible. It would certainly have been morally and legally dangerous to presume otherwise. Thus at that point treating Elrod's burns as effectively as possible was certainly a way of treating Elrod as an end. It might happen, however, that the best techniques for treating Elrod were sufficiently unestablished that the medical team would learn something about burn therapy from treating Elrod's case. Under these circumstances, treating Elrod would also be a means to improving medical knowledge of burn therapy. To such treatment, however, Kant would raise no objection. For although Elrod is being used as a means, he is also being treated as an end, and thus not as a means *only*.

15:5.4   Kant's third formulation of the Categorical Imperative is, "Act according to the maxims of a universally legislative member of a merely potential kingdom of ends." While the language here is complicated, this formulation seems based on the following Kantian reasoning. If individuals are always to be treated as ends and never solely as means, then each person must recognize that all others are morally in an equal position as oneself; they are all moral persons. That is, in effect, to note that all persons belong to the same moral community. Persons who come to this realization recognize two things: (a) they can legitimately pursue those of their goals that do not conflict with the duty to treat others as ends, and (b) they have a duty to facilitate the same possibility for all others. In other words, society should be organized so as to promote each person's freedom and facilitate expressing this freedom within the boundaries of the moral law. Thus, this third formulation of the Categorical Imperative could be read as indicating that persons have a categorical duty to behave in such a way that the principles governing their actions could be adopted by everyone and serve as the basis for a moral community governed by mutual respect.

The case study raises a question whether within a moral community there is a duty to honor serious requests to be allowed to die. Kant did not directly discuss whether there is a right to die. He did sharply oppose suicide. Yet, there is room to ask whether his moral theory, as reflected in the three formulations of the categorical imperative, implies that there is a right to die and a categorical duty to honor it. We leave it to you to consider whether a community where such a right is honored is more or less respectful of persons as morally autonomous ends in themselves than a community where no such right is recognized. Pending further conceptual analysis, what has been said so far might be used to support both views.

Exercises for Module 15: Concepts of Duty

1. Suppose that a given person has earned a certain amount of money by working for it. In such circumstances it is plausible to assert that the person has a right to all of that money. (15:1.1, 15:1.2, 15:2.1, 15:2.2, 15:3.1, 15:3.2)

   a. Describe the payroll deduction of income taxes as showing the defeasibility of that right.

   b. Describe the payroll deduction of a donation to the United Fund (a charity) as showing the alienability of that right.

   c. In the light of *a,* state the characteristics of a defeasible right abstractly, without reference to any particular case of a defeasible right.

    d. In the light of *b,* state the characteristics of an alienable right abstractly.

    e. In the light of *c* and *d,* define the concepts of indefeasible rights and inalienable rights.

2.   Below are three reasons for performing each of two alleged duties. Distinguish the reasons as consequentialist (*CQ*), conventionalist (*CV*), or deontological (*D*). (15:4.1, 15:4.2)

    _____ *a.* If you don't give the kids candies on Halloween, they're likely to soap your windows.

    _____ *b.* Giving the kids candies is respectful and kind.

    _____ *c.* Its traditional to give all the kids candies on Halloween.

    _____ *d.* Bakeries have given thirteen cookies when you buy a dozen for so long that now we just call it a baker's dozen.

    _____ *e.* Customers are likely to come back to a store where they think they're getting something for nothing.

    _____ *f.* A bakery shows its good will towards its customers by making sure that every customer receives a full measure of baked goods for his money.

3.   Suppose you have been invited to a party and your host or hostess has asked you to indicate in advance whether you plan to attend. Provide a consequentialist reason, a reason based on convention, and a deontological reason for communicating your plans in advance. (15:4.1, 15:4.2, 15:4.3)

4.   State three formulations of Kant's Categorical Imperative. (15:5.2, 15:5.3, 15:5.4)

5.   Each of the following actions in some way violates the Categorical Imperative. Explain how.

    a. Tough Tom refused to talk to the cab driver, insisting that all he wanted was a ride and that he was doing nothing wrong so long as he paid for his ride.

    b. Although supplies were limited and his company had instituted a "one per customer" policy, Clever Cal let his fraternity brothers buy two or three. (15:5.2)

    c. Mona told her friend, Lisa, that she had broken up with Al because of how badly he had treated her. She went into great detail about his alleged mistreatment, although it was in fact she who had mistreated Al. (15:5.3)

    d. Despite his daughter's continued interest and even fascination with woodworking, Handy Harry refused to teach her how to use any of the tools. (15:5.4)

e. When Carl, the Cop, saw his friends stuck in one of the lines of the traffic jam, he immediately let that line of traffic go until his friends had cleared the area, while all others remained stopped. (15:5.2)

f. Higgensville Senior High School's policy forbade boys from enrolling in home economics courses. (15:5.4)

Selected Answers to Exercises for Module 15

1. a. The right of the government to collect income taxes, or the right of the society to provide for various needs of its citizens, might override the right of the individual to keep all the money he or she has earned, thereby making his right defeasible.

   b. The individual can renounce his or her right to his or her money by donating that money to some other party, thereby alienating him or herself from that right.

   c. An individual's right is defeasible when, even though the individual has the right, some other party has a right, such that there is adequate justification for the other party to act on his or her right to the exclusion of the original individual's being able to exercise his or her right.

   d. An individual's right is alienable when it is possible for the person to act so as to lose or renounce it.

   e. An indefeasible right is one such that under no circumstances is there an adequate justification for not allowing the person having it to exercise it. An inalienable right is one such that in no way can a person having it lose or renounce it.

2. a. CQ.   b. D.   c. CV.   d. CV.   e. CQ.   f. D.

3. CQ: if I don't announce my intentions, something undesirable will happen: I won't be invited to another party, my host or hostess might embarrass me at the party, there won't be enough food prepared, or whatever.
   CV: etiquette and custom say that a person is supposed to announce whether he or she will accept an invitation.
   D: I have a duty to respect people who have been kind enough to invite me to their party.
   Naturally your reasons may mention different consequences, conventions, or duties from those stated in these sample answers.

5. a. Tom is treating the cab driver merely as a means to his getting where he wants.

   b. Cal is treating his fraternity brothers in a way that cannot be universalized to all customers.

   c. Mona is treating Al solely as a means to trying to create an image of herself that she wants Lisa to have.

d. Harry is refusing to help others to pursue their goals.

e. Carl is treating his friends in a way in which he cannot treat all the people stuck in the traffic jam.

f. The high school is hindering its male students from pursuing goals some of them may have.

Module 16
FOUNDATIONS OF DEONTOLOGY

In Module 14 we analyzed the wide variety of possible rights claims in terms of related concepts, especially that of duty. In Module 15 we examined more extensively the view that there are moral rights that are indefeasible and inalienable. We focused on the Kantian theory that there is, correspondingly, a categorical imperative to honor such rights. In this module we will consider how deontological theorists, such as Kant, might offer justification for their view that some actions are intrinsically right. The guiding questions for the module are these: Why should any rights be taken as indefeasible and inalienable? Why should any duties be taken as categorical? We shall show, then, how the foundations for this deontological theory are imbedded in the concepts of respect, self-respect, and integrity. The concluding section will deal with the Kantian view that acting with proper intention is what makes actions intrinsically right. After reading Module 16, you should be able to

- Characterize respect and self-respect.
- Explain why ignoring each of the three formulations of the categorical imperative implies a lack of respect.
- State the conceptual connection between indefeasible rights, respect for persons, and categorical duties.
- Characterize integrity, comparing and contrasting personal and social integrity.
- State Kant's argument that proper intention makes actions intrinsically right.
- Contrast deontological and consequentialist ethical theories.

THE CASE OF THE IMAGINARY JOURNEY THROUGH SPACE

Come with us on a flight of the imagination to a planet in a far corner of the universe. Envision a world totally devoid of life. You are not there and never will be. It exists in a solar system millions of light-years distant. You will never have any experience relating to this planet in the remotest way. Not only is there no life whatever on this planet, but it also lacks the kind of atmospheric and terrestrial environment that could ever lead to the development of life. The desert landscape of rolling dunes and large, smooth rocks is disturbed only by hot, dry winds. Call this planet Lifeless.

Think now of a different planet, equally remote from you and from Lifeless. Although again there is no life, conditions may allow life some-day to develop there. The proper atmospheric and terrestrial environment, including an abundant water supply, are present. Call this planet Possibility.

Now fly to a third planet. Here atmospheric and terrestrial conditions enable plant life to grow, flourish, and reproduce itself in abundance, save in a few scattered desert areas or in valleys where poisonous gases lie. It is a planet filled with meadows of tall grasses and wild flowers, forests and jungles, plants of all descriptions. Call this world Flora.

Now to a fourth planet, which supports both plant and animal life in advanced forms. Imagine that this is the first of our planets where living things are capable of sensation, awareness of the environment, and move-ment over the surface of the planet and beneath its waters, as well as growth, reproduction and flourishing of animal species are present. The environment is a balanced one, enabling many species to live together. Of course, not all is pleasant. Pain and suffering exist because of the inter-action among the species. The law of the survival of the fittest is opera-tive. There are diseases, storms, floods, droughts, and earthquakes. Call this planet Fauna.

Turn your imagination now toward a fifth planet. Here, intelligent creatures called Groms live together with all of the species found on the planet Fauna. Certain geographical areas on the planet offer that narrow range of weather conditions conducive to Grom life. The presence of Groms makes this the first planet harboring more than the plant and animal functions. The capacity for rationality and rational action are present, so that some behaviors are far from instinctual. We can also imagine that some creatures can choose which of their several potentials shall be pursued and developed. Groms are also distinctive in having the capacity to act autonomously. They can also fail to act autonomously. Self-awareness and self-evaluation are additional new possibílities. With these capacities Groms are able to feel emotions about themselves and about their relations with other beings—satisfaction, exhilaration, confi-dence, care, pride, anguish, frustration, fear, anxiety, shame, and guilt, among others. Some of these emotions do not conduce to the continued flourishing of the Groms involved, whereas others do. In some cases, where some of the more painful emotions or even injuries are suffered, Groms are not flourishing. Feelings of responsibility for themselves and for other Groms are also now possible. Social harmony, mutual respect, cooperation, conflict of interests, war, and exploitation are among the new social potentials found here for the first time. Not only are beings on this planet susceptible to natural catastrophe, but they are threatened as well by environmental abuse. They are capable of destroying the delicate ecological balance vital for the survival of life on the planet. Groms have developed weapons capable of rendering the planet as sterile as the planet Lifeless. Call this planet Precarious.

16:1.1 Deontology and Intrinsically Right Action. This case study illustrates a variety of values that may be realized or realizable within the corners of the universe we have imagined, or for that matter within our own corner of the universe. The conditions and beings found on various of our five fantasy planets illustrate both instrumental and intrinsic values. On Lifeless, for instance, it seems nothing is good or bad in itself. Nothing seems to be of any particular instrumental value either. Weather has no value, since nothing lives on Lifeless that it can be good for or bad for. The most violent storm or earthquake is no "worse" than the mildest of days. On Possibility, at least instrumental value may be present, because conditions on Possibility are good for the development of life. We could add that the destruction of these conditions would be bad, because it would end the potentiality for the development of life there. But be careful—the assumption operative here is that life itself has some value.

In order to determine the values life involves, consider the other worlds in our imaginary galaxy. Each of the remaining planets introduces new levels of potential for living. On Flora, growth, reproduction, and flourishing of an organism are the new possibilities. On Fauna, typical animal functions and potentials, including sensation, awareness of the environment, and movement, are added. Precarious is the only planet described where the potentials of rationality, autonomy, self-awareness, feelings of satisfaction, responsibility for self and others, feelings of fellowship, social harmony, and mutual respect are present.

It is plausible to suggest that each of the potentials found on the various planets has intrinsic value. Some of them, of course, can also be thought of as having instrumental value, making possible the realization of other potentials. Thus, for example, awareness of the environment may be understood as intrinsically valuable and, at the same time, instrumentally valuable, because it is a condition for Groms to be able to come to respect each other.

16:1.2 If the various life potentials on our fantasy planets are considered to have intrinsic value, then it is reasonable to understand the living conditions there to be instrumentally good when they are conducive to the continued development and realization of those potentials. Planetary conditions are instrumentally bad to the extent that they undermine or make impossible the continued development and realization of the various life potentials. Thus, it seems appropriate to think of the weather and the water supply on Flora as instrumentally good; they contribute to the lush growth. But the poisonous gases are instrumentally bad; they kill plant life. The habitable climate of Precarious is instrumentally good, as it allows advanced life such as Groms to flourish; its natural catastrophes, however, are instrumentally bad, for they can diminish the quality of, or even destroy, such life. Other social conditions on Precarious are instrumentally good or bad to the extent that they render possible, contribute to, undermine, or destroy the human potentials for autonomy, social harmony, and the like that exist there.

16:2.1 Respect. In analyzing the case study, we have surveyed some of the capacities that creatures of various kinds enjoy. For these creatures to flourish they must have and exercise these capacities. We have also noted how these creatures can be prevented from flourishing by various planetary and social conditions. This analysis also leads us to a definition of respect. To respect a creature is to *appreciate it for its capacity to flourish.* To respect something is to know and appreciate both its potentials for achievement and its potential ways of suffering. Showing respect for persons, then, amounts to allowing (not interfering with) and perhaps even facilitating their flourishing, or their exercising their capacities that have intrinsic value. In this way respect for persons may be viewed as an *absolute, instrumental value.* The value of respect is absolute because respect is necessary to the intrinsic good of creatures' being able to flourish. It is instrumentally good because it is defined as the means to this intrinsically good end. It could also be argued that respect is *intrinsically valuable.* Consider the possibility that some person is not treated with respect. Not only will this course of action probably reduce his ability to flourish, but it is an act of denigrating the person's value. What such an action says to the person is, "You are not really valuable; how you are treated doesn't matter all that much." This is not only instrumentally undesirable for its impact upon the person's conception of self-worth, but it is intrinsically wrong because of the gap between the implicit judgment concerning the person's worth and the facts about the person that render him or her worthy of respect.

16:2.2   Notice the generality involved in this concept of respect. Essentially we are saying that a being has capacities, the development of which define his or her flourishing. These same beings have limitations, and can, thus, be caused not to be able to flourish. Respect means appreciating both the being's capabilities and the limitations to which it is subject. Respect is broad enough to extend beyond human beings. Animals, for example, clearly have capacities for awareness of the environment, and many are capable of suffering pain. Respect for such beings, then, clearly implies not destroying their capacities for awareness, say by blinding them, and not inflicting pain—except for their own good—upon them.

16:2.3   Respect can be related to indefeasibility of rights. Ethical theorists who maintain that people have indefeasible rights by virtue of their being persons, are thinking of rights to exercise the capacities which we imagined for the first time on Precarious. Beings are intrinsically valuable because of having such capacities. This is the ground for the claim noted in 15:5.3—that to each person there is due, minimally, a higher kind of respect, an inviolable dignity, which is incompatible with his or her being brainwashed, made into a docile instrument for the purposes of others, enslaved, manipulated, or converted into a domesticated animal. If beings have these indefeasible rights, then there is a corresponding categorical duty to respect these beings, in precisely the sense of "respect" delineated in the preceding paragraph. If this is so, then we have uncovered one possible ultimate justification for the deontologists' thesis that there are intrinsically right actions. These intrinsically right actions would be those that are respectful of the potentials and capacities that are intrinsically valuable.

16:3.1   *Self-Respect.*   If it is true that to respect another (person or being) is to permit and even to facilitate flourishing, then self-respect is to do the same for oneself. If we hold that the kinds of attitudes or images a person has concerning himself significantly affect his ability to flourish, then having self-respect will involve having attitudes about oneself that allow oneself to flourish. Self-awareness and self-evaluation first become possible on the planet Precarious. Self-respect also becomes a possibility on that planet. Self-respect includes acknowledging and appreciating the rights that one has by virtue of being a person. Surely no sense could be attached to the idea that a self-respecting person might be unappreciative of his or her own rights as a person.

16:3.2   Self-respect will also be a matter of being prudent, of taking care of one's health, of being aware of one's limitations and strengths and of living within them. It may also involve endeavoring to maximize the development of one's abilities and talents. To better understand the connection of self-respect with development of personal potential, we must take a very important fact into account. Human beings have many capacities. It is impossible to develop all of them, for life is too short, and developing some capacities is incompatible with developing others. For instance, though a person may have the capacities to be both a world class sprinter and a world class swimmer, there is a physical incompatibility between developing both of these capacities. The way one develops muscles and techniques when one is becoming a sprinter makes the body less able to perform as a top-grade swimmer.

Moreover, although it may be possible for many persons to develop various capacities, it may be impossible for all persons to develop the same capacities. We live in a world where specialized labor predominates. However valuable heart surgery specialists may be, it is impossible that everybody should develop the capacity to be a heart surgeon. If everyone who had the capacity to become a heart surgeon took the time to develop it, there would not be time enough left over for people to develop and utilize the abilities to perform other socially useful tasks, such as feeding the population that might someday be in need of heart surgery. These facts about our world and our society constitute limiting factors that self-respecting persons must take into account as they rationally assess their capacities and choose which of them to try to develop.

16:3.3 Self-respect and inalienability turn out to be related in the same fashion as respect and indefeasibility. Whereas defeasible rights can be overridden by the stronger justifications others may have, indefeasible rights cannot be overridden. If one is to be respectful of a person's indefeasible rights, one must honor them. Where indefeasible rights cannot be overridden, inalienable rights cannot be renounced. And just as respect for others minimally involves honoring any indefeasible rights they have, so self-respect minimally involves not denying one's own inalienable rights (the rights one may not renounce). Kant, for example, thought of the development of one's talents as an inalienable right that a self-respecting person would not deny by either ignoring or destroying his or her potentials.

16:4.1 Integrity. Having looked at the concept of respect on both the personal and social levels, let us analyze a related concept, that of integrity, on those two levels. Integrity is a matter of integrating potentialities. Personal integrity is based on the elements of self-respect, such as being true to oneself and living responsibly in the light of one's limitations. Self-respect provides the necessary appreciation of what can be self-enhancing and what can be self-defeating. Beyond this, personal integrity demands a decision concerning which to develop from among the large number and variety of one's potentials. Personal integrity involves a decision to develop a set of potentials that are co-possible, or mutually compatible. This is part of the responsibility for oneself that first appears in the case study on the planet Precarious. One measure of the richness or fullness of particular human lives may then be the comparative extent to which, within those lives, there is a development of a diverse set of co-possible potentials.

16:4.2   The potentiality for individual persons to develop in a variety of ways raises the question of the degree of integrity those individuals attain. It also suggests the same question for societies, or groups of people. Societies can also develop in various ways. In parallel fashion, decisions must be made about which of the potentials attainable in or by a society are to be cultivated. On our imaginary planet Precarious, social development can take several directions, including those that would promote the continued flourishing of the inhabitants and those that could make levels of flourishing forever impossible through destruction of ecological or social balance and harmony.

16:4.3   Some maintain that the best society is the one that develops the social integrity to allow the greatest amount of personal integrity on the part of its members. This view of societal integrity sees virtue in maximizing each individual person's opportunities to achieve the highest degree of personal integrity. Individuals are thought of as if they were independent atoms, each able to find the greatest possible fullness and richness of personal integrity if left, as much as possible, to himself or herself. This view of society is called the *atomistic* view. It can be contrasted with what is called the *organic* view.

In the organic view, society should aim for social integrity measured in terms of its collective accomplishments. Here, individual lives attain meaning by participation in the activity of the larger whole. To achieve this it may be necessary at times to disparage the autonomy of particular individuals. The individual, in fact, might have little choice but to conform to and work for certain societal goals or to be ostracized. (For a fuller discussion of these two views of society, see Module 21.) Given these two possible views of society, and given that integrity has both a personal and a social dimension, one of the most important questions of social philosophy will turn out to be the relationship of the individual to the state. (This question also is addressed in Module 21.)

On Precarious, the feeling of responsibility for others can center upon either of two things. One is each Grom's potential to achieve personal autonomy. This could lead to the development of a society where respect for the indefeasible and inalienable rights of Groms was vitally important. Or the feeling of responsibility for others can center upon each Grom's potential for serving broader social or collective purposes. The same choices are offered on Earth.

16:5.1 Conscience. It could be argued that respect for persons is a matter of respecting (a) all of the human capacities mentioned in the description of the Groms on planet Precarious, and (b) the integrity of persons. In the view of Immanuel Kant, to be true to one's conscience is to act on the intention of respecting persons and, most importantly, respecting their integrity. Kant points out that no one can foresee perfectly all of the consequences of his action. He argues that whether any action is good or bad cannot, therefore, be judged on the basis of something that cannot even be foreseen. However, a person can know the conscience with which he or she acts. This, then, for Kant becomes the basis for judging the rightness or wrongness of the action. If the person acts in good conscience, attempting to respect persons and their integrity, then his or her action is intrinsically right. It is right because of the presence of that intention. Kant is saying that to intend to respect persons is to intend to bring about *as best one can foresee* that people are respected in all of the ways we considered in our analysis of respect above. Thus, in Kant's view, it is the agent's intention that determines whether the action is right or wrong. This is pure deontological moral theory. In contrast, consequentialist theories view the rightness of an action as a function of the consequences it actually produces, such as personal or social benefits.

Exercises for Module 16: Foundations of Deontology

1. *a.* The beings on Fauna and Precarious have characteristics that no beings on Lifeless or Possibility have. List several typical distinguishing characteristics.
   b. When you have checked your list of characteristics against 16:1.1, state more abstractly what it is about characteristics that occur on Fauna or Precarious but not on Lifeless and Possibility that gives rise to the possibility of respect only on the former planets.
   c. When you have checked your answer against 16:1.2, state as clearly as you can what respect is, both in terms of the kind of being towards which respect is possible (the answer from *b*) and in terms of the attitude toward such a being that respect involves. (16:2.1–16:2.3)
   d. What characteristic must a being have in order to have self-respect?
   e. In the light of the answers to *c* and *d,* state as clearly as you can what self-respect is. (16:3.1, 16:3.2)
2. *a.* Suppose Carl the Cop moves his friends' lane until they all have

cleared the area of snarled traffic, in violation of the first formulation of the categorical imperative. (1) State to whom Carl is being disrespectful. (2) Explain what about his action is contrary to the concept of respect. (3) Explain how violation of the first formulation of the categorical imperative involves disrespect. (See 15:5.2 for the first formulation.)

b. Suppose that Mona lies about Al in order to look good in Lisa's eyes, in violation of the second formulation of the categorical imperative. (1) Explain what about Mona's action is disrespectful to Al. (2) Explain how violation of the second formulation of the categorical imperative involves disrespect. (See 15:5.3 for the second formulation.)

c. Suppose that Handy Harry refuses to teach his daughter how to use tools, in violation of the third formulation of the categorical imperative. (1) Explain what about Harry's action is disrespectful of his daughter. (2) Explain how violation of the third formulation of the categorical imperative involves a lack of respect. (See 15:5.4 for the third formulation.)

3. a. State abstractly the way in which persons must be treated if they are to be respected. (16:2.1, 16:2.3)

b. State the grounds for the view that respectful treatment of persons is intrinsically right. (16:2.3)

c. State the conceptual connection between a person's having an intrinsic right to be treated respectfully and the concept of a categorical duty.

4. a. Characterize integrity. (16:4.)

b. Define what it means to say that a person has integrity. (16:4.2)

c. Define what it means to say that a society has integrity. (16:4.3)

d. Compare and contrast accounts of social integrity that view persons individualistically with accounts that view persons as participants in collective social goals. (16:4.3)

5. a. State Kant's argument that actions are not right or wrong in virtue of their consequences.

b. State Kant's argument that actions are intrinsically right in virtue of the intention with which they are done. In your statement include a characterization of the sort of intention that makes an action intrinsically right according to Kant. (16:5.1)

6. Below is a list of statements. Deontological and consequentialist ethical theories can largely be defined by their agreement or disagreement concerning these statements. In the columns labeled *D* and *C* mark T or F for each statement, depending on whether it is true or

false according to the deontologist and the consequentialist, respectively.

	$\underline{D}$	$\underline{C}$

a. Some actions are intrinsically right.

b. Some actions are instrumentally, but not intrinsically, right.

c. Only states of affairs are intrinsically valuable.

d. Being respectful of persons is intrinsically right.

e. Being respectful of persons is something one ought to strive for.

f. Some states of affairs are intrinsically valuable.

g. There are some categorical duties.

h. Some actions are instrumentally wrong.

i. No rights are indefeasible.

j. Being disrespectful of oneself is intrinsically wrong.

Selected Answers to Exercises for Module 16

1.   *d.* Self-awareness is the characteristic it needs.
2.   *a.* (1) Carl is disrespectful of the persons in other lanes, whose right to move along their way is equal to the right of the persons in his friends' lane.
    (2) As Carl focuses on helping out his friends, he is ignoring the capacities of the others, which their circumstances constrain them from using, and he is ignoring the limitations of their time. Appreciating them for their capacities and limitations would imply treating them differently than he is treating them.
    (3) One is disrespectful when one treats persons as if it were false that they all have general capacities and limitations in common. Yet if one treats some persons in a nonuniversalizable way, one treats them as if it were false.
    b. (1) Mona is treating Al in such a way as to ignore his capacities and limitations—in this case, his feelings in particular.
    (2) If one treats a person solely as a means, then one ignores the issue of how one's actions will affect that person's ability to flourish—except to the extent that, if the person does not flourish, he or she may become less useful as one's means.
    c. (1) Harry's action hinders his daughter's development of her potential for using tools.
    (2) When one does not help and maybe even hinders another's development of potential, one constrains the flourishing of the other.
3.   *a.* Your answer should take into account that flourishing is related both to

capacities and to limitations and that respect is related to all three formulations of the Categorical Imperative.

  c. Something is valuable categorically only if it is valuable regardless of circumstances. What is valuable instrumentally may vary with circumstances, but what is valuable intrinsically is valuable regardless of circumstances.

6.

	D	C
a.	T	T
b.	T	T
c.	F	T
d.	T	F
e.	T	T
f.	T	T
g.	T	F
h.	T	T
i.	F	T
j.	T	F

This exercise is intended to be instructive. If you missed any of the items, you should modify your ideas of deontological and consequentialist theories.

Cluster Six

JUSTICE

Questions of the rightness or wrongness of particular actions or policies often turn on whether or not they promote justice. Hence, examination of the concept of justice is an integral part of both ethics and social philosophy. In Module 17 we discuss the varieties of circumstances within which questions of justice arise. We introduce the distinctions among distributive, compensatory, and retributive justice. In Module 18 we analyze what has come to be known as the "formal principle of justice," which is often expressed this way: "Treat persons alike who are alike in morally relevant respects; treat persons proportionately differently to the extent that they differ in morally relevant respects." In Module 18 we examine the relation of the formal principle of justice to the concept of equality. In Module 19 we face the crucial question, "What constitute morally relevant differences among persons?" The cluster's educational goal is to enable you to rationally evaluate claims that justice is or is not being done.

Module 17
SPECIES OF JUSTICE

In this module we shall examine the variety of circumstances within which questions of justice arise. We shall identify the conditions that must be met if a just result is to be attained in such circumstances.

In so doing, we shall consider the significance of issues such as scarcity of resources, conflict of interest, and universalizability as they give rise to and contribute to the satisfactory resolution of problems of justice. We shall then focus on the distinction among questions of distributive, compensatory, and retributive justice, paying special attention to the relation of compensation and retribution to moral responsibility. After reading Module 17, you should be able to

- Distinguish cases in which a question of justice arises from cases in which none is involved.
- Explain this distinction by reference to the cases.
- Define arbitrarily unjust judgments in terms of morally irrelevant characteristics.
- Distinguish cases of compensatory and retributive justice from each other and from cases of distributive justice raised without specific reference to compensation or retribution.

THE CASE OF THE JOBLESS STUDENTS

Mr. Sieth, the high school guidance counselor, smiled as he entered the auditorium of Jane Pitman High. "I've got good news. We were given a special government grant for our Summer Jobs Program. We now have job openings for 50 people. How many of you are interested in applying for a job through our program?"

His heart fell as he saw scores of hands go up. "That must be nearly 150 of you!" he said. "I don't know what we're going to do about this problem. We can't satisfy all of you. I'll take it up with Mrs. Ketting this afternoon. She will make an announcement tomorrow setting the ground rules for who will be eligible to apply."

Later that afternoon Mr. Sieth met with the principal, Mrs. Ketting. "What are we going to do? One-hundred fifty kids want jobs. We can take the applications on a first-come-first-served basis, I suppose."

"That may not be fair, because the seniors are in class for two hours after my announcement time, but the juniors are on free time. The juniors will have the advantage of being able to apply first," said Mrs. Ketting.

"Maybe we can set quotas. Let's reserve 30 jobs for seniors and 20 for juniors. The sophomores and freshmen will just have to wait till next year."

"No, Mr. Sieth. Let's set it at 10 for sophomores, 20 for juniors, and 20 for seniors, and let's say that half of the jobs go to women and the other half to men, depending on which of our young men and women apply first."

"That sounds okay. Will you make the announcement then? Tell them I'll receive applicants in my office."

"Fine. . . . No, wait a minute, Mr. Sieth. Last year we had some trouble with this program. Your predecessor, Bixby, was fired because he altered the numbers on the applications. He made it look like some who really applied late had applied early. He was always playing favorites with the students, and this time he was caught at it. We should make sure that those students who got jobs unfairly last year do not get them this year. We should also make sure that the ones who missed out on jobs because of Bixby's little tricks get jobs this year."

"Yes, I agree, but only up to a point. I agree that we should not mess with the order of the applicants. I also agree that we should first give jobs to those who missed out last year because of Bixby's foul play. But I don't think we should hold it against the kids whom Bixby helped. After all, they didn't ask for favors; and they didn't learn about the matter till well after they were in their new jobs. It wasn't their doing, but Bixby's!"

"Yes," said Mrs. Ketting, "I see your point. We will not hold it against them; except for three of them. You remember, don't you? Armstrong, Tjin, and LaStrada all got jobs by falsifying their applications. This year they should not be eligible."

"I agree."

"Okay. I'll make the announcement. Thank you, Mr. Sieth."

17:1.1 The Concern for Justice. Questions for justice arise whenever there is concern about apportioning benefits and burdens fairly. Such things as appointive offices, welfare doles, taxes, military conscription, natural resources, food, economic and educational opportunities, incomes, punishments, and rewards may be apportioned justly or unjustly. In the case study Sieth and Ketting are concerned about justice; they are concerned about how to distribute job opportunities among the students at Jane Pitman High.

Let us examine two circumstances in which such questions of justice arise—scarcity of resources and conflicts of interest. Let us also examine one of the necessary conditions for the satisfactory resolution of such questions—namely, the universalizability of the resolution.[1]

17:1.2 If *scarcity* of desired materials, resources, opportunities,

[1] Saying "*A* is a necessary condition for *B*" means that *B* cannot happen unless *A* happens. It leaves open the possibility that *A* would happen but not *B*. Other factors besides *A* might also be necessary conditions for *B*.

and the like did not exist, then questions of justice would not arise. If there were a plentitude of available materials, resources, opportunities, and so on, and if there were no way in which others could interfere with a person's taking advantage of that plentitude, then the person would have no interest in justice. Thus, for example, it is the relative scarcity of petroleum in the world, together with there being great stores of it in the hands of a few producing nations, that raises the question of the fairness of practices such as refusing to sell the petroleum (trade embargoes) and setting high prices for what is sold.

Of course it is unrealistic to think of there being an abundance of all of the things in which people can take interest. The finitude of both life and the world's resources precludes it. The case study presents an all-too-familiar instance of scarcity; more students desire jobs than there are jobs available under the government grant to the high school. If there were more jobs than applicants, then there would be no question of the fairness of the procedures for selecting those to get jobs from among job applicants.

17:1.3 Another necessary condition for there being a concern about justice is that there must be a *conflict of interest* in having that which is scarce. That is, given the potential for real scarcity, sufficient numbers of people must be interested in having what is scarce so that not all can be fully satisfied. In such cases it becomes reasonable to be concerned about how to justly allocate the short supply. To see that this condition is an addition to the condition that there must be scarcity, imagine a case of something's being very rare, say iguanas. Suppose that all who seek iguanas for pets are able to have as many as they wish. In this example, the scarcity of iguanas does not suffice to raise a question of justice; there is no conflict of interests in having them as pets.

In the case study there is a conflict of interests among the students who want jobs. Assume that all of the jobs are equivalent, in the sense that none is especially interesting or exciting. The fact that there are only fifty jobs for students at an average-sized high school—the fact that the jobs are "absolutely" scarce—would not in itself give rise to any question of justice. If only ten students raised their hands, there would be no problem. It is the *relative* scarcity (that is, the absolute scarcity in combination with the fact that interested students outnumber job vacancies) that creates a competition of interests. The relative scarcity leads to a need to develop a fair procedure for trying to satisfy the students' interests.

17:1.4 Questions of justice arise under conditions of scarcity where conflicts of interest are present. Just resolutions of such conflicts must be *universalizable* resolutions. A just, or fair, solution to the types of problems we have discussed requires that the persons be respected as persons. Therefore, whatever rules apply to questions of justice must apply indiscriminately to any person. No arbitrary discriminations and exceptions are to be made in favor of, or against, individuals on the basis of morally irrelevant considerations. This universalizability condition should be familiar from Module 3. The point here is that it applies centrally to matters of justice.

In the case study Mr. Sieth and Mrs. Ketting are struggling to discover a universalizable set of rules for proceeding. They do not want to repeat the playing of favorites in which Bixby had indulged the previous year, for Bixby clearly made arbitrary discriminations. They are seeking procedures that can be used indiscriminately in all cases. Where they do see a need to make exceptions to the rules, they endeavor to specify morally relevant differences. When they do make exceptions based on morally relevant differences, they are willing to extend those exceptions to any person who also has the relevant differentiating characteristic. Thus, it is not simply because Armstrong, Tjin, and LaStrada are who they are that Sieth and Ketting want to exclude them from the pool of applicants. Rather, Sieth and Ketting identify what they take to be a morally relevant difference in their case: their past cheating on job applications. They exclude them on that basis. It is reasonable to suppose that they would be willing to universalize this procedure and to exclude anyone else whom they later discover to have cheated.

17:2.1 Justice and Deserts. Questions of justice are questions about what people deserve. They are questions of giving people what is due them under the conditions and in the manner specified in the preceding section. They are, then, in most general terms, questions of the distribution of benefits and burdens. Two special types of cases where distribution comes into question deserve our special attention: (1) cases where persons have been denied deserved benefits or have suffered undeserved hardship, and (2) cases where persons have enjoyed undeserved benefits or have undeservedly avoided their share of a burden. In these special types of cases, questions of just compensation or punishment arise together with questions of responsibility. In what follows we will, therefore, distinguish between the general issue of distributive justice and the more specific issues of corrective justice, compensation, and retribution.

17:2.2 The most general question of *distributive justice* is how to weigh conflicting interests in deciding how to allocate benefits and burdens. It is a problem of comparing the merits of conflicting claims. It is also a problem of devising criteria for making universalizable comparisons. The problem of allocation may (but need not) come into dispute independent of anyone's ever having been undeservedly burdened or benefited in the past. Thus, questions of compensation or retribution for such undeserved burden or benefit are really species of the more general problem of distributive justice.

In the case study Mr. Sieth and Mrs. Ketting confront a question of distributive justice. They must decide how to give out jobs to the students fairly in the light of relevant considerations of what the students deserve. Ketting and Seith compare the merits of the conflicting claims to the jobs and decide upon appropriate general procedures that take into account the students' deserts. If all had an equal claim to the jobs, then a simple first-come-first-served procedure would give all a fair opportunity to apply. The situation is complicated, however, by the facts that some students would be able to come to Sieth's office sooner than others and that people from the upper classes seem deserving of a greater portion of the jobs. Thus, a quota system is devised to take these factors into account. The quota system, you should note, is addressed to the general question of distribution. Unfortunately, factors of past favoritism and past cheating must also be taken into account. They raise the more specific questions of compensation and retribution.

17:2.3   Questions of *compensatory justice* arise in circumstances where there has apparently been undeserved denial of benefit or undeserved suffering of hardship in past distributions of benefits and burdens. The questions have to do with compensation for those misfortunes. In some cases compensation may take the form of restoration of something that a misfortune has cost a person. Thus, if a baseball is stolen, just compensation would seem to be restoration of the baseball or one similar to it. In other cases, however, such restoration may be impossible, so that any compensation must take some other form. For example, if a leg is lost in an accident, there is no possibility of restoring it with a new leg (given the current state of the surgical arts). Instead, compensation must take some other form, such as the gift of an artificial limb, financial compensation, or both.

In the case study a question of compensatory justice is raised. The preceding year Sieth's predecessor, Bixby, had played favorites in allocating a similar set of jobs. As a result, some students were moved down the list of applicants unfairly and did not get jobs. This constitutes an undeserved denial of a benefit that they deserved by virtue of their being on the original list. Sieth and Ketting believe those students are now deserving of some compensation. The current procedure is, therefore, modified in order to ensure that they get jobs this year. In accordance with the ideal of justice, a job this year is seen as at least a rough equivalent of a job last year.

17:2.4   Questions of *retributive justice* arise in circumstances where there has apparently been undeserved benefit, undeserved avoidance of burden, or undeserved infliction of hardship by one person upon another. The questions have to do with what *corrective action* is appropriate to offset such undeserved advantages. Broadly speaking, then, questions of the fairness of punishment are questions of what retribution is due. Given that someone has undeservedly acted at another's expense, what is to be done?

The case study also illustrates questions of retributive justice. Mrs. Ketting first suggests that students who were given jobs unfairly by Bixby the preceding year should be denied jobs this year. This amounts to a suggestion that they benefited unfairly and that proper correction requires that they be denied jobs this year. Mr. Sieth counters by suggesting that their benefiting the previous year was none of their doing and that they do not, therefore, deserve to be punished this year. The offense was Bixby's, and he has been punished with loss of his job. However, Armstrong, Tjin, and LaStrada cheated to gain unfair advantage the preceding year, and Sieth and Ketting agree that they deserve to be denied jobs this year.

17:3.1 Compensation, Retribution, and Responsibility.   The case study reflects not only concern with questions of compensation and retribution, but also an important connection between these questions and those of responsibility. In considering whether retribution is appropriate, much seems to turn on whether the person in question is morally responsible for his unfair advantage or the infliction of hardship on others. It seems appropriate to punish persons only for things for which they bear responsibility. Thus, it seems inappropriate to punish the students who unfairly got jobs last year if they got them because of a factor for which they were not responsible and of which they were ignorant. Similarly, it would seem in principle unjust to visit hardship upon people, as surely punishment does, for such things as their race, their height, their sex, their having been born poor, and the like, where it is clear they bear no responsibility for such matters.

On the other hand, the case of compensation raises a major question for those concerned with justice: Who is to bear the burden of providing the compensation? Where persons can be readily identified as responsible for others' having been unfairly disadvantaged, the answer seems fairly clear. Those who have unfairly benefited should supply the compensation, even though doing so may be burdensome. However, there may be cases where it is reasonable to say that some persons are undeservedly disadvantaged, being neither responsible for their own hardship nor deserving of it, and yet no other persons can be identified as responsible.

Is compensation still due such persons? Who shall be asked to provide it? For example, is compensation due to American Indians? If so, who should provide it?

Exercises for Module 17: Species of Justice

1. Below is a list of statements describing different situations. In some of them a question of justice is raised. Mark each such statement *QJ;* then state what the question is. In some no question of justice is raised. Mark each such statement *NQJ;* then state which factor necessary for questions of justice to arise is missing. (17:1.2–17:1.3)

    _____ *a.* So far 27 children have applied for the 35 openings we have in our Computer for Children program.

    _____ *b.* At least 10 more children are planning to apply tomorrow for the remaining positions.

    _____ *c.* There's only one piece of pie left, but nobody seems to want it.

    _____ *d.* If all the new tax money goes into teacher salaries, nothing will be left to improve the quality of the textbooks the children use.

    _____ *e.* Everybody agrees that Toby should keep the dog he found.

    _____ *f.* With the decline in student enrollments, no student will have to share textbooks this year.

    _____ *g.* Both teams want to have the advantage of the home court in their game.

    _____ *h.* Should Kelly be given the lead for her years of faithfulness to PlayPeople, or should Lori get it for the financial contributions she has collected?

    _____ *i.* Dolores got the job because she was the only one who wanted it.

    _____ *j.* During the next two years, if there is no oil embargo, there will be enough gas for everyone to drive wherever he or she wants.

2. Define arbitrarily unjust actions in terms of morally irrelevant characteristics. (17:1.3)

3. Below is a list of statements describing situations in which a question of justice is raised. If the issue is one of compensatory justice, mark it *QCJ.* If it is one of retributive justice, mark it *QRJ.* If the issue is one of distributive justice raised without specific reference to compensation or retribution, mark it *QDJ.*

_____ *a*. Martha was never paid in any way for the days she took off work while she was having her baby, even though all employees are entitled to sick days with pay. (17:2.3)

_____ *b*. How much money should each employee be asked to contribute to the flower fund? (17:2.2)

_____ *c*. What could be fairer than "first come, first served" at the tennis court? (17:2.2)

_____ *d*. Who should have to pay for town-organized recreational programs? (17:2.2)

_____ *e*. The people who play should be the people who pay. (17:2.2)

_____ *f*. People who abuse the equipment and damage or destroy it should pay to put it back into good shape. (17:2.4)

_____ *g*. Rich people should have to pay more because they are able to pay more. (17:2.2)

_____ *h*. Since people only get rich by taking unfair advantage of others, the rich should always pay more taxes to make up to the poor people what they have been cheated out of. (17:2.3)

_____ *i*. The reason the rich people should pay is because they cheated the poor people in the first place. They shouldn't retain an unfairly gained advantage. (17:2.4)

_____ *j*. Since Martha missed a chance to apply for promotion while she was out having her baby, should she be given a special opportunity to apply now? (17:2.3)

_____ *k*. If we could prove that Charles Mailer Prig moved up the dates for applying for promotion so that Martha would miss them, then we should fire him. (17:2.4)

Answers to Exercises for Module 17

1. *a*. *NQJ:* no scarcity.
   b. *QJ:* of the 37 children wanting to take Computer for Children, which 35 should be admitted to the program?
   c. *NQJ:* no conflict of interest—in fact, no interest.
   d. *QJ:* how should the funds from the new tax be distributed in the school budget?
   e. *NQJ:* no conflict of interest.
   f. *NQJ:* no scarcity.
   g. *QJ:* which, if any, team should enjoy the home court advantage?
   h. *QJ:* who should be given the lead in the play?
   i. *NQJ:* no conflict of interest.
   j. *NQJ:* no scarcity.
2. Actions are arbitrarily unjust when distributions they involve are based on morally irrelevant features. (See 17:1.3.)

3. *a. QCJ.*   *b. QDJ.*   *c. QDJ.*   *d. QDJ.*   *e. QDJ.*   *f. QRJ.*
    g. QDJ.   *h. QCJ.*   *i. QRJ.*   *j. QCJ.*   *k. QRJ.*

MODULE 18
JUSTICE AND EQUALITY

Our basic sense of justice is disturbed if we discover that, as benefits and burdens are distributed, two apparently similar persons are treated quite differently. Our sense of justice is satisfied only when we are presented with reasons why the persons are different in some morally relevant respect. The basic principle underlying this sense of justice has come to be called the "formal principle of justice." It requires that persons who are alike in morally relevant respects ought to be treated alike, and that persons who differ in morally relevant respects ought to be treated differently in proportion to the differences between them. In this module we will analyze this most fundamental principle of justice. We will learn why it is considered to be a "formal" principle and distinguish its *formality* from the *materiality* of other principles. We will also analyze an ambiguity in the notion that justice requires equality of treatment, showing that on the one hand this notion may be identified with the formal principle of justice and on the other hand it may be taken as an implausible material principle of justice. We will then examine two presumptions for justice that derive from the formal principle, contrasting the implications of each. After reading Module 18, you should be able to

- Distinguish formal from material considerations of justice.
- Distinguish different meanings that "equality" may have, explaining why, on each meaning, equality is either a formal or a material principle of justice.
- Distinguish formal and material principles of justice from the presumptions of justice.
- Explain the conceptual connection between the presumptions of justice and human ignorance.

THE CASE OF THE JOB VACANCY NOTICE

"Come in here, Olafson, would you?"

"Yes, Mr. Carp, I'm coming. What is it?"

"I'm trying to write a job vacancy notice for the position of office secretary. Tell me how this sounds to you so far." Carp began to read from his yellow pad. "Wanted—Capable and experienced woman, age 25 to 35, for full-time secretarial position. Pay rate: $3.25 per hour. Job entails typing, filing, stenography, using standard office machines, handling crates up to 30 lbs., composing routine letters and memoranda."

"I'm not sure I would specify the age and the sex in the job description. Besides, why *not* consider a male for the position?"

"Come on, Olafson. Men are called 'administrative assistants,' and they get paid $4.80 an hour. I want a sharp, good-looking young woman."

"Well, then, you want a playmate, not a secretary."

"No, not really."

"Admit it, Carp. Administrative assistants and secretaries do the same job around here. For you to specify age and sex is unfair to many people who are able to do the work you want done. What happened to giving everyone an equal chance? You have to treat people equally unless you can find some reason why they are different."

"That's silly, Olafson. I treat people who seem different as if they are different unless I find a reason to treat them equally."

"Well, Carp, in my view sex discrimination is wrong. It's out of step with the times."

"Hang on there, Olafson. Women, especially young ones, are better looking than men—at least to me! Besides, women are not as strong or as bright as men, so they don't deserve the same jobs or the same pay."

"I think they're just as bright, and besides looks just aren't important, given your job description."

"Looks count with me, Buster. And what about the differences in strength?"

"Strength makes no difference on this job. If they can lift 30 pounds, they are strong enough. You know very well that the union agreement requires we call in a freight man for any heavy moving or for lifting crates that weigh more than 30 pounds. Any woman who can lift a four-year-old child can handle the strength requirement you have in mind. The job is really no different than the administrative assistant's job that pays $4.80."

"Well, if you insist, Olafson, I'll take that business about age and sex out of the vacancy notice. But I can't be held responsible for what special factors I might consider as I review applications or conduct interviews."

"I think you can zero in on the factors that count if you put your mind to it, Carp. But if you have trouble, why don't you let me interview people with you?"

"We'll see. Thank you, Olafson. That's all for now."

18:1.1 Formal Justice. The ultimate or first principle of distributive justice is to treat relevantly similar cases similarly and to treat relevantly different cases differently in proportion to the difference(s) between them. This principle entails that injustice is done when similar persons are treated differently or when persons who are different are treated similarly. It is called a "formal" principle *because it does not specify what respects are to be counted as relevant similarities or differences* among persons. No two cases or persons will ever have absolutely all characteristics in common, but that does not answer the question of whether they are the same or different with respect to morally *relevant* characteristics.

As an illustration of the formality of this principle of justice, consider how ready you are to accept the idea that if two students do the same work, they should get the same grade, and that if one does much better work than the other, then he should get a much better grade than the other. Note that this seems intuitive, even though it assumes that students' grades should be based on similarities or differences in their work rather than on other similarities or differences, such as eye color, family lineage, race, sex, or the like.

18:1.2   Many theorists believe that the formal principle of justice suggests that some characteristics are not even potentially relevant differences among persons. Many have suggested that characteristics for which no one can bear any responsibility, such as eye color, race, sex, native ability, and the like, are not to be counted as relevant similarities or differences when justice is being considered. As an example, consider a proposal to give welfare assistance only to the first illegitimate child. It could be argued that such a proposal is unjust on the grounds that there is no relevant difference between the first illegitimate child and a second or subsequent illegitimate child. None of the children is responsible for being first, second, third, or later. In effect the argument is, then, that the only difference that generally obtains between such first- and later-born children is one for which these children are not responsible. Therefore, this difference cannot be counted as a relevant one in their treatment.

The entire discussion in the case study is based upon what appears to be the shared acceptance of the formal principle of justice by both Olafson and Carp. They are both concerned about whether there are relevant differences in the potential male and female job applicants. Carp seems uncertain about what the relevant differences and similarities might be in assessing applicants for the job, but he and Olafson never waver from the view that the relevant characteristics should be identified, so that any difference in treatment can be based on differences with respect to those characteristics. Olafson presses Carp to be specific, and

Carp somewhat begrudgingly acknowledges that it is important to address Olafson's questions. Another question raised in the case study, but never handled thoroughly, concerns the justice of the differences in salary between secretaries and administrative assistants—two apparently identical jobs. If you experience a lingering concern about this, it indicates that you, too, accept the formal principle of justice and feel a need to specify relevant differences where persons are treated differently.

18:1.3 Besides highlighting the importance of identifying some relevant similarities and differences among persons, the formal principle of justice requires that any differences in treatment be directly proportional to the relevant differences. Thus, for example, if one person were slightly more deserving, given slight differences in relevant characteristics, it would be an injustice to treat that person much differently from the others with whom he or she is compared. Likewise, slight difference in treatment is unjust if there is a great difference in desert.

To illustrate, consider the issue of justly proportioning punishment to offenses. Those who commit crimes differ from those who do not. It is commonly believed that we should relate the severity of the punishments to the seriousness of crimes. We also believe that some forms of punishment should be rejected as cruel and unusual. It used to be that pickpockets were put to death. That practice appears unjust in terms of the requirement that differences in treatment be directly proportionate to differences in desert. While pickpockets may well deserve different treatment, it seems implausible that their relatively slight offense justifies so great a penalty. On the other hand, many today suggest that white collar crime and crimes committed by privileged classes are among the most serious of offenses, greatly affecting many lives. Some argue that there is a real injustice in allowing such criminals to be punished only slightly if at all. [Note that throughout this discussion no specific (material) criteria have been specified for determining what makes crimes minor or serious; the discussion has remained formal.]

The case study poses a question of the justice of a major salary difference between secretaries and administrative assistants, when there is only a slight difference, if any at all, in the jobs. If there is a difference in the jobs, is it so great as to justify a wage difference of $1.55 per hour?

18:1.4 While the formal principle of justice does not tell us what makes a person *deserving* or what sort of *distribution* he or she ought to receive for that desert, it does suggest the relationship of the desert to the distribution. To see this relationship, imagine an absurd practice in which it would be violated. Imagine that persons who worked hard and were very productive were therefore penalized. The harder they worked and the more they produced, the more severe their punishments. Similarly imagine that people who caused other persons pain, hardship, and suffering were rewarded, with the greatest rewards going to those causing the most damage and pain. Would these arrangements be just or not? Direct proportionality is maintained here—but rewards are directly proportioned to the creation of burdens, and punishments to the creation of benefits. These practices, even though they maintain proportionality, run contrary to the concept of justice. Why? Because the concept of justice involves distinguishing between benefits and burdens, rewards and punishments, so that rewards go to those who create benefits (things of positive value) and punishments go to those who create burdens (things of negative value). To conceive of the treatments in our imagined cases as just would require imagining that pain has a positive value and productive work a negative value.

18:2.1 Equality.   Often the concern for justice is identified with the concern for equality. Great care must be taken in doing so, however. At least three things can be meant by the claim "Everyone should be treated equally," and two are misleading if not mistaken. In the first interpretation the concern for equality is identical with the concern for justice as captured in the formal principle of justice. Indeed, another way of phrasing that principle is to say that those who are equal in relevant respects are to be treated equally and those who are unequal in relevant respects are to be treated unequally in proportion to the relevant inequality. The concern for equality can remain quite formal, inasmuch as none of the important respects in which persons may be equal or unequal is specified. In this sense of "equality" the discussion in the case study is focused as much upon equality as upon justice.

18:2.2   In a second and nonformal understanding, "equality" becomes a disguise for a material principle of justice (that is, one that specifies some characteristic to be morally relevant for deciding that people are to be treated similarly or differently). To see how this can happen, consider a possible discussion about treating wage earners "equally." Suppose we have two families of different sizes with one wage earner each. Someone might maintain that treating equals equally means that since each worker is one worker and each does one job, then each should be given an equal salary. Someone else, however, might note that the first worker is working to support eight people and the second to support two people. This person might argue that treating equals equally and unequals unequally here requires that the one worker receive four times the salary of the other, since this is the proportion of the inequality between them.

Reviewing the last paragraph, can you see how the two evaluations of what is to be done in allocating salaries invoke more than a formal conception of justice in their talk about equality? The evaluators are implicitly invoking their views on the material respects in which equality is to count. What are the relevant respects, in other words, for two parties to count as equals? One invokes the principle that salary is to be proportioned to work done, and the other that salary is to be proportioned to the different number of people to be supported. It would be better in such discussions if talk proceeded explicitly in terms of the material principles invoked and their relative merits, rather than in a disguised manner where both speak of "equality" but each means something different by it.

In the case study the issue of equal pay for equal work is implicitly raised when it becomes clear that men are paid $1.55 more than women for a job involving virtually the same work. You can probably pick out the material elements in this practice, if you recall that the formal assertion of equality would not go beyond the idea that persons who are equally deserving should receive equal distributions. Material elements enter the picture when we say that equality in work makes persons equally deserving, and equality in pay means that they have been equally rewarded.

18:2.3   A third and also nonformal understanding construes "equality" in the strict sense of the word. When the concern for equality is invoked in either of the manners discussed above, it is about what has come to be called "proportional equality"—that persons are to be treated differently only *in proportion* to their inequality. Advocates of "strict equality," however, are interested in having it accepted as a *material* principle of justice. Strict equalitarianism would require that *all benefits and burdens be distributed equally* to all persons. Typically this equalitarianism is based on the belief in the equal humanity of all persons. While it is often maintained and acknowledged that such an equal humanity secures to all persons certain rights (see Module 16), it is quite different to claim that being human qualifies a person for an equal share in the distribution of *all* of the benefits and burdens individuals or societies can bestow.

Taken literally, the strict-equality principle is absurd, since in addition to whatever common humanity people enjoy it is clear that they differ in important respects. It would be utter folly, for example, and surely an injustice, to subject all persons to open-heart surgery when only a few need it. The absurdity of such cases may lead a strict equalitarian to argue that he has been misunderstood; what he advocates is each person's being given an equal share of society's resources in order that the differing needs of each may be met. Similarly, all persons are to carry equal burdens or responsibilities. Opponents reply that even this version overlooks the obvious fact that some needs of some people (such as the need for open-heart surgery) are far more expensive than others, and strict apportionment of wealth would make meeting those needs impossible. Similarly, since some people are much more able than others, equal burdens might well imply burdening the less able with "responsibilities" beyond their capacities. If the equalitarian replies that benefits ought to be distributed in proportion to need, or burdens proportioned to abilities, then strict equality has been abandoned and a concern for equality proportioned to need or ability has taken its place.

18:3.1 Presumptions of Equality and Inequality.   Let us go back to the first understanding of concern for equality as presented in 18:2.1, the one that identifies concern for equality with concern for justice as specified in the formal principle of justice. Even when it is agreed that equality is to be understood formally, a problem arises, because often we must make decisions of justice in a state of at least partial ignorance. We may be uncertain whether people are alike or different in morally relevant respects. Many equalitarians think that justice requires, given such uncertainty, that persons should be presumed to be equal and, thus, treated equally, until it is shown that they differ in morally relevant respects and are, therefore, deserving of different treatments. They acknowledge that people are not strictly equal in all respects but suggest that the "burden of proof" falls upon those who would treat people differently to provide an account of their reasons for doing so. In this view, only exceptions to *equal* treatment require justification.

Yet, the formal principle of justice would seem to indicate that a second presumption is also possible and sometimes reasonable: that where people are seemingly different, they should be treated differently until it is shown that they are alike in morally relevant respects. Once their likeness is demonstrated, they can be treated equally. In this view, some exceptions to unequal treatment require justification.

18:3.2   The question of which presumption is to be operative in a given set of circumstances depends upon what is believed or known about the respects in which the persons involved are alike or unalike. Thus, if persons are believed to be alike in some relevant respects, then the first *presumption of equality* would seem to apply: the burden of proof or justification would fall upon those who wish to treat the persons differently. On the other hand, if persons are believed to be unalike in some relevant respects, then the second *presumption of inequality* would seem to apply: the burden of proof or justification would fall upon those who wish to treat the persons alike.

As illustration of both of these principles in operation, consider two pairs of students who have completed an assignment. The first pair has come to the assignment with similar abilities, and the quality of the essays they have handed in is equally high. Given what is known in this case, it is safe to presume that each will be given the same grade. If it turns out that one receives an A and the other an F, the burden of proof would seem to fall on the instructor to justify the difference in treatment. One possible justification would be that the F grade was given because the student was caught cheating. Consider now the second pair of students. They are known to differ greatly in ability, and their essays more than reflect that difference. One essay is of extremely high quality, the other is a disaster at best, reflecting not only poor ability but in fact little effort to use it. Given what is known in this case, it is reasonable to presume that different grades will be given. If it turns out that both essays receive an F, the burden of proof would seem to fall on the instructor to justify the equality of treatment of two such different essays. Again, the F for the outstanding essay might be a result of the student's having been caught cheating.

In the case study Olafson and Carp confess that they are operating on these two different presumptions of equality and inequality. Olafson says, "You have to treat people equally unless you can find some reason why they are different." Carp calls Olafson's presumption silly, saying, "I treat people who seem different as if they are different unless I find reason to treat them equally." In this particular case, Olafson's presumption is more appropriate, given what we know about how strength and good looks are rarely relevant respects for distinguishing men and women as applicants for this job and especially what we know about their irrelevance for distinguishing between secretaries and administrative assistants. But if we did not happen to know these things, if the facts were quite different, if we knew that strength and good looks were often extremely relevant and indeed crucial in distinguishing between secretaries and administrative assistants, then the opposite presumption, the presumption of inequality, would be the appropriate one.

18:3.3 You should be very careful here about whether presumptions of inequality or of equality are culturally relative. If you will reflect a moment about part of the history of women in our culture, you will get a clearer view of this question of relativity. There was a time when (a) many secretaries were required to lift up to 100 pounds or more, and (b) women were widely believed to be substantially less bright than men. Given that, for whatever reason, most women were then unable to lift 100 pounds, and assuming that believing women intellectually inferior to men was at least plausible, it would be reasonable for any person, on these bases, to presume that women are relevantly different from men with respect to a job requiring significant strength and intelligence. However, when the job changes so that lifting no more than 30 pounds is required, then, objectively, the strength to lift 100 pounds simply becomes irrelevant to the job. And when the empirical evidence that women are certainly not the intellectual inferiors of men has already become quite clear, it is objectively no longer reasonable to presume women relevantly different from men with respect to this job; contrarily, it is reasonable to presume them relevantly similar.

18:3.4   Let us look at two spheres where the presumptivist principles of justice we have been talking about do seem to operate in our everyday thinking about what is fair, and where the presumptions do seem to make a difference. Consider first the presumption in our American judicial system that all who are charged with crimes are innocent until proven guilty. This may be taken as an instance of the first principle: people should be presumed equal until it is established that they are not so. In this case it is presumed that all are alike in being innocent, and the burden of proof falls on prosecutors to establish guilt beyond a reasonable doubt. It is obvious that the presence of this presumption as an *operating procedure* makes our judicial process quite different from other possible systems where no such presumption of innocence is operative. The contrast is even greater if a system is imagined to hold the opposite presumption—where persons charged with crimes are presumed to be guilty until they are able to prove themselves innocent.

By contrast consider a case where the presumption of inequality is operative. In our society parents treat their own children differently than they treat the children of others. Parents make differential distributions of the benefits they have at their disposal. It would not seem odd at all if parents invested in piano lessons for all of their children and did not send their neighbors' children to take similar lessons. Here parents presume that their children are unequal to their neighborhood peers, in that the parents are related in an especially important way to their own children. It would seem odd, and even unfair, if parents denied their children piano lessons that they could well afford because they could not provide lessons for children not their own.

Exercises for Module 18: Justice and Equality

1.   Below is a list of statements that some treatment is for some reason either just or unjust. Distinguish those statements invoking formal principles of justice *(FPJ)* from those invoking material principles *(MPJ)*. When a formal principle is invoked, also distinguish whether it is that of treating similar cases similarly *(SS)* or of treating dissimilar cases dissimilarly in proportion to the differences between them *(DD)*. (18:1.1–18:1.4)

_____ *a*. Since both boys worked equally hard, they earned the same money.

_____ *b*. They were treated the same because there was no difference between them.

_____ *c*. Mary and Alice should not have been assigned such different jobs, since there's only a small difference between them.

_____ *d*. Mark and Bill need the same money for food, since their appetites are equally large.

_____ *e*. Sally should have been the more highly praised, since she tried the hardest.

_____ *f*. Merideth deserved to win, because Alison used an illegal stroke.

_____ *g*. A reward policy that makes no distinctions between very unlike persons cannot be just.

_____ *h*. Greater privileges should normally be given to older children.

_____ *i*. People shouldn't make distinctions in how they treat people, unless those treated differently are really different.

_____ *j*. The darker a person's skin, the better he should be treated.

2. *a*. Below is a list of statements that employ some concept or another of equality. Distinguish the use of a formal principle of proportional equality (*FPPE*) from the use of a material principle of proportional equality (*MPPE*) and from the use of a material principle of strict equality (*MPSE*).

_____ (1) If Jonas and Zeb are going to be treated equally, then Jonas should be given the greater reward, because he did more work. (18:2.2)

_____ (2) Since these entering freshmen are all equal, one no different from another, they should all take the same courses. (18:2.3)

_____ (3) When two groups are equal, they ought to be treated equally; that's only fair. (18:2.1)

_____ (4) If the Abbotts and the Babbitts are only a bit unequal, while the Abbotts and the Cabots are very unequal, then the differences between the treatments of the Abbotts and the Cabots should be greater than the differences between the treatments of the Abbotts and the Babbitts. (18:2.1)

_____ (5) Dorothy's pay should not be the equal of Kevin's, because he has his whole family to support whereas Dorothy is only supplementing her husband's income. (18:2.2)

b. State what distinguishes a principle as formal in contrast to material.

3. Below is a list of statements. Some state a principle of justice, either formal or material. Mark those either *FPJ* or *MPJ*. Some state a presumption of justice, either a presumption of similarity (*PS*) or a presumption of dissimilarity (*PD*). (18:3.1, 18:3.2)

_____ a. In general, persons' backgrounds should be considered similar until proved dissimilar.

_____ b. Persons known to have passed organic chemistry, however, should be considered different unless known to be similar.

_____ c. Equals should always be treated equally.

_____ d. You can't assume that a person should be licensed as a doctor until he or she proved qualified.

_____ e. We assume that our customers in good standing can meet their debts until experience shows that they cannot.

_____ f. Larger contributions should be expected from persons of greater abilities.

_____ g. More help should be available to persons with greater needs.

_____ h. The difference in treatment between two persons should be proportioned to differences between the persons.

_____ i. Whites should be assumed to be as intelligent as blacks until proven otherwise.

_____ j. Persons from similar backgrounds should be given similar opportunities.

4. Abstractly state the circumstances in which no presumptions concerning similarities or dissimilarities would be appropriate.

Answers to Exercises for Module 18

1. a. *MPJ.*
    b. *FPJ, SS.*
    c. *FPJ, DD* (problem is one of proportionality).
    d. *MPJ.*
    e. *MPJ.*
    f. *MPJ.*
    g. *FPJ, DD.*
    h. *MPJ.*
    i. *FPJ, SS.*
    j. *MPJ.*
2. a. (1) *MPPE.*   (2) *MPSE.*   (3) *FPPE.*   (4) *FPPE.*   (5) *MPPE.*
    b. In a formal principle the similarity or dissimilarity of treatment is

related merely to similarity or dissimilarity of the people treated, without specifying the respects in which the people are similar or dissimilar because of which they deserve to be treated similarly or dissimilarly, respectively. A material principle, in contrast, includes a specification of the characteristics of people in virtue of which they ought to be treated similarly or dissimilarly.

3.   *a*. PS.
   b. PD.
   c. FPJ.
   d. PS: persons should be presumed to be unfit to be licensed as doctors until proved otherwise.
   e. PS.
   f. MPJ.
   g. MPJ.
   h. FPJ.
   i. PS.
   j. MPJ.

4.   If, with respect to each of the characteristics that were relevant to how people ought to be treated, one *knew* which characteristics each person had, then one would *know* whether the people were similar or different in each of the relevant respects. Under that condition, there would be no need at all for presumptions of similarity or dissimilarity. Thus, human ignorance about which of the relevant characteristics each person has is a necessary condition for its being appropriate to make presumptions of similarity or dissimilarity.

Module 19
STANDARDS OF MATERIAL JUSTICE

In Module 18 you learned that the formal principle of justice does not tell us which characteristics of people are morally relevant in deciding how to treat people. Proposals suggesting which factors are relevant are called "material principles of justice." In this module we examine various material principles of justice. We shall consider the range of criteria proposed as marking significant differences among persons. The principal criteria to be examined in some detail are related to *work* and to *need*. We shall examine circumstances where it is plausible to suppose that these criteria apply and others where it is implausible. The concluding section will be devoted to a contemporary view, that of philosopher John Rawls, to the effect that social policy should work to the benefit of the disadvantaged. After reading Module 19, you should be able to

- Distinguish ability, productivity, effort, and need as standards of material justice.

- Match the justifications traditionally provided for each of these standards of material justice with the standard it attempts to justify.
- Match possible social circumstances with the standard of material justice each tends to make appropriate.
- Compare and contrast circumstances of overabundance and extreme scarcity as they bear on the virtue of justice.
- Identify states of affairs that are not matters of justice or injustice according to Rawls.
- Show how Rawl's concern for intergenerational justice employs the presumption of equality.

THE CASE OF THE SENATOR AND THE SOCIAL WORKER

"The Senate Committee on Labor and Welfare special hearings on welfare reform are now in session. Please be seated." The familiar words of the committee chairperson rang through the hearing room. "The chair recognizes Senator Judith Dexter for the purpose of questioning Mr. Lestroff, the special witness representing the Social Workers for Reform Association. Senator Dexter."

"Thank you. Now, Mr. Lestroff, you testified yesterday concerning three programs: The Food for Children Program, which assists with hot lunches in schools and day care centers; the Job Retraining Program, which prepares middle-aged people for midlife career changes; and the Unemployment Compensation Program, which is basically a free ride for those too lazy to go out and find work. I can support the first two programs; but the third one stinks. There is no reason to pay these people. Work is available in this country. They are able to work, aren't they? The work pays well enough. So, it is my judgment that those who are unwilling to use their talents to take these jobs are at fault. They don't have any handouts coming to them, especially when the money comes from the pockets of hard-working taxpayers. If they fail to find the work that is out there to be done, or if they fail to perform satisfactorily at jobs they are qualified for, then that's their problem—not the government's. Their needs could be met by their own honest effort, and we should not step into the picture. Don't you agree, sir?"

"I might agree, Senator, except for certain problems. First, in some areas of the nation there is not enough work; or if there are jobs, they are jobs for which the people in this program are not qualified. You cannot turn an out-of-work college professor into a health-care professional overnight. Even given that some of these people can be retrained in time to take advantage of job opportunities, there are others who simply lack the mental or physical skills to hold the more demanding jobs required by our technological society. These untrainables need support. They are misfits in our society through no fault of their own. Second, there are some jobs, especially for unskilled workers, that just do not pay enough to support an individual. Some jobs are seasonal, others are only part-time, some just pay too little and are useful only as second-income jobs. Third, given the government's unwillingness or inability to move unemployment below the 4 percent level, there always will be people who need this program. Fourth, some people are in need of this program because they cannot work owing to handicaps or to their responsibilities to care for their children or other dependents. Until we adequately fund day care centers, there will remain a large number of single parents who are physically able and willing to work but who could do so only by neglecting their children. No, Senator, on balance I cannot agree with your assessment of the need for this program."

"Thank you, Senator and Mr. Lestroff. Are there any further questions for Mr. Lestroff before we call the next witness?"

19:1.1 Material Principles of Justice. Finding adequate material principles of justice is crucial if the formal principle of justice is to be fleshed out and made fully usable. Without material principles there would be no specification of which characteristics of persons are to count as morally relevant in making decisions about the distribution of benefits and burdens. The formal principle of justice cannot do all the work necessary in this regard.

Before going on to consider in greater detail the prime candidates in the field—the work and the need criteria—you should note that certain criteria that would determine desert on the basis of characteristics over which people have no control and about which they can do little are widely regarded as unacceptable. Thus, it is clearly possible, and too often true, that persons may be treated differently because of their caste, class, race, sex, or age. Yet it is widely recognized that practices such as elitism, classism, racism, sexism, and agism amount to arbitrary discrimination and constitute some of the most blatant cases of injustice known.

19:1.2 By contrast, both the work and the need criteria may be understood as having a greater initial plausibility. In the case of the work criteria, it is reasonable to suppose that people are being held responsible for something over which they can exercise some control, namely their own labor. In most cases persons can be held responsible for the development of their abilities, the quality of the work they do, or the amount of effort they put into their work.

In the case of the need criterion, it is reasonable to suggest that persons are strictly equal as persons. This means they all have some very basic human needs, such as nourishment, shelter, and the like. On this criterion people are equally deserving of having these needs met. They are easily met in an affluent society. Though it is not reasonable to suppose that people are responsible for their having such needs, neither is it reasonable to suppose that whether a person's needs are met is morally neutral. Moreover, people *can* typically, do something about seeing to it that their needs are satisfied, whereas nothing can be done, with rare exceptions, about one's caste, class, race, sex, or age.

19:2.1 The Work Criteria.   One of the two principal contenders as a material principle of justice is the work criterion. Many have argued that it is reasonable to distinguish among persons in the distribution of benefits and burdens in terms of equality or inequality of their work. You should notice, however, that this is really no simple criterion but rather a cluster of criteria, all somehow being work-related characteristics of persons. Thus, in order to treat the subject responsibly, we need to break it down into at least three subcriteria relating to (1) ability to work, (2) productivity in work, or (3) effort invested in work.

19:2.2   Consider first the work criterion relating to *ability*. This criterion gains its plausibility from the obvious differences in the abilities required to perform various tasks, the importance we attach to what can be done with some abilities, and the relative rarity of the development of those abilities. Thus, if there is a rationale for the high earnings of doctors or judges, it seems not to be a function of either their higher productivity or effort, although it is recognized that both must invest much effort in cultivating their special abilities. It would seem, rather, to be much more a function of the importance we attach to their abilities and to health or satisfactory resolutions of legal problems. Similarly, garbage collectors tend to receive a low salary, again because of the value we place on the service they provide and because the ability needed in their work is not very specialized, sophisticated, or scarce. In the case study this difference in rewards for jobs as a function of the skills required to do them is mentioned by Mr. Lestroff. The legitimacy of assigning salaries in accord with such considerations is never questioned by either the social worker or the senator.

Some question the ability criterion, holding that it is most important that persons be treated differently only when they can reasonably be held responsible for the differences between them. While one can be said to be responsible for how well one develops the abilities one has, people do not have much control over the abilities they have to begin with. This has been taken as arguing against distributing *benefits* on the basis of abilities. There is another side to the question of distribution, however: the issue of the distribution of *burdens*. Where this is the primary concern, few have taken exception to the notion that it is reasonable to hold persons responsible for developing and performing to the best of their abilities. Those who work to less than their full potential have been thought less deserving than those who work as best they can. Some people argue that it is only fair that those with rare and useful abilities be asked to develop them.

19:2.3 Many view the second work criterion, *productivity* or *contribution*, as more satisfactory. It seems that people can more easily be held accountable for the amount of work they do. Thus, many think it is fair to pay fully productive persons, or persons who make significant contributions in their field, more than relatively unproductive or lazy persons, who make little if any significant contribution. In cases where piecework is being done, it is clearest that payment is being made in a manner strictly proportional to the productivity of the workers. Hourly wages and distinctions between salaries for part-time and full-time work may reflect differences in productivity over differing periods of time. One possible reading of the senator's concern in the case study is to take it as a concern that the Unemployment Compensation Program unfairly rewards nonproductive workers who could be productive if they would simply go out and do the work that, in the senator's view, is waiting to be done. In her view unemployed persons not only are unproductive but are responsible for not doing productive work.

It becomes difficult to measure productivity or contribution when we go from thinking about the kind of work done on assembly lines or by manual laborers in other fields to thinking about the kind of work done by administrative staff, executives, or workers in fields such as science, education, art, entertainment, athletics, theology, government service, or health care. Just how is productivity in such fields to be conceptualized? How are contributions of persons in such fields, including some of the greatest achievements in history, to be compared with and rewarded proportionately to the productivity of the average laborer who puts in a full day in an auto assembly plant? Moreover, there seems to be a connection between making contributions in such fields and the having of abilities to make such contributions. Besides, it is also true that at times good fortune or unusual developments beyond one's control play a big part in making such contributions or achievements possible. Given these facts, some argue that not everyone has an equal opportunity to make these contributions. They argue that people are not accountable for these differences of opportunity between them and that, therefore, differential treatment on this basis is not just.

19:2.4   One work-related matter where there does seem to be equal opportunity and where it is, therefore, more plausible to hold people responsible is the *effort* that people invest in whatever work they do. It is because of this advantage over the ability and productivity criteria that some have defended effort as a standard of material justice. On this criterion, hard-working manual laborers, health-care professionals, executives, ministers, and artists all would be compensated equally for their efforts, and less hard-working people in whatever field would be compensated to a proportionately lesser degree. Thus, a lazy doctor or judge would be paid less than a hard-working garbage collector. Another reading of the senator's concern in the case study is to take it as a concern about the difference in the efforts of those who work regularly and those who are unemployed and served by the Unemployment Compensation Program. She mentions that it is unfair to treat "lazy" nonworkers as deserving of the same rewards as hard-working taxpayers who are making genuine efforts to meet their own needs.

While effort is in some ways the strongest of the work criteria of material justice, it also has weaknesses. The clear but unhappy possibility is that, through lack of ability or knowledge, the productivity of a person may be very low even though his or her effort is great. According to the effort criterion, such a person's efforts would yield great rewards. Yet such rewards seem problematic in two ways. First, from whose labors are these great rewards to come? Clearly, the more productive workers will have to prop up these hard-working, but less productive workers. The intuitiveness of the productivity criterion argues against this solution. The second problem is more abstract. You will recall that questions of justice arise because of conditions of scarcity. If benefits become too scarce, however, no just distribution will be possible, for there will be little or nothing to distribute. Here some thinkers invoke the value judgment that it is better for conditions to remain such that just distributions are possible than for conditions to become so bad that questions of justice become irrelevant in a sea of misfortune. Their point is that using the effort criterion of material justice is in tension with securing the conditions under which justice remains a virtue. The more resources are expended on persons whose efforts are insufficient to meet their own needs, the less resources can be reserved to protect against catastrophe.

19:3.1 The Need Criterion.   The principal alternative to work as a proposed material principle of justice is human need. In this view it is thought just to treat people differently in proportion to their needs. Indeed, many think it part of the concept of respect for persons that their particular needs be understood and appreciated. (For a discussion of this concept, see Module 16.) The concept of human need is a complicated one, however, and it is important for us to analyze it. Let us say that a person needs something if he would suffer without it. Some needs may be called "survival needs"; they are so basic that without them a person's survival would be threatened. The needs for such things as food, water, shelter, minimal health care, and the like are generally recognized as falling into this category and as being needs that all have equally by virtue of their being persons.

As society becomes more complex, it may well be that other things are needed in this most basic sense, such as transportation (so that one can get to work) or education (so that one can manage one's life in a sophisticated and rapidly changing social environment). In the cases of other needs, even though survival would not be threatened, the quality of people's lives would be compromised significantly if what they needed were not available to them. Thus, various things are necessary for the accomplishing of particular goals or purposes that people come to believe to be important as giving meaning to their lives. Failure to meet such needs can make people very unhappy.

In the case study Mr. Lestroff, the social worker, is much concerned about the need criterion. He is especially concerned about the needs of untrainable or handicapped persons as well as persons who, in his view, are locked out of the sophisticated economy where they could earn sufficiently to meet their needs. Their needs, as he sees them, remain deserving of serious attention.

19:3.2   It is important to note in discussing both the work and the need criteria of material justice that there is a distinction to be drawn between what a person has *earned* and what a person *deserves*. In all foregoing discussion we have focused primarily on what a person deserves. This leaves open the question as to whether his deserts depend on what he has earned. The most fundamental question of material justice is why persons *deserve* anything, or, put another way, "What is the basis for their deserving whatever they do deserve?"

Only one of the several most frequent answers to this question is that they deserve what they earn. It is obvious that those who defend work criteria, especially the productivity and effort criteria, are concerned that persons must earn their deserts. Yet, it is equally clear that need is a strong contender as a possible standard of material justice and that, however deserving a needy person may be, persons do not, in any sense, earn their needs. As an example, consider educational opportunities. People generally believe that children deserve these opportunities. The earlier such educational opportunities come in the course of a child's life, the less plausible it is to suggest that the child has earned them.

19:4.1 Work, Need, and Social Circumstances. Work and need have been shown to be standards of material justice with a great deal of plausibility. The work criterion derives its plausibility at least in part from the idea that persons deserve what they earn. On the other hand, the need criterion gains its plausibility from the idea that there are some basic needs that all persons have in common by virtue of their being persons. These needs are deserving of attention if we are to remain respectful of human beings. Let us now consider how differences of social circumstance may be understood as influencing the applicability of these criteria.

First, consider social circumstances where all of the following conditions are met: (a) there is sufficient work so that there are jobs for all who need them, (b) the jobs available to each person include jobs that the person has the abilities to perform, and (c) the jobs pay well enough so that whenever a person takes one, it will enable him or her to earn enough so that his or her needs are met. Many would argue that in circumstances such as these, people have a responsibility to do the work. They hold that people are at fault if they do not work and, therefore, do not earn enough to meet their needs. In circumstances such as these the work criterion in some version appears completely applicable, and there is nothing unjust about not meeting the needs of persons who are capable of meeting their own needs but simply choose not to do so.

19:4.2 Now consider how social circumstances can differ by not meeting the conditions specified in 19:4.1. (a) It may be that there are fewer jobs than there are people who need them. (b) Persons may be unable to perform the jobs that are available owing to simple lack of ability, handicap, or other obligations, such as the obligation to care for a child. The lack of ability may be socially dependent in the sense that skills that people do have can become outmoded and no longer needed in a rapidly changing and technologically progressive society. Or it may be that in a nation as a whole there are sufficient jobs to match the abilities of the people, but the people with the abilities are not located where the jobs are, and inadequate provision is made for getting the people and the jobs together. It could also be that some are denied opportunities to do the work for which they are qualified owing to various forms of job discrimination. (c) It may be that the jobs for which some people qualify, or that they are able to handle given their other responsibilities, simply do not pay well enough to meet their needs. The wages may be extremely low, or the work may be part-time or seasonal. It is plausible to suggest that the greater the extent to which the conditions specified in 19:4.1 are compromised, the more reasonable the application of the need criterion becomes.

In any of the varieties of circumstances just described it is difficult to fault a person for being unable to meet his or her own needs. If the proposition is accepted that there are basic needs that all persons, as persons, deserve to have met, then justice requires that those needs be met where persons cannot meet them for themselves.

19:4.3   It is precisely the applicability of the work vs. the need criterion that is at issue between the senator and the social worker in the case study. There are two ways of understanding their dispute, the one more charitable to the senator than the other. On one reading, the less flattering, the senator is simply unwilling to accept the principles that underlie our present discussion. That is, she can be understood as holding that only persons who earn their own way are deserving of having their needs met. "If people are not capable of earning their own way, then let them perish," is an implication of this way of thinking. On the second reading, the senator accepts the principles that underlie our discussion but disputes the social worker's account of the social circumstances that obtain in the nation. That is, she may be willing to admit that persons who are unable to earn their own way are deserving of having their needs met; she may simply disagree that there is inevitable unemployment in the economic system as presently constituted, or that some are truly unable to work, or that some jobs do not pay sufficiently well.

It is clear that the social worker accepts the underlying principles in our discussion and holds that social circumstances are such that the work criterion is not always strictly applicable. He believes there is a real need for the Unemployment Compensation Program for this very reason.

19:4.4   One kind of circumstance, which we have not yet considered, makes it clear that not all cases of failure to meet basic human needs are cases of injustice. That circumstance is one of *extreme* or *sudden scarcity*. If there simply are not sufficient resources available to meet such basic needs for all people, then it is impossible to do what justice requires. It may be better to say that the principles of justice cannot be applied, since the judgment that justice was not done presupposes that it could have been done. Justice is a virtue that can only exist in circumstances where benefits exist to be distributed and the burdens are not simply overwhelming. If crops fail because of drought that irrigation cannot overcome and food becomes extremely scarce, it is certainly a misfortune that some starve. But the simple fact that some starve does not by itself constitute an injustice. The human capacity to provide alternative deserts, which might then be weighed as more or less just, was lacking in those circumstances where food was not available to be distributed to the population.

Conditions of relative scarcity can lead to some very difficult questions. Suppose there is not enough food to feed everyone, but there is enough to feed some. At this point questions such as these might arise: Should we feed only those whom we select to contribute labor toward securing more food? Should we feed only those who are closest to death or otherwise in greatest immediate danger of starvation? Should we feed only those who have large numbers of dependents? Should we feed only those who are young and strong enough to be able to survive the present disaster? Since we cannot feed everyone, we cannot meet the need criterion for the whole community. Since there are more who can work than we can feed, we cannot meet the work criterion for the whole community. However, once we decide which group to try to feed, whether that turns out to be everyone or only a subgroup of people, we can then apply one of the two material principles to that subgroup.

19:5.1 Needs and Disadvantage.   The alternative criteria of material justice we have been discussing may be construed as defining sets of rules for the enactment of policies within a society. John Rawls, a contemporary philosopher, holds that the just social policy must take into account that resources will be available to different persons and families within a given generation in different measures. He believes that it is neither just nor unjust that persons are born into circumstances of relative wealth or poverty. But he also notes that social policies will tend to make it easier or harder for those born to wealth or poverty to meet their needs and to pursue their aims. The implication here is that persons are initially advantaged or disadvantaged by circumstances not of their own making, but social policy should reflect both a recognition of the equality of desert arising out of common basic needs and the disparity in the abilities to meet these needs due to social circumstance. Rawls argues, therefore, that the presumption of equality among persons dictates that social policy should work to the advantage of those who are disadvantaged. The kinds of social policies that might be justified, given this reasoning, include inheritance taxes that would tend to equalize the distribution of wealth in future generations and special education programs designed to aid the poor in overcoming their economic disadvantages.

Exercises for Module 19: Standards of Material Justice

1. Below is a list of statements employing different principles of material justice. Mark those employing an ability principle *A,* those employing a productivity principle *P,* those using an effort principle *E,* and those using a need principle *N.*

_____ *a.* Anybody with the hands and mind to be a great surgeon should be led into a career in surgery. (19:2.2)

_____ *b.* Let's give a big cheer for Amos and the long, hard hours he worked to make homecoming a success. (19:2.4)

_____ *c.* A child shouldn't have bad teeth because his parents can't afford a dentist. (19:3.1)

_____ *d.* We are gathered here tonight to honor Mickey Spillane as the greatest of mystery writers, for he has published more mystery stories than any other writer. (19:2.3)

_____ *e.* You will be paid 20 cents for every quart of strawberries you pick. (19:2.3)

_____ *f.* It's only fair to let the fastest swimmers swim in the meets. (19:2.2)

_____ *g.* Any kid who works out faithfully at every practice should be included in the meets. (19:2.4)

_____ *h.* If a man needs twice as much money to support his large family, then he should work twice as much and earn the money. (19:2.3)

_____ *i.* There ought to be special classes for any kid with potential like Wanda's. (19:2.2)

_____ *j.* In respect for the community leadership they have provided and the fine parents they have been, senior citizens should pay less for hospitalization than those who have yet to prove themselves. (19:2.3)

2. Below is a list of eight arguments, each of which attempts to justify or discredit the use of a particular principle of material justice. Use *A, P, E,* and *N* to designate arguments concerning the ability, productivity, effort, and need principles, respectively. Then use *J* or *D,* depending on whether the argument attempts to justify or discredit the use of the principle you have designated. (19:1.1–19:3.1)

_____ *a.* A child deserves the opportunity for substantial education, for without it he or she will suffer misfortune for which he or she cannot be held responsible.

_____ *b.* Of the great, great things must be asked. Society, after all, could not survive without their great contributions.

_____ c. The cost of hospital care for the elderly must be higher than for younger people, because the elderly require more hospital services.

_____ d. Wanda didn't do anything to deserve to be so bright. Benefits should not be based on mere good fortune.

_____ e. Johnny tried as hard as Mary, so how can you give him less credit? All you can really ask a person to do is to try.

_____ f. If Johnny didn't do as well as Mary, that's because boys his age don't have the maturity girls have. But since Johnny can't help his inability, it's not fair to judge him on success.

_____ g. If you don't get the strawberries picked, I can't sell them and make money. If I don't make the money, how am I supposed to pay you? Don't tell me you worked hard.

_____ h. Everybody has the same needs. So when resources are inadequate to meet everyone's needs, then some other way must be found to determine who is deserving.

3. Below is a list of four sets of social circumstances. Each tends to justify one of the principles of material justice to the exclusion of the others. Mark each set of circumstances *A, P, E,* or *N* depending upon which principle it tends to justify.

_____ a. In this desperate society the labor of productive workers is sufficient to meet only their own needs.

_____ b. The society as a whole and the variety of kinds of people within it can enjoy a higher standard of living if everyone does work that utilizes his or her talents and capacities than if some or all persons work using less than their scarcest talents.

_____ c. Although some persons' best efforts are insufficient to meet their needs, the ability to meet the needs of all is amply met within the society as a whole.

_____ d. The society as a whole and the variety of kinds of people within it can enjoy a higher standard of living if everyone works as hard as he can than if some or all persons make only lesser efforts.

4. Compare and contrast circumstances of overabundance and extreme scarcity as they bear on the virtue of justice. (17:1.2 and 19:4.4)

5. Below is a list of states of affairs. According to Rawls some of them are, but some are not, matters of justice or injustice. Mark them *MJ* or *NMJ.* (19:5.1)

_____ a. The social class into which one is born.

_____ b. The kind of job that is open to one.

_____ *c*. The generation into which one is born.

_____ *d*. The wealth or poverty into which one is born.

_____ *e*. The education that is open to one.

_____ *f*. The possibility of improving the status of the poor.

_____ *g*. Whether one's interests count equally with others on public issues subject to community decision.

6. Rawls is concerned to improve the quality of justice over the course of generations. Show that this concern presumes equality by showing how the assertion of the existence of injustice would be discredited if an opposite presumption were made.

Selected Answers to Exercises for Module 19

1.   *a. A.*

    b. E.

    c. N.

    d. P.

    e. P.

    f. A: the swimmer's ability is the basis for including him or her, although it may be assumed that performance can be predicted on the basis of ability.

    g. E.

    h. P.

    i. A.

    j. P.

2.   *a. N, J.*

    b. A, J.

    c. P, J: the argument is that the elderly should pay more because the medical staff must produce more in order to keep the elderly healthy.

    d. A, D.

    e. E, J.

    f. P, D: Johnny's inability is used as the basis for discrediting considering his productivity.

    g. E, D.

    h. N, D.

3.   *a. P:* the society will not survive if the needs of the unproductive are met.

    b. A: each using his or her abilities benefits each and benefits all.

    c. N: the society can meet the needs of all its members, and those unable to meet their own needs are presumably not responsible for being unable.

    d. E: each making his or her best efforts benefits each and benefits all.

5.   *a. NMJ.*   *b. MJ.*   *c. NMJ.*   *d. NMJ.*   *e. MJ.*   *f. MJ.*

    g. MJ.

6.   If we presume that people are sufficiently different, then we can argue that all differences in the ways burdens and benefits are distributed to them are deserved. Rawls's presumption of equality functions in his argument to rule out such differences.

Cluster Seven

SOCIETY

What is a society? When is a society a state? What are the legitimate purposes of government? Where does the ultimate authority over actions reside? What are the limits of that authority? Should the state serve the interests of the people or the people serve the interests of the state? What would a group of rational people do if they could establish a governmental organization? These questions, and others like them, have been the focus of intense philosophical concern from Plato's time until our own. The various answers given have been used to sponsor tyrants, spawn revolutions, and serve as the justifications for all manner of governmental institutions from totalitarian fascism to representative democracy to socialism and anarchy. The educational goal of this cluster is for you to examine the range of possible answers to these questions. Module 20 presents some basic terminology and then raises the question of sovereignty: "Who does have the ultimate authority over actions?" Module 21 contrasts opposing views of the state, one seeing the state as an atomistic collection of individuals, the other as an organic whole, in some sense more than the sum of its individual parts. Module 22 raises the question of the legitimate purposes of government, contrasting various views of government's proper role and examining a range of possible purposes.

MODULE 20
THE QUESTION OF SOVEREIGNTY

We begin this module by defining key terms such as "society," "state," and "authority." Then we will focus on the question of sovereignty: "Does any person or group of people have the authority to secure the cooperation needed to pursue and so attain their fundamental shared human purposes?" This complex question demands a careful and thoughtful response. We will explore the three major responses offered by philosophers to this question, the theories of "dictatorial sovereignty," "popular sovereignty," and "individual sovereignty." After reading Module 20, you should be able to

- Characterize a society and explain what a state, as a kind of society, is.
- List some of the purposes that people might view as those common fundamental human purposes that define a state.
- Distinguish between authority and power, and between derived and underived authority.
- Compare and contrast the theories of dictatorial sovereignty, popular sovereignty, and individual sovereignty.
- Explain how the question of sovereignty can be answered in part by appeal to different domains of concern.

THE CASE OF LAMBDA SEVEN, PART I

Lambda Seven was one of 15 exploratory space vehicles sent to various sectors of the universe to search for inhabitable planets. It had crashed on an uncharted planet, The craft was destroyed, and only a little of its life-support equipment could be salvaged. Many of the 500 people aboard died either during the crash or from infections and strange diseases encountered in the alien environment. All hope of rescue and return home being lost, the 120 Lambda Seven survivors met to discuss their common future. They would call themselves the Lambda Seven Colony. The first question they faced was who should have ultimate authority over the colony.

Subcommander Gonzales spoke first. "I will be the leader and judge. I am next in command after the late Captain Frazlo and, according to official military regulations, I unquestionably must assume command."

"Now hold on there, Gonzales," said the director of the research team, Quale. "My research people are the ones with the know-how to save all of us. We should be in charge of the group. We'll select a subcommittee of scientists to see to governmental decisions, and the rest of the research people can lead various community programs and survival operations." From near the rear of the crowd came the voice of Fran Zoflewski. "There are only 120 of us left, we are all in this thing together, so we should all have a say in major decisions. The military rules apply only in the space craft. So, Gonzales, if you want to be in charge of the wreck, you can be; but we're talking about building a home for ourselves now. As for you and your experts, Quale, we need your knowledge, but that does not give you the right to make up laws and dictate policy. No, the people should rule. We'll have to find a way to share the chores of government."

"A fine speech, Zaflewski, but not too practical," came the reply from Walsh, the one nurse who had survived. "Nobody is going to tell me what to do, not Quale, not Gonzales, not you, Zaflewski, not even the whole 120 of you. You people do not have the right to force me to cooperate, and if I don't like what's happening, I'm not going to cooperate. That's my prerogative. And, remember, I'm the only medical specialist left alive."

20:1.1 Society and the State.   Let us begin by defining our terms. A *society* is a group of people who engage in cooperative behavior for the sake of a common goal. There are plenty of examples of societies in our culture: amateur teams, fan clubs, social groups, lodges, partnerships, corporations, military forces, charitable organizations, political parties, guilds, unions, and professional associations. At times a society will maintain a place of common residence, a meeting hall, or a headquarters. Religious orders, churches, labor union locals, and country clubs usually establish permanent facilities of this sort. When the members of a society start to regularly reside together or take meals together, the society can be called a *community*.

In order to exist, societies identify and maintain focus on shared goals. However, they do not necessarily engage in formally adopting laws or formally empowering a governing board or ruler. A family is a typical society. A family can exist without formally adopting its own internal set of laws. The cooperative behavior that a society's members engage in is not, however, random or unorganized. Usually from their very earliest days societies fall into, or adopt, behaviors that become, for them, custom or norm. For instance, imagine a fan club regularly meeting to hear records and write letters to their singing idol. Accomplishing this purpose requires a number of cooperative arrangements. Someone must be responsible for bringing the records for the meetings. Someone must provide the phonograph. If letters are to be written, then paper and pens must be available. If members are to know when meetings are being held or when there are changes in plans, then internal organization and communication must occur.

Such customary practices are sufficient to establish *division of labor* and create *mutual expectations* and *responsibilities* that ensure the more or less adequate achievement of the purposes of society. This sufficiency is, however, based upon the presence of environmental factors that may or may not be within the total control of the society. Without the needed financial, human, and technological resources no society could sustain itself. In order to listen to records, the fan club requires not only some sort of sound system but also the power supply to run it.

Thus, although its cooperative behavior need not be governed by official rules or laws, a society is at least bound by its norms or customs. Through these, its members cooperate to achieve their shared purposes, given the limitations of the environment within which the society exists.

20:1.2   The state is a certain kind of society. The *state* can be defined as a society such that the cooperative norm-bound behavior is directed toward a special set of shared purposes. Those shared purposes are the fundamental purposes of human life. To have a clear idea of what the state is, we must clarify what makes a particular human purpose *fundamental*. Otherwise we might take the word to express only the intensity of a person's emotion about a certain purpose, without objectively characterizing that purpose in any particular way.

What makes a purpose fundamental? One fairly clear meaning is that it is a purpose the achievement of which is *necessary* to the achievement of other purposes. Then the most fundamental purposes of human life will be those such that without their achievement life itself would not be possible. Thus, *survival* and *safety* could be listed as fundamental human purposes. The notion of fundamental purposes of human life, however, is ambiguous, because it can refer to the life of the individual, the life of the group, or the life of the whole human species. The two views that have become dominant focus on the individual and on the group. We will examine the controversy between these two orientations in the next module.

Whatever the resolution of that controversy, whether we focus on the individual or the group, there remains still another controversy. Some thinkers wish to limit the idea of the fundamental purposes of human life to those *without which survival is endangered or made impossible*. Others contend that the idea should be broader, that the state should be organized around those human purposes *without which life would not be worth living*. This notion has proved very difficult to define in any clearly objective manner, though the clearest attempt is made by those who advance the "organic" theory of the state. We shall discuss this theory in Module 21.

   20:2.1 Sovereignty. Beyond the controversies listed in 20:1.2, one question is more basic and ultimately even more important. It is the question of sovereignty: "Which members of the state, if any, have the authority or the right to require and secure the cooperation needed to pursue and attain those fundamental purposes for which it was formed?" In order to develop a precise understanding of this question, you should grasp certain preliminary distinctions. First is the distinction between the *ability to control* and the right or *entitlement to control*. A homeowner, for example, has the right to control who comes into his or her home. A thief may have the ability to gain entrance, even though he or she lacks the right. *Power* can be defined, in this context, as the ability to control, in order to distinguish it from *authority*, defined as the right to control.

   Once we have distinguished power from authority, a further distinction of two kinds of authority becomes crucial. For authority can be either a derived or an underived right. That is, authority might be given or delegated from another authority, as when the president delegates authority to particular administrators, agencies, and governmental operatives. Instances of delegated authority are very frequent in our culture. Corporations delegate authority to their boards of directors. The board delegates to the corporate presidents, who in turn delegate authority to vice-presidents, managers, executives, directors, and so on, depending upon the hierarchy within the particular business. The question of sovereignty is not one of delegated authority; it is, "Who has *un*derived or *un*delegated authority?" Once lawful authority has been established, it can be delegated; our concern is not with delegation. We want to ask, "Who has the underived right to establish all subsequent authority?"

   20:2.2   There have been a number of answers to the question of sovereignty. They can be classified into roughly three theories: (a) dictatorial sovereignty, (b) popular sovereignty, and (c) individual sovereignty. The theory of *dictatorial sovereignty* holds that some identifiable subgroup in the state, perhaps one identifiable person, has the underived authority to rule the state. This authority is often regarded as complete and absolute, although it need not be viewed as absolute. Saying it is *complete* means that the authority extends to every aspect of the life of the group and the lives of its members. Saying the authority is *absolute* means that no act based on it can be legitimately challenged by any other person or agency in the state.

Dictatorial sovereignty is usually argued for by appeal to one of three basic theories. The first is that the dictatorial ruling class, or oligarchy, has the right to rule because *those whom the gods ordain to rule should rule*. This is often called the theory of the "divine right of kings." The important question of how we know that this particular person or group has been divinely selected to rule is not answered by this theory. There are two traditional responses to this question, however. The will of the gods is thought to be manifest either in the assumption of power of a particular dynasty or through the approval of the state's religious institution. Whatever the answer offered, the question of how people know the will of the gods is crucial to the success of the divine right theory. Anyone can claim the divine right to rule. Only a clear procedure for finding out whose claim is legitimate can save the dictatorially organized state from the political turmoil and civil war that result from conflicting claims of would-be rulers.

An alternative theory is that dictatorial authority belongs to any person or group with the power to seize it. This is the theory that "might makes right." If someone is able to put together the military power, political support, and popular appeal, then the person can take over control of the state. It often happens in human history that such a person gains control of the government and, after a time, is recognized or acknowledged to be the official ruler. An important problem is associated with this theory, however. The theory that might makes right does not explain why the person who has seized power *ought* to be acknowledged as the rightful authority. There are practical reasons, such as the fact that resisting could bring severe punishment. But the difference between power and authority we mentioned in 20:2.1 raises the question of the *right* of the person to rule. Historically this question has led rulers deposed by dictatorial powers and their followers to go into exile still claiming the rightful authority to govern. It has led them to seek to regain the control of the state by encouraging war and popular rebellion against the dictator who has seized rule by force.

The third theory offered in support of dictatorial sovereignty is that those who are experts should rule. This can be called the "rule of the wise" theory. It is based on the view that experts who can see what is really in the state's best interest should have the authority to rule, even if the remaining members of the state do not agree with them. Wisdom is, according to many thinkers, the highest virtue, which uniquely qualifies someone for the role of ruler.

In our country this argument is accepted to some extent. People are usually appointed to executive agencies on the basis of their presumed knowledge. This theory is, like the others, also open to question. How shall we determine who is the wisest among us? What is the relationship between wisdom and technical expertise?

20:2.3   In the case study the colonists from the Lambda Seven are debating the question of sovereignty. The military subcommander proposes that he should be dictator. He appeals to military regulations in a way that is as least reminiscent of how a would-be king might appeal to a divinely inspired document as the source of his authority. The research director, Quale, argues for a dictatorial oligarchy of experts. Her appeal is that the scientific knowledge of the research team best qualifies them to lead. Zaflewski responds to both of them by appeal to what is called the theory of popular sovereignty. Nurse Walsh takes a more radical position, advancing a version of the theory of individual sovereignty. Let us look at these latter two theories.

THOMAS JEFFERSON (1743–1826)

One of the strongest and most influential advocates of popular sovereignty was Thomas Jefferson. His political views can be traced to the English philosopher John Locke. Like Locke, Jefferson advocated a wide range of civil liberties for all men, including rights to life, liberty, property, and the pursuit of happiness. He opposed slavery and insisted on a free press and religious toleration as essential to a democratic society.

Jefferson expressed these political views in many of his writings, including the Declaration of Independence (1776). Further, he put his theories into practice as a leader in the American Revolution, as governor of Virginia (1779–1781), and as the third president of the United States (1801–1809).

Jefferson felt that guaranteeing the continuance of popular sovereignty and democratic institutions involved preparing people to govern themselves and supporting democratic leaders and governments abroad. Thus he advocated life styles that fostered diligence, self-reliance, clear thinking, and local self-government. He also directed U.S. foreign policy toward the support of countries that themselves were establishing democratic governments. He advocated a strong government with limited purposes and careful provisions for checks and balances.

20:2.4   The theory of *individual sovereignty* maintains that each person is sovereign over himself or herself. Each person, in other words, has the underived authority to act as he or she chooses. No one else has a right to interfere. The theory is typically supported by persons who give priority to individual self-determination. The individual is entitled to be free to make his or her own life, to choose his or her own values, to follow the dictates of his or her own conscience, and to adopt his or her own life style.

20:2.5   The theory of *popular sovereignty* maintains that the people as a whole—the group of people composing the society—have ultimate authority. In the state the people are thought of, under the theory of popular sovereignty, as having the ultimate right to express their collective will, which is itself the ultimate authority. Like the various versions of dictatorial sovereignty, this theory leaves important questions unanswered. How is the collective will of the people to be recognized? How do the people, taken as a group, manifest what they, as a group, desire or decide?

You will get some insight concerning both the difficulty of recognizing the will of the people and distinction between individual sovereignty and popular sovereignty by examining the concept of voting. Within the United States, although not only here, the people as a whole are thought of as having the ultimate authority to protect citizens against harm caused by others. Our governments make laws against a wide variety of such harms. The lawmakers gain their authority to make such laws by having been elected as lawmakers. Thus, when a person votes for a legislator, the individual person is not understood as delegating to the legislator the *individual's authority,* for the individual is not understood as having the authority to make any laws or regulations. Instead, the individual by voting is understood as helping to clarify what the people as a total society want. In elections, the idea of "majority rule" is that the will of the people is shown, or determined as best it can be, by whatever the majority of people vote for. Sovereignty is understood, throughout, as residing with the people, not as delegating individual sovereignty.

It seems that these two theories are compatible. One could maintain that the collective is sovereign over those purposes that are shared by everyone, but that each individual is sovereign over those purposes that are his or her own personal concern. But, as the case study shows, this division will not work. Nurse Walsh may want to maintain his own individual sovereignty, but he is the community's chief and only medical resource. They need his knowledge and cooperation. If he is sovereign, they cannot rightfully claim it. If they are a sovereign collective, then they can rightly claim that he is obligated to render medical aid when needed.

20:3.1 Domains of Concern. One way to overcome problems like the one cited above is to define domains of concern. A *domain of concern* is a group of purposes. We might now decide that different theories of sovereignty apply to different domains of concerns. *Complete* sovereignty, in other words, would not be of any one type—dictatorial, popular, or individual. The experts might be sovereign over concerns such as military security or technical management of resources. The population as a whole could be sovereign over concerns such as establishing rules and laws to regulate interpersonal and commercial interaction. Each individual could be sovereign over such concerns as his or her own optimal health and happiness. This idea holds promise, but serious problems remain in determining each of the ranges of concern. Perhaps chief among these is deciding who has sovereignty over the *life* and *labor* of each member of the state. This question will be brought into sharper focus in Module 22.

Exercises for Module 20: The Question of Sovereignty

1. Describe two groups of people in such a way that one group clearly is a society and the other is not. (20:1.1)
2. Below is a list of purposes, each of which some group of people is cooperating to achieve. If that purpose has traditionally been suggested as characteristic of the state, mark it *ST*. If it is not a generally shared or common human purpose, mark it *NC*. If that purpose has not been regarded as fundamental, mark it *NF*. Note that some purposes are neither common nor fundamental. (20:1.2)

_____ *a.* To prevent cruelty to animals.

_____ *b.* To play soccer.

_____ *c.* To have sufficient food for every citizen.

_____ *d.* To make mobile homes safer from fires.

_____ *e.* To minimize the hazards of the natural environment.

_____ *f.* To maximize individual freedom.

_____ *g.* To provide a sense of dignity and meaning for human life.

_____ *h.* To make each individual happy.

_____ *i.* To provide educational opportunities.

_____ *j.* To find a cure for diabetes.

_____ *k.* To defend against military attack.

3. Below is a list of reasons why a certain something ought to be done. Some of these reasons are appeals to power. Mark them *AP*. Others are appeals to authority. If an appeal is to derived authority, mark it *DA;* and mark it *UA* if it is an appeal to sovereignty or underived authority. (20:2.1)

_____ *a*. If you don't do it, Robbie, Mommy is going to spank.

_____ *b*. Young man, I do outrank you in this army.

_____ *c*. You don't want to spend the next three weeks on KP, do you?

_____ *d*. The people of this nation have a right to an army that can defend them.

_____ *e*. By the power vested in my exalted office, I now declare you a Third Rank Schnutz.

_____ *f*. This is our lodge, you know, so we can make whatever rules we want for it.

_____ *g*. I'm entitled to swim any stroke I please because this race is designated as "free style."

_____ *h*. I'm entitled to swim any stroke I please for my own pleasure.

_____ *i*. What justification can there be for arguing with her? We know she's the expert.

4. Below is a list of assertions about sovereignty. Different ones of these assertions are true on different theories of sovereignty. On the right are columns marked *DS, PS,* and *IS* for dictatorial sovereignty, popular sovereignty, and individual sovereignty, respectively. Mark a *T* or an *F* in each column beside each assertion depending on whether the given assertion is true or false according to each of the three theories of sovereignty. (20:2.2, 20:2.4, 20:2.5)

	DS	PS	IS
a. Every person is sovereign over his own actions.			
b. When the actions of an individual affect the purposes of the state, the individual is not sovereign.			
c. A person's sovereignty may be based on his wisdom.			
d. A person's authority may be based on his wisdom.			
e. When everybody is affected, or can be affected, by an action, the ultimate right to decide rests in common hands.			
f. If an individual has the power to enforce his will, then there may be no higher right to decide.			

DS   PS   IS

   g. The circumstances of a person's birth cannot establish the right to decide.

   h. The right to decide can be distinguished from the power to decide.

5. *a*. State what it means to say that sovereignty is *complete*.

   b. Use this concept of completeness in order to characterize a domain.

   c. Describe any two domains in such a way as to support the assertion that one sort of sovereignty holds in one domain and another sort in the other.

   d. Abstractly state how the concept of domains might be used in order to make the three theories of sovereignty compatible with each other. (20:3.1)

Answers to Exercises for Module 20

1. You have correctly described a society if you have clearly stated a purpose that the members of the group share and you have described their acting cooperatively in order to achieve this purpose. Your other group will fail to be a society if it has no common purpose (as, for instance, people listed on the same page of the telephone book seldom do), or if they do not cooperate to achieve it (as, for instance, when a mob is pushing and shoving to see a celebrity).

2. *a*. *NC, NF*.

   b. *NC, NF*.

   c. *ST*.

   d. *NC:* since some people have no involvement with mobile homes. It is a fundamental concern, since it is a concern for survival.

   e. *ST:* this concern is similar to the one above, but it is general enough to be common.

   f. *ST*.

   g. *ST*.

   h. *NF:* although perhaps a state could regard this purpose as fundamental.

   i. *ST*.

   j. *NF:* like the mobile homes.

   k. *ST*.

3. *a*. *AP*.   *b*. *DA*.   *c*. *AP*.   *d*. *UA*.   *e*. *DA*.   *f*. *UA*.   *g*. *DA*.

   h. *UA*.   *i*. *UA*.

Notice that throughout this exercise the assertions are judged on the basis of what is *claimed*. No comment is being made about whether each of these authorities is derived or underived as claimed. (See 20:2.1.)

4.
	DS	PS	IS
a.	F	F	T
b.	T	T	F
c.	T	F	F
d.	T	T	T
e.	F	T	F
f.	T	F	F
g.	F	T	T
h.	T	T	T

g. (According to IS, it is the *fact* of one's birth, not its circumstances, that make one sovereign.)

5. a. To say that sovereignty is complete is to say that it extends to every aspect of every action.

b. A domain is defined by some sort of action or some aspect of actions. Thus, if sovereignty is confined to a domain, it is not complete.

c. A good answer to c meets two requirements. The domains should not overlap; if they do, conflicting claims to sovereignty will arise. And the domains should be so described that traditional theories of sovereignty make it plausible that each sort of sovereignty should hold in one of the domains but not in the other. Your answer to d should be framed around these two requirements.

MODULE 21
THEORIES OF THE STATE

In Module 20 we mentioned the conflict between the interests of the individual and those of society. This module examines that conflict. The resolution of the conflict depends on one's view of the state, which depends upon what one takes to be the fundamental, shared, human purposes for which the state exists. We will examine various theories of the state, defining and distinguishing each in terms of different views about the fundamental, shared, human purposes. The theories we will look at are classical liberalism, socialism, and fascism. Finally, we will look at the social contract theory as one approach to resolving the problem of the conflict of interests between individuals and the state. After reading Module 21, you should be able to

- Describe the conflict that arises between the interests of the state and those of its individual members.
- Compare and contrast atomistic and organic theories of the state.
- Compare and contrast fascism, socialism, and classical liberalism for their views of fundamental, shared, human purposes.
- State the elements of the social contract theory.
- Explain the intended function of social contract theory.

THE CASE OF LAMBDA SEVEN, PART II

Nurse Walsh's challenge did not go unheeded by the others of the group. Everyone saw the danger in his threat to withhold his medical expertise if he didn't like the way things were going. Gonzales, seeing the implications of the problem, spoke up first. "Walsh, suppose I were to withdraw my military forces if I didn't like a particular decision. In that case you and all the others would be totally undefended. But why should my soldiers risk death to defend you? Why, especially if you claim the liberty to withhold your ability as a nurse?"

Quale picked up the theme quickly. "If we all held out, cooperating only when it was to our own selfish interest, then the whole bunch of us could end up quite dead. Nobody here has yet proved that the good of each is the same as the good of all. Individual interests, claims of personal liberties, and special exemptions could be a disaster for the whole community. These claims could destroy our cooperative spirit. They could prevent even those who wanted to cooperate from having access to the resources and talents needed to survive. We are a unit! We must think as a unit. We must act as a unit. None of us is more important than the survivial of the group. No personal interests can be tolerated."

"I'm not sure about that," said Sharma the agriculturalist. "We have enough people to form three or four small communities. We can separate into these smaller groups and still be self-sustaining. Some of the discord we now experience would be minimized because we would not be so conscious of differences in class or occupation. We could all work and share in the production of our own communities, when possible taking turns at various community jobs and more or less equally benefiting from the work."

"We would still need a centralized leadership group," said Gonzales. "What about a defense against common enemies, and what about sharing ideas for increasing production?"

"Not necessarily," replied Sharma.

At this point Walsh broke in again. "One big group, four little groups. I don't want either. I claim there are limits to what can be demanded of any of us. I'm not willing to say that soldiers must fight and die any more than I'm willing to say that I must practice medicine. We are nothing more than a bunch of unfortunate people thrown together here. That does not give any of us, nor any group of us, the right to demand something of any other person or group. What we decide to give is up to us individuals to determine."

"I, for one, am willing to negotiate," said Zaflewski. "Let's see if we can't agree to surrender some of our individual prerogatives in order to form a pact or agreement of some kind. Perhaps by mutual consent we can form a contract that specifies some of our mutual liberties as well as our community obligations."

21:1.1 The State and the Individual.   The interests of particular individuals are often in conflict with the interests of the state. Criminals are denied their liberties. Workers are taxed. Property is reclaimed from individuals by laws of eminent domain. Scarce resources are rationed. The question must be asked: "How far can the state go in this?" To answer this question, we will have to look more closely at what the state is.

In Module 20 we defined the state as a society that is concerned about fundamental, shared, human purposes. In order, then, to get a clearer idea of what the state is, we must find out what those fundamental, shared, human purposes are. We can begin by distinguishing *purposes* from the *means* used to achieve them. Purposes are goals, such as survival, security, economic wealth, wisdom. Means are ways of achieving goals. Accordingly, when we think of something as a means, we are focusing on its value only as instrumental. You can acquire wealth in several ways—through work, inheritance, theft, or gift. Our concern is not with particular ways that states might use to achieve their goals but with what those fundamental, shared purposes themselves are.

Second, among goals having intrinsic value, we should distinguish fundamental goals from derivative or secondary goals. Survival is a fundamental goal. Enjoying a game of volleyball is a secondary or derivative goal, even though it might be argued that the enjoyment of the game is intrinsically valuable. But we must be careful here. The difference between what is fundamental and what is not is a matter of degree. We can recognize examples at both extremes, but there is a grey area in the middle. Some goals, such as having friends, being healthy, and being protected from certain diseases, fall in the middle. Some would be inclined to call them fundamental; others would not. Some would argue that the state should work to make human relations more harmonious and friendly, to provide programs that improve the health of its citizens, and to seek ways to protect the citizens from dangerous diseases. Others would argue that these goals, while important, are beyond the scope of the state's legitimate concerns. In other words, everyone can agree that purposes that are not necessary for human life are not fundamental, even if the achievement of these purposes is intrinsically valuable. The difficulty for the definition of the state comes about because people disagree about what purposes are necessary. The contrasts developed in 21:1.3–21:1.6 between classical liberalism, socialism, and fascism help to elaborate why these disagreements exist.

21:1.2   Let us look at three theories that seek to specify the relationship of the individual to the state: *classical liberalism, socialism,* and *fascism.* In effect, by examining these theories, we are trying to answer the question, "What concerns are fundamental?" They represent three different ideals of the state and of the scope of its purposes. In practice, some nations combine these ideals in various ways at various times in their histories. It is also possible that different ideals are used when considering different domains of concern.

21:1.3   *Classical liberalism* defines the fundamental purposes of the state as those of particular individuals. If focuses on the interests of the individual as opposed to the interests of the collective. Thus, in saying that survival is a fundamental human purpose, the classical liberal is talking about the survival of individual people, not the survival of the community or the state.

The classical liberal views the state as a tool aimed at guaranteeing that individuals can go about their private business, see to their own concerns, and do so with a minimum of interference either from other individuals or from governments. The state, then, in this view, serves to protect the individual from harm while allowing him or her as much freedom as possible. Individuals are to be left free to pursue their own goals, unhindered by others.

This theory sees people as potential threats to each other. It says that the state exists to protect us from each other but otherwise not to interfere with our personal goals. Our social, economic, religious, educational, moral, artistic, and recreational interests are our own concerns. The state must not, in this theory, interfere with our freedom to dispose of our wealth as we choose.

Some liberal thinkers are willing to introduce an ethical limitation on this freedom. They say that classical liberalism does not allow complete freedom to do what one wants, but only the legal freedom to do what one is allowed to do. In other words, the fact that private drunkenness cannot be outlawed under this theory does not mean that people are morally free to get drunk. These thinkers distinguish classical liberalism as a theory of state from other normative theories that may specify one's personal morality. Such thinkers typically argue that if behavior does not cause harm to others, it should not be prohibited by the state, even though it may be morally wrong.

Many classical liberals hold the theory of individual sovereignty. In the case study Walsh argues for classical liberalism. You will recall that he held the theory of individual sovereignty in the case study for

Module 20. Some classical liberals hold the theory of popular sovereignty. They hold that the people have the right to prohibit individuals from harming others.

21:1.4   Classical liberalism is often called an *atomistic* theory of the state. It sees the state as a collection or group of individuals. A theater audience, for example, is a collection of people. Each is seeking to enjoy the show; they have that purpose in common. They come together for that purpose. When the show is over, each goes about his or her separate business. This is how atomistic theories, such as classical liberalism, see the state. Of course, if the people in the audience feel that their individual enjoyment depends on talking with their companions during the show, then the resulting noise can ruin the show for everyone.

Let us look at this problem implicit in talking at the theater more closely. It has been called the *tragedy of the commons,* and it is often advanced as a criticism of atomistic theories and specifically of classical liberalism.

Imagine a theater full of people watching a play. This audience is composed of a large number of small groups of people who have come to the play together. Either because of difficulties in understanding the play or because of wanting to share the enjoyment of the play with friends, you can imagine that each of the small groups of people would find it advantageous to talk within itself from time to time about the play. Moreover, if only a very few people talk, it is probable that the actors will be heard over this talk and nobody will be greatly disturbed by it. However, if almost everybody, realizing the advantage to be gained by such talk, begins to talk during the performance, the result will doubtless be that no one will be able to hear the actors. Small groups, or individuals, each planning what is best on the small scale, may make and carry out plans that are disastrous for the group as a whole. The tragedy of the destruction of the common goal occurs when everybody acts in pursuit of his or her own interest, since no one is given specific responsibility for maintaining what is good for all.[1]

In the case study Quale tells Walsh, "Nobody here has yet proved that the good of each is the same as the good of all." Quale is bringing up a serious objection to classical liberalism: If each person pursues his or her own interests, the common good will not necessarily be served, in fact it may be harmed. Consider our natural resources, such as lumber. Over the course of time, lumber can be replaced. So, even though the supply

---

[1] The term "tragedy of the commons" and our discussion of it are derived from ecologist Garrett Hardin's presentation in his now-famous article, "The Tragedy of the Commons," originally published in *Science,* December 13, 1968, vol. 162, pp. 1243–48.

is limited, if it is managed it can be made to last. As some is used, new forests will come to maturity. But suppose each of us uses just a small bit more than his or her share. We can justify our individual excess because of the importance (to us) of our goals and because we have only used a small amount more than is our due. But what happens to our resource? With millions of us overdemanding lumber, the resource is depleted, and all of us are then frustrated in our aims because of its absence. As another example, we all value defense. But it is not in our interest, as individuals, to join the armed forces, go to war, and risk death; our individual interest dictates that we avoid the risk. But the collective interest in national security will be frustrated if everyone waits for the other person to go out and do the job. Even in our society, which is heavily based on an atomistic theory of the state, we take a collectivist or group approach to defense. When volunteers are not forthcoming, we impose conscription.

21:1.5 *Socialism* is a theory of the state that emphasizes the value and importance of *cooperation*. It emphasizes the importance of collective work, careful planning for group needs, and cooperative work in securing those needs. This emphasis on cooperation can be interpreted in either of two very different ways. For cooperation can be understood so as to be compatible with an atomistic understanding of the state, or it can be understood so as to imply an organic understanding. Since the cooperation of centralized planning is essential to socialism, we will do well to grasp how cooperation can be interpreted either atomistically or organically.

Suppose we approach the need for cooperation simply from the perspective of the tragedy of the commons. To return to our theater example, probably each group will soon realize that everyone had better be quiet so that all can hear. Any group that is slow in coming to this realization is also likely to be prodded by the shushing that surrounding groups will quickly supply. The outcome is that all groups are likely to become fairly quiet as they watch the play. In an atomistic sense, the members of the audience are cooperating. By that we mean, first, that they are cooperating. They have a common goal of wanting to hear the play. And each is employing the means of keeping quiet in order to achieve their common goal.

In saying that their cooperation is *atomistic*, we mean foremost that the only goals are the goals of the individuals. The audience members must cooperate, in their means, so that they can achieve their goals, but each member of the audience establishes his own goals, which can be exclusively for himself or herself goals, we could say, completely of self-interest. A secondary point in saying that the cooperation is atomistic is that there need be no interaction among the members of the audience in order for them to employ their means (each can shut his or her own mouth) and thus achieve their goal.

When persons cooperate, however, it is not necessary that their goals will be atomistic. A sports team may cooperate to defeat the opponent, but team spirit may develop out of their interaction as they cooperate, and the members of the team may enjoy the team spirit as much or more than they enjoy winning. Moreover, many would argue that an individual team member might pursue the development of team spirit not only to help the team win and not only to enjoy that spirit himself or herself but also for the non-self-interested reason of helping or allowing other team members to enjoy themselves. Such relationships are likely to exist also, for example, in a harmonious family or harmonious orchestra.

In these relationships there certainly is cooperation. The cooperation, however, is not easily interpreted atomistically. The alternative interpretation, called the *organic* interpretation, is that cooperation is a means not simply to self-interested ends, not merely to provide the planning necessary to avoid a tragedy of the commons, but a means toward creating and then maintaining a new unity, the team or the family, which has new goals of its own, beyond the original goals of the individuals. The team seeks to develop, to maintain, and to exhibit its spirit, as well as to seek the victories the individuals might originally have sought. The family seeks harmonious relationships among its members, not merely so that the members are not hampered by their family membership, but also because they find that their interrelating harmoniously is intrinsically enjoyable.

In summary, then, in the case of organic cooperation, cooperation is seen as intrinsically valuable, the goals of cooperation will include goals of the group or collective, and, typically, interactions between group members will have the potential for developing a sense of group unity, spirit, or harmony. In contrast, in the case of atomistic cooperation, cooperation is seen as valuable only instrumentally, the goals of cooperation will exclusively be those of the cooperating individuals, and interactions between members of the group will be valued only as instruments toward the realization of individual goals, not toward any new, collectivistic goals to which the interactions might give rise.

While cooperation, at least in order to prevent tragedies of the commons, is central to socialism, the nature of that cooperation, as atomistic or organic, is usually not defined in socialist thought. Thus socialism can develop with either an atomistic or an organic view of the state.

21:1.6   *Fascism* is clearly an organic theory of the state. It includes a broader selection of goals as fundamental, shared, human purposes. Not only would it include the survival and safety of the community, as does socialism, but it would add the pursuit of a sense of the significance of the state, of community spirit, and the continuity of civilization. The individual is viewed as gaining a sense of the meaning of his or her life by seeing it as part of a whole, a unity, a large, important, and ongoing purpose—the health and growth of the state. These are included in the concept of fundamental, shared, human purposes because, in the fascist view, they are necessary for survival—the survival of the state. To survive, the state needs a sense of mission, scope, grandeur, and importance. From this the people can derive their individual significance. Their lives can become meaningful as they see how they contribute to the ongoing collective organism, the state. Next to this the individual's life is petty and momentary. Accordingly, without the state's having such stature, the individual's life would be meaningless on account of its insignificance. Since without meaning life is seen as not worth living, belonging to the state is seen as a fundamental purpose, if not to the survival, at least to the worth of the survival of the individual.

In fascist theory the state is a living totality. Divisive special-interest groups and petty personal individuals cannot be tolerated. Under fascism all social institutions, religion, morality, commerce, law, education, transportation, resource development, and so on are to be totally coordinated for the long-range good of the people viewed as a whole. A fascist state philosophy usually seeks to uphold virtues of personal integrity, cooperativeness, self-sacrifice, heroism, loyalty, and patriotism. It strives explicitly for a comprehensive *totalitarianism*—that is, state control over all aspects of the lives of its members that may affect the collective good. Centralized authority located in an individual, a central committee, or a strong ruling party helps to make possible more complete organization, integration, and cooperation. Fascism, correspondingly, regards pacifism, unwillingness to self-sacrifice, and individualism as vices. Often a measure of austerity, self-denial, and personal discipline is deliberately built into a fascistic model of society. Fascist thinkers feel this helps people avoid the laziness and selfishness often associated with lives of pleasure and self-indulgence. In a fascistic theory of the state the individual is given no special privileges or exemptions, unless those exemptions serve the collective good. There are in principle no limits to the state's legitimate authority over the labor or life of the individual. The state can ask anything of anybody. The individual does not have the right to refuse, but rather the duty to obey. Although fascism has been racist or nationalistic in some of its historically prominent forms, the sketch of fascism here presented shows that it is not an essentially racist or nationalistic theory. In the case study Quale advocates fascism.

He speaks of the importance of acting as a unit. He is not tolerant of personal interests.

21:2.1 Contrasting Classical Liberalism, Socialism, and Fascism. The difference between classical liberalism and fascism is the difference between atomistic and organic views of the state. The atomistic view sees human needs in terms of individual needs. Thus, classical liberalism defines the fundamental human purposes as the survival needs of the individual. On the other hand, the organic view focuses on collectivist needs. Thus, fascism defines the fundamental human purposes in terms of the survival of the state.

Underlying these two theories are differences in their concepts of human survival needs. Classical liberalism thinks of these needs in terms of the individual. Fascism thinks of them in terms of the state.

Socialism differs from classical liberalism in that collective planning is valued highly, at least instrumentally to avoid the tragedy of the commons and, also, to thereby ensure the survival of the state. Socialism differs from fascism in that only under fascism is the life of the individual totally to be focused on the goals of the state, since only participation in the achievement of those goals is thought to give meaning to the life of the individual.

21:3.1 Social Contract Theory. In order to understand how people, acting rationally, could decide among alternative theories of sovereignty and among such other notions as classical liberalism, socialism, and fascism, many thinkers have presented versions of the *social contract theory.* This theory says that people in effect form agreements between themselves and the other members of the community. These agreements, or contracts, call for the surrendering of certain individual prerogatives, in return for which the community will address itself to meeting the individual's fundamental human needs, however these needs are defined. Social contract theorists do not always hold that people actually sat down and wrote out or agreed to such contracts as a matter of historical fact. In fact social contract theory is best understood not as making assertions about actual human history at all. Rather, the theory is addressed to the hypothetical question, "If a rational group of people were going to try to frame the best sort of social organization and government possible, for any people whatever to live under, no matter what those people's interests or particular psychological characteristics might turn out to be, what would rational people decide under these circumstances?" Regardless of whether you have studied the cluster on Rights and Duties, you might profit now by reading the case study for Module 16. You should notice how that case study has characteristics in common with social contract theory: (1) your reflection proceeds independent of your self-interest, and (2) the attempt is made to reach a rational conclusion about what ought to be done on the basis of the characteristics of the beings involved.

The conflicts among liberalism, socialism, and fascism seem very difficult to resolve in theory, because they are based on such different ideas about human needs. The social contract theory, however, suggests a practical solution. It asks, "What individual liberties are you willing to part with in order to be guaranteed that your fundamental needs will be satisfied?" In effect it allows the individuals to reason with each other —in a hypothetical sense, of course—about what their fundamental needs are and what sacrifices of personal liberties they are worth.

21:3.2 In the beginning of this fictitious negotiation everyone is thought to be under the "veil of ignorance." That is, initially nobody is in a position to know where his or her personal self-interest lies. Under the veil of ignorance people take an objective look at their shared needs; nobody is biased by knowing that once the state is formed he or she will or will not have certain economic or political advantages. This starting point for reflection is called the initial position. The case study only partially illustrates people in the initial position. They are under the veil of ignorance. Nobody knows yet who will rule, who will be called on to sacrifice his or her life, who will benefit most or least from the state they are about to form. Thus they are able to enter into their social contract without concern for unshared interests.

21:3.3 Many social contract theorists move from this stage to the support of one or another of the theories of the state discussed earlier. John Rawls, a twentieth-century theorist, urges that the next step in the reflection should be a conservative one. He argues that since we do not know that people will turn out to be friendly or benevolent, it would not be rational nor prudent for us to be too trusting. We should, rather, make provisions to prevent ourselves from harming each other. Thus, while cooperation is advantageous, it should take second place to security. On the other hand, if adequate guarantees for personal security can be arrived at, then the advantages of collective defense and centralized economic planning should be pursued.

From the seventeenth-century British philosopher Thomas Hobbes on down to contemporary times, few contract theorists have been fascist. On the one hand, they have seen clearly the atomistic possibilities for fulfillment in human life. On the other hand, they have been either implicitly or explicitly skeptical of the existence and the absolute value of organic human purposes. Their strongest skepticism, however, has been of the comparative value of organic purposes. Because they have attributed a positive value to an individual's freedom from interference by others ("negative freedom") and to setting and pursuing one's own goals ("human autonomy"), and because they have seen that these values would have to be sacrificed in a dictatorial, totalitarian state, where it would not be clear that the result of this sacrifice would be anything beyond the fulfillment of the dictator (at the expense of everybody else), social contract theorists have judged that the values of negative freedom and human autonomy should not be sacrificed or even jeopardized for the sake of a possible organic fulfillment.

The social contract theory, once it is freed from being viewed as a statement of historical fact, can be seen as a normative theory. It tells us how rational people could and should resolve problems of conflicts of interests. They should resort to contractual agreements, charters, constitutions, or other forms of mutually agreeable, binding accommodations. In the case study it is Zaflewski who invites the others to be rational about the resolution of their disagreements. Her invitation does not determine which theory of the state they will select; it does not define their fundamental, shared, human purposes. But it does indicate how to begin to identify these purposes and decide what losses of personal liberty or personal freedom they are worth.

Exercises for Module 21: Theories of the State

1. a. State the minimal list of common, fundamental purposes of all individuals.
    b. State the minimal interest of the state.
    c. Describe the kinds of circumstance in which conflict may arise between a and b (21:1.1)
2. a. State the purpose of the state according to the organic theory of the state.
    b. State the further purposes of persons that this purpose of the state theoretically fulfills.
    c. Explain the further kind of conflict that would arise between a state that pursued 2a and a person who accepted 1a but not 2b.
    d. Explain why according to organic theory this conflict dissolves. (21:1.5)
3. Below is a list of assertions about what the common, fundamental, human purposes are. Different ones of these assertions are true according to the classical liberal, the socialist, and the fascist. On the right are columns marked CL, S, and F, for these three views. Mark a T or an F in each column beside each assertion depending on

whether it is true or false according to each of these three views of the common fundamental purposes. (21:1.3 through 21:2.1)

<u>CL</u>   <u>S</u>   <u>F</u>

a. Agreements to cooperate should be enforceable.

b. Full human dignity must extend the significance of an isolated individual's life.

c. Harm caused by others should be avoided.

d. Planning should be sufficient to prevent the disruption of the state.

e. The rights of individuals not to be interfered with so long as they are in turn not interfering with or harming others should be guaranteed.

f. The state is justified in pursuing goals other than those of individuals when it is necessary in order to prevent individuals from indirectly harming each other.

g. The state is justified in pursuing goals other than those of individuals because the citizen's identity is completed and his life fulfilled only by participating in the achievement of these greater goals.

h. The state is justified in pursuing goals other than those of individuals when it is either necessary or helpful in order to provide a dimension of benefits individuals would otherwise lack.

4. a. State the assumptions of social contract theory about the conditions under which the social contract is made.

   b. State the function that the theory is intended to serve.

   c. State why it is supposed that if the assumptions are true, the function will be fulfilled. (21:3.1, 21:3.2, 21:3.3)

Answers to Exercises for Module 21

1. a. The minimal common fundamental purposes are to survive and to ensure continued survival.

   b. Minimally the state's interest is in surviving and ensuring its survival.

   c. When the state's survival is in question (because of attack, say, or because of food scarcity threatening the breakdown of society), sacrificing or endangering the individual's survival may help ensure the survival of the state.

2. *a.* According to the organic theory the state sets lofty goals, such as advancing culture or civilization, with which citizens can identify.

    b. Individuals, divorced from the state, are insignificant and isolated. The goals of the state theoretically provide citizens with significance and meaning for their lives through identification with and participation in the goals of the state, which transcend the limitations of individuals.

    c. Such individuals would feel constrained, forced against their own will, to accept and pursue goals with which they did not identify.

    d. According to organic theory, this conflict dissolves, because persons cannot fulfill themselves as individuals. The greatest satisfaction possible for persons, according to organic theories, is to participate in the development of culture or civilization, the goal of the organic state. Thus theoretically only "brainwashed" persons would experience the conflict at all.

3.

	CL	*S*	*F*	
a.	T	T	T	
b.	F	F	T	(Socialist theorists need not accept this if they take an atomistic approach.)
c.	T	T	T	
d.	F	T	T	
e.	T	F	F	(Such is the importance of planning, according to the socialist and fascist.)
f.	F	T	F	(The classical liberal finds it unjustified: the fascist finds the interference justified but not for the reason given here.)
g.	F	F	T	
h.	F	T	T	

4. *a.* The condition is hypothetical, not historical; it is assumed that society does not exist, the "original position" obtains; it is also assumed that the "veil of ignorance" holds: nobody knows his or her own interests, nor anything else that would allow him or her to infer what those particular interests would be.

    b. The theory is intended to provide a rational demonstration of what sort of society, state, and government is best for human beings.

    c. It is supposed that if people were to reason about the desirable conditions for human beings to live under, they would be able to agree with each other as long as each was not pursuing his or her own particular interest.

MODULE 22
THE PURPOSES OF GOVERNMENT

The contrasts among classical liberalism, socialism, and fascism arise out of differences in what each sees as the fundamental human needs. These differences yield very different views of the purposes of the state.

The government is the organizational structure charged with carrying out the state's purposes. The government, then, is viewed as having different legitimate purposes depending upon your theory of the purposes of the state. In this module we will examine the range of government purposes people have thought to be appropriate. First we will clarify what a government is. We will then examine the relationship between the concepts of government and of sovereignty in order to identify the possible purposes of government. After reading Module 22, you should be able to

- Define "government" and give examples of possible governments for a variety of societies.
- Compare and contrast the theories of anarchism, limited government, and totalitarianism in terms of the purposes of government.
- Define and state the difference between participatory democracy and representative democracy.

THE CASE OF LAMBDA SEVEN, PART III

Walsh and Quale were returning to their quarters after the earlier discussions. Quale asked, "Walsh, what exactly do you think a government should try to accomplish?"

"Ha! Nothing, frankly! My real view is that no government at all is the best. People should act voluntarily without any of the constraints of governmental authority. I don't like majority rule, I don't like being represented by somebody else. I want to speak for myself and be my own boss."

"It seems to me that some governmental structures are absolutely necessary," responded Quale. "I might agree that the government's functions should be limited to simply resolving conflicts of interest between citizens and generally providing for the security of the people. I cannot agree that we can accomplish these goals in a purely voluntary system. We need government to establish and enforce laws that protect people."

"Look, Quale, once it starts, it gets away from you. First government is just a security force, then it gets involved with resources, transportation, and communications systems. After that comes further encroachment into private industry, regulation of business, and control of the economy. Then government moves into education and medical care. It can even get involved with organizing morality, religion, and recreation. No, Quale. It's a slippery slope; once you establish a government you have already started to slide."

"Honestly, Walsh, I'm not sure that government should avoid being involved in those aspects of life."

"Well, I am! Worse than that, what about controlling the government? There are bound to be abuses of power, failures to do what the people really want done, and finally a total inability to recognize when it has outlived its own usefulness. How do we control it, once it gets started?"

Quale was about to reply, but Walsh seemed to prefer to leave the question open. He smiled and walked into his room. Quale thought about following him but decided not to. He would wait until the community met again before he tried to answer Walsh's question.

22:1.1 Government.   An organization having the authority to pursue a society's purposes is called a *government*. The government's task, by definition, is to try to achieve the goals of the society that forms it. For example, the shareholders of a corporation are a society. They share a common interest—that of making a profit through the success of the corporation. To this end they form a government, a corporate board of directors, which concerns itself with the interests of the corporation with a view toward its making a profit.

A government, in order to achieve its goals, must often work to secure the cooperation of various people. Often these people are the members of the society the government is serving. Also the government must decide on divisions of labor, making sure that all of the necessary jobs are being done and, so, the good of the society is being served. For example, the captain of an amateur team must secure the cooperation of the team's members and must decide who shall play each position so that the team is best able to achieve its goal, whether this be winning, having fun, or both.

Governments establish regulations in the attempt to direct the conduct of people toward the goals of the society. These regulations can take the form of laws, policy statements, executive directives, or suggestions. Whatever their force, their aim is the same—to guide people's behavior. The state's government articulates its regulations by means of legislation. Governments of states make laws to regulate the activity of the members of the state whenever this activity might have a positive or negative effect on the achievement of the state's purposes. That is, governments of states pass laws to prevent people from doing things that work against the state's goals. They also pass laws to require people to do things that are useful in achieving the state's goals. To prevent harm to people there are laws against violence. To achieve goals such as adequate health care or adequate education there are laws requiring people to pay taxes, which are used to meet these ends.

22:1.2   In the case study Walsh comes out against the whole idea of having a government. He seems to be asking a question that is very common: "Why do we need all of the rules, regulations, political leaders, and officials that a state's government involves?" The response has already been suggested. In a large, anonymous society in which different groups of people have different customs, mores, and traditions, the purposes of the state are endangered without government and law. We need the mechanisms to work for these goals. Yet the rules, officers, bureaucracy, fines, and imprisonments can sometimes become quite an obstacle to seeing the overall necessity of some form of government. As government pursues the goals of the state, it develops agencies, structures, bureaus, departments, and any number of things that seem to make it more an obstacle to human goals than a servant.

This problem of the growth and proliferation of government and governmental structures is not too serious in many societies, because most societies are voluntary. People can sell their stock, quit the team, drop out of the club, and, in general, disassociate themselves from societies if they don't like their governments. Disassociation, however, is less feasible in the case of states. It is almost impossible to find a place to live that is not governed by some state or other. Immigration laws, financial penalties, cultural ties, and friendships make it much harder to quit a particular state. Another reason why state governments are much more difficult to do without lies in the purposes they serve. Their purposes are the state's purposes—the meeting of people's fundamental human needs. So long as we have these needs and see their being satisfied as reason to form a state, we have reason to accept some state and, if it has such, its government. We can do without some societies, but as humans with shared fundamental needs we cannot easily do without states.

22:1.3   We are not saying that governments are necessarily good. At times they can become rather serious threats to the state they have been created to serve. This occurs either when governments take on purposes that are not legitimate purposes of the state or when they seek their own preservation even to the possible harm of the state. As an example of the first, some people point to the U.S. involvement in Indo-China. Some claim that our government had no business there, because we, as a state, had no national interests at stake there. As an example of the latter, people often point to the failure of the German Third Reich to negotiate a surrender toward the end of World War II. This is seen as a conflict between the interests of the Nazi government and those of the German state.

22:2.1 Sovereignty and Government.   Earlier we reviewed the argument that states need governments. The argument comes to this: We have shared fundamental needs. Take personal survival as an example. To meet this need we must ensure our safety from the violence of each other and from the violence of people who are not members of our society. The mechanism to serve even this very limited goal is a government. It serves to organize us in case we must band together for our common defense. It sets up the laws needed to prevent us from doing violence to each other. It enforces these laws and punishes those who break them in order to ensure that even if violence does occur, it is stopped, peace is restored, and a repeat of the crime by the same criminal is rendered less likely.

If this argument holds, then total individual sovereignty in all domains of concern will not be appropriate. This argument is also used by critics of the theory called *anarchism*. In the case study, Walsh advocates classical anarchism. Classical anarchist theory advocates voluntary cooperative social arrangements free from any of the authority or constraining forces of government. The anarchist view is that people can naturally be fair to each other, keep promises, and work cooperatively. They do not need governments to make and enforce laws. The anarchist typically believes in complete individual sovereignty, and he or she values individual liberty more highly than any of the possible advantages of even limited government. Anarchism has come to be associated with terrorism and, to some extent, with ethical nihilism. But these connections are no part of anarchist theory. Some anarchist theories are pacifistic, others not. Some are socialistic, others are individualistic. Considering what Walsh said in the earlier case studies in this cluster, he could be called an individualistic anarchist.

22:2.2   In contrast to Walsh, Quale advocates some form of *limited government*. In this case study he begins by saying that government should provide security, prevent harm, and perhaps adjudicate internal conflicts, but that it should not do anything positive such as improve transportation, health care, education, or living standards. Later, Quale seems to suggest that governmental interests can extend to these other areas. We cannot tell from this case study, or even the earlier ones, whether Quale would want government to establish standards of morality, regulate artistic and literary activity, or moderate religious practices. All of these are possible purposes of government.

22:2.3   The argument in favor of limited government can be developed beyond what has been said in 22:2.1. Considering the complexity of a typical society, governments can serve two further purposes beyond providing security and securing the people's cooperation in pursuit of the fundamental purposes. These two further purposes are securing agreements between people and providing for differences in needs and abilities. Let us look at them more closely.

In a complex society such as our nation we often need to enter into agreements with strangers. We use the government to make these agreements secure. When you order a book or record by mail, when you buy a car, when you pay tuition, you are entering into contractual agreements with people whom you do not know, whom you may not trust. The government stands behind these contractual agreements to make sure that both parties live up to them. Laws regulate how contracts are made and what their terms may be. The government enforces the contract on all parties by its power to penalize any who fail to fulfill their part of the agreement. Without this guarantee we would be forced, out of practical necessity, to limit our dealings to those whom we knew and personally trusted. It is not likely that any highly industrialized and complex nation could survive if contractual obligations were not backed up by the power and authority of governmental law.

Second, our complex society leads to high degrees of specialization. Each of us depends on many others in order to live. Some grow food, others process it, others deliver it, and still others sell it. Other groups are involved in the production and delivery of energy resources or in transportation, communication, health care, or education. People argue that we need some governmental mechanisms to regulate and coordinate all of these activities, so that they all come together for the good of the state.

In this argument the distinction between what we need for survival and what we need for our well-being is very vague. Communication, transportation, health care, and education are all needed for survival in certain ways. But also they all lead to a greater enjoyment of life, to recreational outlets, to improved health and diversified interests and entertainment. These make life more enjoyable and enhance our well-being. For example, health care leads not only to survival through cure, but also to a healthier, happier life through preventive medicine and the control of dangerous diseases.

22:2.4   Whatever the strength of the argument for some form of limited government, Walsh's fear in the case study must be addressed. How will the government itself be controlled? Often the government itself is charged with the function of controlling the government. This crucial function of self-regulation can be accomplished in a variety of ways, such as building checks and balances into the government structure; providing for separation of legislative, enforcement, and judicial powers; providing for regularized changes of the persons in leadership roles; providing for impeachment and recall procedures; allowing for a free press with the liberty to criticize governmental activities; limiting secrecy, privileges, and special prerogatives to only those necessary for the security of the state. Each of these proposals has its strengths. Walsh might well reply that all of these are still not adequate. The temptations of power are great, and leaders throughout human history have fallen prey to them. They have found ways to use government to their own personal advantage. There are so many examples of the abuse of governmental power, of favoritism and bribery, that the problem is not identifying the limited purposes of government but keeping the government limited to only those purposes. Conflicts between the leaders' purposes of self-interest and the interests of the state are almost inevitable.

Plato (427 B.C.–347 B.C.) suggested a way to resolve the problem of corruption and the problem of government's taking more and more power to itself. His proposal ran something like this: Select potential leaders at a very early age. Separate them from the business and military sectors. Train them to be strong, well-informed, wise, and just. Supply their human needs and grant them absolute power. The idea is that although they have tremendous power, their wisdom and virtue will guide their use of this power; they will use it for the good of the state.

22:2.5　Plato developed his ideas not in support of limited government but in the service of a *totalitarian* and dictatorial concept of government. Gonzales, who in the case study for Module 21 advocated fascism, might be inclined to push for a totalitarian, dictatorial form of government. Government, in this view, could legitimately become involved in all human purposes. It could strive to assert governmental authority into every aspect of society. For example, it could strive to improve communications by developing and regulating a postal system, a government press, and government-operated telecommunications systems, such as government radio and television networks. It could strive to regulate all forms of commerce and manage the production and distribution of food, energy resources, and health care. It could seek to improve the health, education, welfare, and moral character of the people by regulating the programs presented in schools, churches, and the entertainment media. It could centralize social planning and seek to control the distribution and exercise of economic and political power in the society.

The concern in dictatorial theory is not with how to limit government authority but with how to acquire, maintain, and strengthen it. Regulating the press and other media, establishing secret security forces, relocating the population into smaller, more rural communities, rewarding governmental loyalty, and imposing mandatory indoctrination programs on all citizens have been used along with imprisonment or other severe penalties as tools toward this goal. Given the fascist concept of the state and fascist ideas about the fundamental human purposes, these governmental measures are desirable. Similarly, given a theory of dictatorial sovereignty, the goals and measures suggested above could all be accommodated. Given the views of classical liberal theory and the theory of individual sovereignty, these goals are mistaken and these measures are outrageous. Given a concept of popular sovereignty and a socialist view of fundamental human purposes, many of the goals listed above are worthy, although some of the measures suggested may be viewed as severe or extreme.

22:2.6   In our nation we combine a variety of theories of sovereignty. We allow for individual sovereignty in certain domains of concern, such as morality and religion. We generally advocate popular sovereignty in domains such as the regulation of education, basic health care, and the production and distribution of goods and services, in that all of these are topics about which our legislatures make laws. In normal times the president's authority over matters of foreign trade, foreign policy, and the use of military force, however absolute or limited, is derived from the people who have elected him. But we also allow for complete dictatorial sovereignty in the case of national emergency. If the president proclaims a state of emergency, then he or she has the authority to make policy and issue executive orders that can affect any aspect of our social lives. Thus, not only do we allow for different concepts of sovereignty in different domains, but we allow special circumstances, such as an immediate military or economic danger, to expand or contract the domains of concern.

22:2.7   We have indicated the argument against the individual sovereignty theory and the dictatorial (authoritarian) sovereignty theory. The first leads to anarchistic theories of nongovernment, which may fail to adequately provide for our survival needs. The latter leads to governments that threaten individual liberties. The argument against popular sovereignty is that it demands that the government not only work for the purposes of the people taken as a whole, but also work to discern the will of that people taken as a whole. This creates the problem of how to learn what the will of the people is. The problem has two chief aspects: First, is there really a single collective will of the people? Second, if there is, how can the leaders learn what its desires are? There is also a third, less-discussed problem: What should the government do if it believes that the will of the people as expressed on a particular issue is in conflict with either the long-range good of the society or the will of the people as expressed on another issue? As an example, consider the government's dilemma in the case of forced school bussing. As a people we are on record in favor of equal opportunity in education and against racially segregated schools. As a people we are, by and large, opposed to bussing.

which has been identified as the only effective way to desegregate schools and provide for equal opportunity in education. A problem of this sort is usually resolved by holding that the will to heed is the one that indicates the general goals (equality and desegregation), and the will to disregard, or put in second place, is the one that criticizes the means (bussing). In other words, we operate as if the will of the people concerning goals were more important than their will concerning means. But what if there is a conflict of the will of the people with itself concerning goals? This problem might be handled if we could find out which goal the people viewed as more important. This leads us back to the more basic problem of how we find out the will of the people in the first place.

Defenders of the theory of popular sovereignty, and of government based on that theory, suggest two ways. The first way is to presume that some person or group of people can be trusted to know and act on the will of the people. The person might be a divinely guided dictator, a popular and charismatic leader, or someone wise enough to know what the people would choose if they were to be able to express their choice in the light of their own long-term interest. The group might be some combination of such people, or it might be selected to represent a particular interest group and express its point of view. The second way is to provide means for the people to express their own opinions. These means might include letter writing, elections, demonstrations, or town meetings, where the presiding officer tries to express a group's concensus on an issue.

22:2.8   In the United States we use both ways. We try to settle some issues through *participatory democracy*—that is, we use town meetings, open hearings, and public referenda. We also use *representative democracy,* which provides for people from various geographic regions to elect representatives to speak in councils, legislatures, and congress on their behalf. This creates a significant normative problem for the person who is elected. He or she has to determine whether to speak the point of view of the people who elected him or her, or to become more informed on issues so as to exercise his or her own judgment. If the representative does the former, he or she is acting like a reporter, but one that is less accurate than a good public opinion poll. If the representative does the latter, he or she risks taking a position that the constituency would view as alien to their own point of view or interests.

There are reasons to question these defenses of popular sovereignty. First, we cannot be sure that the individual selected to lead or represent us actually knows our collective will. Second, voting as a way of revealing our collective will may not be adequate either. Should we require that all votes be unanimous? This entails practical difficulties, because unanimity is very rarely possible. If not unanimity, what percentage should we agree to? Should different percentages be needed for different kinds of issues—say, a plurality to win an election, a two-thirds majority to amend the Constitution? But if we reject unanimity because it is rarely possible, how can we claim that the collective will is being expressed? In a recent election a president was selected who received only slightly more than half the votes cast. If you totaled the people who cast against that president with the number of eligible people who did not vote at all, then nearly 65 percent of the people had not expressed a desire to have that person be president.

Exercises for Module 22: The Purposes of Government

1. *a.* A lodge or a club is an example of one sort of society. The owners of teams of professional athletes in a given league and a given sport exemplify another society. Either describe the governmental functions that these societies would want because of the kind of societies they are, or begin from your own examples and describe the governmental functions that those societies would desire. (22:1.1 and 22:1.2)

   b. Define government, checking to see that your definition fits the governments you have described. (22:1.1)

2. *a.* State how anarchists and advocates of limited government agree or disagree about the reasonableness of placing into any hands power sufficient to prevent harm caused by others and to ensure maximal individual freedom. (22:2.1 and 22:2.2)

   b. State the assertions about the value of freedom to which anarchists and advocates of limited government agree.

   c. Explain why totalitarian government is acceptable and congenial to the organic theory of the state. (22:2.5)

3. *a.* Cite a real example of participatory democracy in some society.

   b. Cite an example of representative democracy in some society.

   c. Characterize participatory democracy by stating (1) the theory of sovereignty under which it operates, (2) what involvement the sovereign has in formulating a rule or law, and (3) whether the authority of those formulating the rule or law is derived or underived. (22:2.8)

   d. Characterize representative democracy in these same ways.

Selected Answers to Exercises for Module 22

1. *a.* A lodge or club may want to define who can become a member, what members' responsibilities are, who can become officers, and what officers' responsibilities and powers are. A lodge or club may also need to define who has the authority to take over when an officer is unable or unwilling to fulfill his responsibilities. Enforcement powers and judicial roles may not need to be specified in voluntary societies, especially if there are no strong conflicts of interest. A society such as professional sports team owners, however, is very likely to experience conflicts of interest. Therefore, regulations granting enforcement and arbitration powers to league authorities (say, the commissioner) will be appropriate.

    b. A government of a society is any organization that has the authority to pursue the goals of the society.

2. *a.* Anarchists find such a practice unreasonable and objectionable because they fear that the power granted to prevent harm and ensure freedom will be used to cause harm and restrict freedom, resulting in a net loss to individuals over a situation where no governmental authority existed. Advocates of limited government believe that with a careful system of checks and balances, individuals can experience a net gain in liberty and suffer less harm.

    b. According to both anarchists and advocates of limited government, the freedom of the individual from constraints imposed by the interference of others is desirable and ought to be as great as it possibly can be.

    c. It is not at all surprising, and it may be helpful, to have government involved in all aspects of life (totalitarianism) if the most satisfying life for the individual is one that is totally involved and absorbed in the goals of the state.

3.

	c. Participatory	*d.* Representative
(1) Theory of sovereignty	Popular	Popular
(2) Involvement of sovereign	Directly formulate rule or law	Elect representative to formulate rule or law
(3) Authority of formulators	Underived	Derived from those electing them

LAW

A wide variety of laws regulate many of the most important aspects of our social lives. There are laws concerning politics, business, education, taxation, safety, land use, and health care, to name just a few. This fact raises many questions. What are the advantages of the rule of law for society? What conditions make possible the rule of law? Module 23 will take up these questions. In Module 24 we will analyze the concept of a legal obligation. We will ask how law relates to morality and how it relates to the penalties imposed on those found guilty of breaking the law. We will question what makes such penalties appropriate. The educational goal of this cluster is for you to understand the potential advantages of the rule of law, the conditions needed for the development of the rule of law, and the relationships between the law and morality and between the law and legal penalties.

Module 23
THE RULE OF LAW

Laws regulate conduct by telling us what things we are legally obligated to do and not to do. Although laws do not affect every aspect of our lives, they do exert a major influence over our conduct, especially in some of the more socially important areas. In this module we shall examine the rule of law in order to discover its advantages over reliance on social mores, customs, and traditions. In our civilization governments make laws, enforce them, and settle disputes concerning them. We can think of the group of laws developed by any given governmental authority as a *legal system*. Several legal systems affect our lives, for governments at all levels—national, regional, state, and local—make laws. In this module we will ask what conditions are necessary for the development of legal systems and the rule of law. The answer will involve a combination of factors: what issues the laws in question cover, how the laws are made and amended, how they are enforced, and how disputes of law are adjudicated. After reading Module 23, you should be able to

- List the theoretical advantages of the rule of law over the rule of social custom.
- List the four types of conditions necessary for the rule of law, and distinguish which specific conditions fall under each.
- Given example laws or situations, identify the conditions for the rule of law that are unmet in them; also, explain how the example law or situation could be changed to fulfill the unmet condition.
- Supply examples of laws or situations that fail to meet each of the conditions of the rule of law. Identify the unmet condition and explain how your example law or situation fails to satisfy it.

THE CASE OF PLANGTON HEIGHTS

Judith Franllow, 14-year-old daughter of Vern Franllow, quietly approached the old man who sat in the rocking chair on the wooden porch. He perked up as she climbed the steps. He knew Vern Franllow was the richest and most politically influential of the new group of land developers, real estate people, and industrialists who had caused the population of Plangton Heights, N.D., to swell from 486 to 24,000 in just ten years.

"Good morning, Mr. Thorntwister. What have you been doing today?"

"Nothing, Judy. Just remembering: remembering what Plangton Heights used to be like before it got to be a city."

"What was it like?"

"Well—that corner where the new library stands used to be the only crossroads for over ten miles. There was only eight families living around here when my father brought us in. We all were farmers except for old man Green. We worked the farms and went to the crossroads every weekend for entertainment. There was one store, one stable, a school that doubled as the town hall, and one church. Didn't have no mayor or no sheriff even. Didn't need 'em, you know. If anybody got difficult we just ignored 'em, or my father would ride out and calm 'em down. We all grew up together, you know. Everybody sort of knew what they could and could not do."

"But what about outlaws?" Judith asked.

"Oh, there weren't no outlaws in these parts. We knew everybody for miles around and they all knew us. We just lived our lives and when there was a cause, we would work together to build a new school or put out a fire."

"But how did you collect taxes? Who built the roads? Who hired the teachers? Who decided cases when people disagreed about property lines or traffic accidents?"

"Well, we didn't have most of these here complications that you see nowadays. No taxes, 'cause we just pitched in and worked together. Except none of us farmers cared about building roads to open up old man Green's forest for logging. Land was all over the place and there was no problem telling yours from mine cause nobody seemed to care. There was more than any of us knew what to do with. My father was sort of the judge till he died, and then Mr. Grownker, the storekeeper, just took over. I remember that 'cause there was no real problems with Mr. Grownker except when somebody—Mrs. Barcon, I think—felt that she was cheated on the price of bacon or flour. Grownker wouldn't even talk to her about it and nobody else had acted as judge for so many years that we all just let it go. Poor Mrs. Barcon left town after that.

"Judy, it was good in those times, but these strangers started coming in and causing trouble. We elected a sheriff to keep the peace, but he said he needed to know the laws. So we would get together in the town hall to make up laws. The strangers wanted to put up fences and build railroad yards, mills, and even a small factory. There was dissension and bitterness. They said our sheriff was always arresting their workers, but was leaving us farmers alone. It was hard times. One night they burned down the church; none of them strangers came to fight the fire. We called in a federal judge, but nobody was ever convicted of that crime."

"Then what happened?"

"We all got over it. But we came out of it with more laws, lawyers, and politicians than I care to count. At least when it was over we all knew where we stood. We had the law to tell us what we could do and what we couldn't do. Once we learned what the laws was, that was it. Everything started getting all legal-like. Why, you couldn't even buy a horse without exchanging papers and going to the courthouse. When I was a kid we bought our whole farm just by a handshake. Now you need title searches, registers of deeds, your credit is checked, and their ain't no end to all the things people do 'cause they can't trust each other."

23:1.1 Advantages of the Rule of Law. When we say that a society is governed by the rule of law, we mean that it has established the governmental authority to (a) make laws, (b) enforce these laws, and (c) resolve disputes over these laws. We can call such governmental authority—the legislative, enforcement, and judicial systems—its *legal institutions.* By saying that a society lives under the rule of law we further mean that the laws are designed to regulate the conduct of all its members by indicating what is permitted, what is forbidden, and what is required in that society. When we say that a society is governed by social customs, mores, or traditions we mean that only customs, traditions, and generally accepted ways of acting serve to guide conduct. In such a society there may be no official governmental authority that is responsible for making, enforcing, or adjudicating laws. Plangton Heights started off that way in the case study. It had no mayor or city council to make laws, it had no sheriff to enforce its laws or even its customs, it had no officially elected or appointed judge to handle disputes. Plangton Heights ended up under the rule of law. The people elected a sheriff to keep the peace. They had town meetings to agree on laws. They brought in the territorial judge to settle disputes. They did these things in order to establish the rule of law in Plangton Heights. Much of this module is devoted to detailing the specific conditions that must be met if the rule of law is to exist.

For Plangton Heights the transition time from the rule of custom to the rule of law was one of great turmoil and difficulty. Plangton Heights was, in a way, suffering growing pains. For several reasons the growth of Plangton Heights made the rule of law progressively more desirable for its people, while custom, mores, and traditions became increasingly inadequate and ill-suited to govern their society. The remaining subsections of 23:1 will explain those reasons separately.

23:1.2   One of the possible advantages of the rule of law is *social stability.* Laws tell people what is expected of them and what they can expect of others. Laws create regular methods for handling one's affairs. Thus, even if you wished to buy a house from someone you did not know, you could rely on the laws to lend a regularity to that business transaction. The laws specify what selling a house requires and what buying a house requires. Selling houses is a stabilized activity in our society. As our legal system grows, we introduce stability into more and more aspects of life. In the United States we are engaged in stabilizing health care delivery systems, education opportunities, and the treatment of persons who apply for jobs.

23:1.3   A second advantage of the rule of law is that it *allows for cultural diversity.* Customs may differ from group to group. In the case of groups with different ethnic, racial, economic, or religious backgrounds, the cultural differences could be rather great. To rely on these customs as a basis for social interaction would be to invite chaos. Laws can cut across these differences in customs and traditions. You may not share the customs or traditions of some other members of our society; nevertheless, you and they are still bound by the law to act or not act in certain ways. In this way the cultural richness of a pluralistic society need not lead to a conflict because of incompatible traditions and social mores. Pluralism is possible because the important social interactions among people of all heritages and backgrounds do not depend on their individual customs but on the rule of law. If you tried to live in Plangton Heights in its early days, you might have faced the problem of either adopting its life style or living in relative isolation like old man Green. He wasn't a farmer, and his neighbors, all farmers, would not pitch in to build a road to allow him to log his forest.

23:1.4 *Social complexity* is also provided for more adequately by the rule of law. Custom and tradition tend to be less adequate as society becomes more complex. New interests arise in society, new goals are developed, new people with differing backgrounds come on the scene, entering into new relationships with each other. Laws can be made that account for these diversities and social complexities. Consider, as just one example, the federal income tax law. It tries to account for a wide variety of personal differences in how people earn and spend money, while still seeking an equitable tax from each. It also tries to account for differences in people's needs and in their abilities to pay taxes. It is a complex law, because our economic interrelations are complex. The law, rather than trying to minimize the complexity and neglect the differences among people, tries to accommodate this complexity and these differences. Although it may not fully succeed, it does far excel any unwritten traditions or customs concerning what constitutes a fair tax burden for each individual.

23:1.5 The fact that the law is institutional brings a number of potential advantages. There are regular procedures for updating laws and for writing new ones to cover new needs. On the other hand, there are usually no regularized ways to update or expand custom or tradition. Also, laws are usually collected into codes or statute books. Thus they can be more easily made public; they can be transmitted from generation to generation with less chance of being altered by failures of memory; they can offer more specific guidance to police forces in terms of telling them exactly what conduct is not to be tolerated, and they offer a firmer basis for judges to rely on in determining whether or not a crime has been committed and punishment is deserved. These can be called the *procedural advantages* of laws. A number of procedural conditions are necessary to realize these advantages. We will be looking at these conditions in a moment.

23:1.6 A final advantage of the rule of law is that it liberates us and *creates new opportunities* for us. In a complex society such as ours the law allows us to conduct business even without knowing or coming to trust those with whom we have dealings. The law relieves us of the burden of having to personally get to know and trust everyone that we depend upon. You probably do not know all the people who grow your food, deliver your fuel and energy, build your homes, educate your children, or operate your transportation and communications systems. You can buy stock in a corporation, realize a dividend, vote on a corporate policy, and sell that stock, all without ever meeting another shareholder or visiting the place of business. Our rule of law makes that possible. This liberates us to do more of what we would like to do; it also provides opportunities for us to do things that otherwise we would not dare to do. The rule of law allows us to live together even if we do not come to trust each other, but it does presume we all more or less trust the law and have confidence that the government can make others live up to it. In a sense, trust has not become irrelevant; it has been changed into a trust in our legal institutions. We must, then, concern ourselves with whether or not they deserve our trust. Without this trust the rule of law could collapse.

23:2.1 Conditions for the Rule of Law. In reviewing its advantages, we have suggested some conditions that make the rule of law possible. Let us now develop a more careful list of these conditions. Some relate to the issues the law addresses. These are called *substantive conditions*. Others relate to how the laws are made and how they are adjudicated. These are called *procedural conditions*. Another group relate to how society responds to the laws and how the laws are enforced. These are called *material conditions*.

In part we can evaluate and compare legal institutions and systems by determining how well they meet these three sets of conditions. A good part of what makes one law, legal system, or legal institution (legislative, police, or court system) better than another is how well they compare in terms of the conditions we are about to list.

23:3.1 Substantive Conditions for the Rule of Law. People can decide to make laws to regulate almost any aspect of their lives. But if they neglect certain of these aspects, then, many have argued, their society will not be able to endure. Their laws must ensure their society's survival by providing for the peaceful and rational coexistence of its people. When a society grows in such a way that (a) it becomes normal for persons to have dealings with others whom they do not know and cannot personally trust, and (b) subgroups within the society have different and even contrary customs, mores, and traditions for regulating interpersonal dealings, it is plausible that law must (come to) function where custom and the like will no longer be adequate.

Minimally there are three areas where laws are necessary to insure peaceful, rational coexistence, giving us the three substantive conditions for the rule of law:

(1) Laws must provide people with security from the violence of others.
(2) Laws must provide people with access to and control over the resources necessary to live.
(3) Laws must provide enforcement for contractual obligations made between people.

23:3.2 Let us look at the reasons for each condition. Physical, economic, or political power gives one person an advantage over another. This could lead to people's achieving their goals at the expense of harming other people. In order to prevent the abuse of physical power, laws usually rule out overt violence. Some legal systems also regulate

---

H. L. A. HART (1907–   )

Herbert Lionel Adolphus Hart is one of the foremost philosophers of law of the twentieth century. He was educated in the classics at Oxford, where he later taught jurisprudence and philosophy. He practiced law from 1932–1940 and then served in the War Office until 1945. His distinguished career in education and legal theory led to many visiting professorships and honorary degrees. He wrote *Causation in the Law* (1959), *The Concept of Law* (1961), *Law, Liberty and Morality* (1963), *The Morality of the Criminal Law* (1965), *Punishment and Responsibility* (1968), and many other works on Jeremy Bentham and on legal philosophy.

Hart was one of the first legal theorists to apply the philosophical method of conceptual analysis to legal concepts. Rather than look for what a legal term such as "contract" or "corporation" referred to, he tried to discover the conditions under which it was properly used. He also was one of the first to argue that legal language was not purely descriptive, but rather that it often was used to create rights and ascribe responsibilities. He carefully distinguished law from morality, arguing that it often may be neither necessary nor desirable to use law to enforce society's moral standards.

economic and political power in order to minimize their potential for harm. The traditional argument for these regulations is that without them society might become little more than a human jungle, where only the strongest would survive.

Since resources are limited and since people need them to meet their needs and pursue their aims, some form of regulation and control of resources is crucial to society. Laws guaranteeing property rights are an obvious example. The scarcity of a given resource requires a more systematic regulation of its distribution and use.

The importance of guaranteeing that contracts not be violated arises out of the great utility of entering into binding contracts to achieve one's basic needs and secure one's goals. In contemporary society none of us is self-sufficient. Contractual relationships allow us to survive and flourish in the midst of social complexity. But laws are needed that will guarantee that agreements are kept. As we said earlier, in our society we often must deal with people whom we do not know and may not fully trust.

23:4.1 Procedural Conditions for the Rule of Law: Legislative. Even the best set of laws can be the source of injustice and difficulty if certain procedural requirements are not met. These procedural requirements fall into two groups, those relating to the making of the laws and those relating to the adjudicating of the laws. We will take up the judicial conditions in 23:5.1. Let us turn now to the legislative conditions:

(4) The laws must be general.
(5) The laws must not be retrospective.
(6) The laws must be free from contradiction, ambiguity, and vagueness.

23:4.2 Let us consider the reasons for each of these legislative procedural conditions. That laws should be general means they should apply to groups of persons, or to everyone who meets certain conditions. This is especially important, for it makes laws universalizable. Further, it would not be equitable to make laws that aim to hinder or advantage specific individuals. Thus, for example, a state can make a law requiring all those who operate rest homes to install smoke detectors, but it would be unfair if the state made a law requiring one specific rest-home operator to install smoke detectors while allowing other operators not to install them.

Retrospective legislation is problematic, because it puts people under obligations to have done something in the past without their having had the knowledge that they were under such an obligation. This would be unfair, because it would not allow them the opportunity to control their conduct in the light of that obligation. Consider the unfairness involved if a state made a law today requiring smoke detectors in rest homes for the past ten years and then penalized rest-home operators so many dollars per year per rest home for noncompliance. The rationale for laws' not being retrospective also means that those who come under obligations by new laws must be given a reasonable time to comply. If a court orders bussing, the court, if it is being reasonable, must give the school district involved adequate time to implement the bussing order, which in such a case could be a matter of several months.

The requirement that the laws be free from contradiction, vagueness, and ambiguity means that they should avoid obscurity and aim for precision. Obviously a law should not contradict itself. But laws do not exist in isolation; they are incorporated into a system of laws. No law in a legal system should contradict any other law in that system. A state law requiring smoke detectors in rest homes might, for example, contradict another state law prohibiting the installation of electric devices in rest homes. Similarly, overlapping jurisdictions can lead to contradictory legislation. A city may require a certain method of waste disposal, but the state or federal government may prohibit it.

Ambiguous laws are susceptible of two or more differing interpretations. Many people criticize income tax laws because they find them ambiguous. For example, travel expenses involved in going away from home to earn income are deductible. But there is ambiguity in the concept of "home." Some view it as the place where a person's family resides. Others interpret it as the place where one lives while one is working. So, if you live with your family in New York and travel to work in Chicago, your travel is a business expense. But, on another interpretation, if while you work in Chicago you live in a motel, then travel to and from New York to see your family is personal recreation and is not deductible. This ambiguity led the federal government to define "tax home" as the place where you live while you earn your income. Such definitions, happily, can overcome the problem of ambiguity.

Vague laws are obscure, because it is not clear that the law applies in a given case or what precisely is required by law. If a state required "that those who operate nursing homes install smoke detectors," it would be unclear whether that law applied to those who operate "rest homes," which might be distinguished from "nursing homes." Further, it would not be clear whether the obligation could be satisfied by installing one smoke detector in each home, one on each floor of each home, or one on each wing of each floor. Ambiguity and vagueness lead to obscurities that provide loopholes for the unscrupulous. They leave our legal obligations unclear; thus, we can be victimized by others. Because our obligations are not clear, we also may find it more difficult to plan our lives.

23:4.3   Two other procedural conditions apply to those who make the laws. These are:

(7) The laws must be publicly promulgated.
(8) The laws must be easily accessible.

Both of these requirements allow for people to better understand their legal obligations and, in turn, better organize and plan their lives in their light. Further, people need access to the law so that they can know what they can legally expect of others as well as what others expect of them. Without promulgation and accessibility the rule of law tends to break down. The confusion in Plangton Heights was not resolved just by adopting laws; the laws had to be promulgated and made known to the citizens. When laws are not promulgated or easily accessible to the population, it is easy to come to view the government as capricious or arbitrary. People will not know what their duties are, what they can expect from others, or what actions will lead them to be in violation of the law and subject to penalty. Rulers can then use such secret "laws" to victimize enemies.

23:5.1 Procedural Conditions for the Rule of Law: Judicial. When laws are violated or when disputes arise, the judicial system comes into play to determine guilt, apply a penalty, adjudicate disputes, and, at times, issue orders requiring or prohibiting further actions. For the rule of law to be fully in effect a fair and impartial judicial system is necessary. This calls forth the judicial conditions for the rule of law:

(9) Judges must be free from conflicts of personal interest in the matters before them.
(10) Judges must be unbiased and objective in considering the matters before them.
(11) Judges must allow all the disputing parties to present arguments concerning matters of law and matters of fact.

23:5.2   The reason why a judge must not have a personal interest in the case before him or her is that it could lead him or her to be unfair. The judge might be moved to be sympathetic to the side he or she has an interest in. Or the judge might be moved to be overly harsh to that same side in order to ensure himself or herself that impartiality has not been compromised. In the case study the storekeeper-judge, Mr. Grownker, seemed to lose his impartiality when Mrs. Barcon's case against his operation of the store came up.

The requirement that judges be unbiased and objective means that they should not allow prejudices or irrelevant factors to influence their decisions. Suppose that a group of citizens brought suit against a rest-home operator for not installing smoke detectors in rest homes that served black citizens when he or she had installed them in all his or her homes serving whites. A judge who was prejudiced against blacks might rule in favor of that operator because of that prejudice, but justice would not thereby be served.

Injustices can also be done if an unbiased judge hears a case. A judge who refuses to let all parties present their side of the dispute is being unfair. Mr. Grownker tried to cover his conflict of interest by refusing to hear Mrs. Barcon's side of the dispute. There was no rule of law in Plangton Heights at that time, and so there was nothing for Mrs. Barcon to do but accept the injustice or leave town.

23:6.1 Material Conditions for the Rule of Law. Even given wise laws that satisfy the substantive and procedural conditions listed, it is still possible for the rule of law to be undermined in a given society. To further ensure the rule of law, three more conditions must be met. These conditions relate to the readiness of people to accept the law and to how the laws are enforced. They are:

(12) The community must generally obey the laws.
(13) The enforcement of one law must not require the violation of another.
(14) The laws must be regularly enforced without regard for who may be in violation.

23:6.2 Let us look at the reasons for each of these requirements. First, it is financially impossible for the vast majority of societies to employ, train, and equip enough law enforcement officers, judges, and prison guards to enforce the laws, to run the courts, and to operate the prisons unless most of the population generally obeys the laws. If most people ignore a law, then it becomes unenforcible. For example, prohibitions against alcohol are thought to have failed largely because the public widely violated them. Moreover, widespread disapproval of specific laws tends to undermine public respect for the rule of law.

If the enforcement of one law means the violation of another, then the police force will be rendered ineffective in that enforcement. Drug laws are hard to enforce because violations tend to occur in private places such as homes. Thus law enforcement officers are hindered from apprehending violators by other laws concerning entering and searching private residences without warrants. Or, if detecting violations of the law requires wiretapping, then this may be a closed option, because in some cases wiretapping violates the right to privacy guaranteed by other laws.

Notice that in the cases discussed here, the laws are not themselves in conflict. Everyone can refrain from use of illegal drugs—*obeying* those laws, that is—while everyone is also respecting others' privacy. The problem is to *enforce* the drug laws without violating the privacy laws.

The respect for law is quickly undercut if laws are selectively enforced. If the police generally do not arrest their friends, or if they enforce certain laws in the inner city but neglect the violations in the suburbs, respect for law deteriorates. It seemed that the sheriff in Plangton Heights created discord by showing favoritism to the farmers over the newcomers. The universal scope of the legislated law (see condition 4) is undermined if the law is enforced only selectively.

Exercises for Module 23: The Rule of Law

1. List the theoretical advantages of the rule of law over the rule of custom (23:1.2–23:1.6)
2. *a.* List the four types of conditions necessary for the rule of law.
    b. After checking your answer to *a,* list each of the following 14 specific conditions under its appropriate type: (i) the community must generally obey the laws, (ii) there must be laws providing for security against human violence, (iii) the laws must be free from contradiction, ambiguity, and vagueness, (iv) judges must be free from conflicts of interests in the cases they judge, (v) laws must not be retrospective, (vi) laws must enforce contractual obligations, (vii) judges must be unbiased and objective in considering cases, (viii) laws must be publicly promulgated, (ix) the enforcement of one law must not require violating another, (x) laws must be easily accessible, (xi) judges must allow all disputing parties to speak to all matters of dispute, (xii) the laws must not be selectively enforced against any particular groups, (xiii) the laws must be general, (xiv) there must be laws providing people with access to and control over resources. (23:3.1, 23:4.1, 23:4.3, 23:5.1, 23:6.1)
3. Below is a list of situations or laws in which some condition for the rule of law is unmet. (We refer here to the numbered listing of conditions in the text, not in 2*b* above.) For each item on the list, state what condition is unmet. Then modify the item so that the condition is met.

    a. The police officer stops two drivers for going 55 mph in a 45-mph zone. The 30-year-old woman driver is warned but not ticketed. The 18-year-old boy is both warned and ticketed.

b. Middleton county's hospital is barred by county regulations from accepting children under the age of three months, while the state requires local government units to provide facilities for all persons with congenital hydrocephalus.

c. In Whoseincharge, no legal obligations are involved in the signing of agreements between persons about what each will do for the other under various conditions.

d. When the judge assumed the bench, he sold all his Agribusiness stock, but he never wavered in his view that there's no place for the small family farm in modern America.

e. Most department stores are open on Sundays despite laws to the contrary.

f. Three years after Nixon's resignation the legislature enacted a statute requiring that the seller of any piece of real property after January 1, 1960, provide the buyer with a title search.

g. To enforce a law against unnatural sexual acts, a police laboratory developed an infrared movie camera that police could install and hide in the bedrooms of suspects.

4. Supply examples of laws or situations that fail to meet each of the conditions of the rule of law, identifying the unmet condition. Use the abstract language of unmet conditions to describe how your examples of laws or situations fail to meet each of the conditions. Your examples should follow the pattern of those in Exercise 3, and your descriptions should be like those given in the answers to Exercise 3.

Selected Answers to Exercises for Module 23

2. a. Substantive conditions, legislative procedural conditions, judicial procedural conditions, and material conditions.

3. a. Condition 14, enforcement of the law against all violators equally, would require ticketing all persons going a given speed and ticketing no one for going at lesser speeds.

b. Condition 6, keeping the law free from contradiction, would involve (a) making an exception in one of the two existing laws, or (b) repealing one of those laws.

c. Condition 3 provides for laws to govern contractual obligations. In Whoseincharge such laws still need to be written.

d. Condition 10, that the judge should be unbiased and objective, is violated, even though Condition 9, that the judge should have no conflict of interest, has been met. At least the judge should be disqualified or disqualify himself from hearing cases involving small family farms or farmers.

e. Condition 12 is unmet because the laws are widely violated. Only greatly changing citizens' attitudes about the acceptability of stores' being open on Sunday will make the laws enforceable.

f. Condition 5, that laws should not be retroactive, is unmet. To meet the condition the requirement should be imposed only on future sales—and people in the midst of selling real property either should not be forced to comply or should be given reasonable time in which to do so. Alternatively, the law could read that those having sold property since January 1960 must within 90 days from the date the law takes effect provide a title search of that property.

g. Condition 13, that the enforcement of one law should not involve violating another, is problematic here, since police officers would presumably lack the legal right to install or use such cameras.

MODULE 24
LAWS AND SANCTIONS

Having reviewed the importance of the rule of law and examined the conditions needed for its development, we can turn to one of the foremost questions of jurisprudence and the philosophy of law: "What is the law?" In this module we will approach this question through the idea of legal obligation. Our analysis will yield the two theories that dominate much of the contemporary thinking about the law. One theory sees the law as establishing a set of moral duties or obligations for people to meet. This raises the question of the relationship of law to morality. The second theory sees the law as predicting the penalties that will be imposed on those who violate its statutes. These penalties are called legal *sanctions*. The second theory raises the question of why we use legal sanctions. It also suggests the further question of the appropriateness of the use of specific sanctions when one takes into account the criminal, the crime, and the harm done to those wronged by the crime. In this module we will examine these issues. After reading Module 24, you should be able to

- Distinguish predictive and normative interpretations of given example laws.
- Given an example law, supply both a predictive and a normative interpretation of it.

- State the difference between the predictive and the normative interpretations of the law.
- State the reasons cited to justify the imposition of legal sanctions.
- Distinguish the factors having to do with the potential criminal, the criminal, the person wronged, and society as a whole that influence the appropriateness of the sanction to be applied.

THE CASE OF SMOKE DETECTORS

Jason Industries owns and operates a number of rest homes in several midwestern states. Indiana has passed a law that requires smoke detectors in all rest homes. The corporation's lawyers, Phelps, Ross, and Ramkin, are debating the question of compliance.

Lampson Phelps popped a pumpkin seed into his mouth and began to chew and talk at the same time. "We have to send a memo to the vice-president in charge of operations explaining why we are obligated to comply with the Indiana law. What do you think we should say?"

"Explain that failing to install the devices in our homes in Indiana will mean we will very likely have to pay fines of about $500 per home, per year," said Ross.

"Hold on, Ross," said Lucille Ramkin. "I know that vice-president; she will not respond to the threat of a small fine. She would probably not install the smoke detectors because the installation costs are greater than the penalties for not putting them in. I propose to tell her that the law imposes a duty on us. We should comply because it is immoral to neglect one's legal duties unless some other overriding moral principle is being violated by doing that duty. The state has the authority to impose this safety requirement on rest homes. So, if we want to operate rest homes, we are morally bound to comply with these regulations."

Ross was about to reply, but Phelps interrupted: "Maybe we should just give her both opinions. Now, let's look at this Indiana statute itself. What precisely does it require? How long do we have to show compliance? How is it going to be enforced? What precisely are the penalties for nonfulfillment?"

Ramkin said, "There is more to this business of penalties than Ross indicated before. Ross spoke about the possible fines we would have to pay Indiana. But there may be lawsuits brought against us by people injured in fires in our rest homes. Suppose these homes are not equipped with smoke detectors. We could end up paying negligence damages running up in the millions. So, besides the cost of the fines we risk significant other costs."

Ross broke in, "Look, Ramkin, there are costs no matter what. We have to buy and install all the smoke detectors, and that isn't going to be free."

"I'm surprised at you," Ramkin said to her colleague. "The purchase and installation costs of the detectors are not penalties we have to pay, even though they are expenses. It could happen that we pay penalties for noncompliance, pay damages for injuries resulting from negligence, and then still have to pay the expenses of purchase and of installation. The smart thing to do is to install the smoke detectors right away. At least that way we can hold our costs down to the purchase and installation expenses, and not incur the fines and sanctions."

24:1.1 Legal Obligations.   What does emerge from our study of the proposed purposes of law is that people feel certain goals are worthwhile enough to make laws in order to achieve them. That is, people are willing to put themselves and each other under some form of *obligation* in order to achieve certain purposes. Let us focus on this idea of obligation under the law.

Our effort to understand what the law is uses conceptual analysis on the idea of law, specifically on the idea of a legal obligation. At this point we encounter the problem that Phelps faces in the beginning of the case study: we have to explain what "being under a legal obligation" means.

A legal obligation is an imposition made by law on conduct. The law does not physically prevent us from doing something, nor does it make us do something. Thus the law is not a limit in the way that a wall is a limit, preventing us from moving, nor is it a stimulus that forces us to react without deliberation. The imposition tells us what we are obligated to do or not do. Further, it tells us that failure to comply will result in some form of penalty. A legally binding contract, for example, creates legal obligations. Certain things must be done, and certain things not done, by each party. Failure to live up to one's part of the contract will result in some form of punitive action.

Our analysis of legal obligation, thus, yields two different ideas. First there is the idea of an obligation or the creation of a duty of some kind. Second there is the idea of the penalties to be suffered if the obligation is not fulfilled. The case study illustrates these two interpretations. The first one, which focuses on our duty, is called the *normative interpretation of law.* Ramkin articulates this view when she says that the law imposes a duty that it is immoral to neglect. The second, which focuses on future penalties for noncompliance, is called the *predictive interpretation of law*. Ross presents this view in the case study when he cites the potential fines for noncompliance. Let us look at each view in more detail.

24:1.2   The *normative* interpretation views the law as creating duties for people. The argument for this view points to the right or authority of the lawmaker to put people under obligations with respect to certain things. The normative interpretation takes note of some important similarities between being moral and obeying the law. The law tells us what we *ought* to do. The connection between law and morality is very close in those cases where people view the law as the embodiment of moral goals, such as respect for persons or justice. Living morally and living by the law are both seen as rule-guided ways of living—that is, using rules or precepts to govern or guide one's conduct. For many people in normal circumstances being moral means, at least in part, living according to the laws.

These similarities raise the question of the precise relationship of law to morality. Some would argue that the law and morality are the same. However, strong counterarguments exist. First there are cases where laws are unfair or unjust, such as laws requiring religious or racial discrimination and persecution. In such cases it could be immoral to follow the law. Moreover, morality is often used to improve laws. We can measure the justice of our legal systems only if we view morality as an independent standard. Only when morality is distinct from law can we criticize law and seek to make it more just or show greater respect for people. Further, some aspects of morality are not codified into laws, such as the possible moral obligations to keep verbal promises or share equally in routine housekeeping chores, or live in accordance with one's own conscience—which may include aesthetic and religious values. We cannot say that our moral obligations begin and end with our legal obligations.

There are basically two reasons why the law cannot be identified with morality. The first lies in the potential conflicts that can arise between the law and morality. The second arises out of how people generally respond to situations where enforcement powers break down, as in cases of riot or war. These are seen as situations where there is no law. In such cases of lawlessness morality can remain, but that morality is not the unenforced law, but rather some usually less articulated sets of values and personal moral codes.

24:1.3   According to the *predictive* interpretation, to assert that something is the law is to predict that if a person acts in some way contrary to the dictates of the law, then that person will in fact suffer certain penalties. The fact that people often view the breakdown of law enforcement as an occasion when there is no law suggests that the operative interpretation of the law, at least for those people, is the predictive interpretation.

This predictive interpretation views legal obligations in terms of penalties that will result if they are not met. Thus, the predictive analysis focuses on something that almost everyone views as an important practical consideration: How much, if at all, will I suffer if I am detected disobeying this law? The predictive interpretation avoids the problems associated with identifying legal obligation with moral duties. On the other hand, the predictive view is criticized for being too broad. There are many circumstances in which we can predict harm for noncompliance, yet the items to be complied with are not laws. The child can predict discipline for not being obedient to parents, yet many of the procedural requirements for the rule of law (23:4 and 23:5) are not met by the parents' directives. A kidnap victim or the victims of extortion can predict harm for not complying with the will of the kidnapper or extortionist, but this does not give commands of a kidnapper or extortionist the force of law. People can predict being criticized for violating group norms, but this social penalty does not mean these norms are laws. So, to say that noncompliance with legal obligations will yield penalties is to say that, in this respect, laws are norms or commands that are backed up with the threat of force. In other words, to say that we know what will happen to us if we do not fulfill our legal obligations is not the same as saying that we understand what legal obligations are. We know that if we do not eat, we will die. That does not mean that we understand the biological processes that will culminate in our deaths.

24:1.4   We have looked at the two chief views concerning what law and legal obligations are, the normative and the predictive, and we have reviewed the objections raised against both. Sometimes when people try to combine two theories, they end up with a third theory that has all the weaknesses of both. Sometimes the combination is a successful compromise. In this case we may be able to successfully combine the two views. The normative view emphasizes our duties, while the predictive view motivates by warning of the practical consequences of noncompliance. Some see in this combination an equal emphasis on what the law means (the creation of obligations) and what it intends (the warning against failure to obey).

24:2.1 Sanctions.   The predictive interpretation of the law, with its focus on penalties for noncompliance, raises several questions about those penalties. What kinds of penalties can be imposed? Who can justifiably impose them? For what reasons are they imposed? Penalties imposed on those found guilty of breaking the law are called *legal sanctions*. The concept of a legal sanction includes three elements: the kind of penalty, the source of the penalty, and the reason for the penalty.

Sanctions can take the form of financial penalties (fines) or the restriction of personal liberties (imprisonment, probation). Some societies use sanctions that include various forms of torture and even death.

24:2.2 The source of the sanction is also important. Legal sanctions can be imposed only by legitimate authorities. Legitimate authority lies with the government. It is the government's legal authority to frame laws, promulgate them, enforce them, and apply sanctions to those guilty of breaking them. It is not up to the typical citizen to apprehend and punish criminals. Citizens in general do not have the legal authority to do those things. People who take the law into their own hands (vigilantes and self-appointed "security guards" or "citizen police forces") are acting without proper authority if they seek to punish lawbreakers. In many societies these groups themselves are outlawed. (For a fuller discussion of governmental authority, see Module 22.)

Although governments have the authority to impose sanctions, not all governments do impose them. Some systems of law, such as international law, do not always involve sanctions for failure to comply. In other words, it is possible to have laws that carry no sanctions. However, the majority of laws that we encounter or that apply to our daily lives carry sanctions. Sometimes the precise sanction is established by the legislation itself—for example, five years in prison for using a hand gun in committing a felony. Sometimes the sanctions are left to the discretion of the judge or jury within certain limits—for example, one to ten years in prison for auto theft.

24:2.3 A sanction may be imposed for failing to do what one is legally obligated to do (filing a tax return) or for doing what one is legally obligated not to do (speeding). However, not every expense, inconvenience, or restriction of liberty imposed on us by law is considered a sanction. Ramkin in the case study points this out to Ross. The expenses Jason Industries must incur in order to conform to the law are different from any sanctions imposed for not complying. A tax imposed by legitimate authority is not a sanction, for by definition a sanction is imposed *to penalize* people for having broken a law. However, failure to pay a tax is failure to comply with a law. The government may, then, collect both the tax and a penalty for the original failure to pay.

24:3.1 Reasons for Sanctions. The basic reason why a sanction is imposed is that a law has been broken. While the reason is clear, there is considerable question about the consequences of sanctioning people and about the justifications for penalizing lawbreakers. In Module 23 we detailed many of the advantages of the rule of law. Among other things, the laws make our important social obligations clear. They allow us to better understand and anticipate consequences of noncompliance. The importance of making sure that people abide by the laws is a direct consequence of the value of the rule of law.

Sanctions applied to those who break the law are intended to play an important role in guaranteeing that the laws are kept. A person may be disinclined to obey even a very clear and important law that is not backed up by the threat of a sanction, because no obvious penalty would arise from disobedience. In the case study Ramkin notes that the vice-president might decide not to obey the smoke-detector law because the attached sanction is so small as to be meaningless to a big company like Jason Industries. For many years antipollution laws were disregarded for similar reasons.

24:3.2   The reasons for sanctions relate to the potential wrong-doer, the criminal, the person wronged, and society as a whole. From the point of view of the *potential wrongdoer* sanctions are meant to deter. They are intended to serve as a coercive force that makes people think twice about breaking the law. In the case study the weak sanction did not seem able to serve this function. From the point of view of *society as a whole* sanctions are meant as security. By imprisoning criminals society protects itself from them; they are prevented from threatening public peace and security by being removed from the community. From the point of view of the *criminal* sanctions are thought to serve two functions. Some see sanctions as a way of forcing the criminal to repay to society his "debt" for having violated its laws. This debt is exacted in terms of money, pain, or denial of liberties. A second view is that sanctions can serve to rehabilitate the criminal. They "teach the criminal the lesson" that society will not tolerate certain conduct. Further, during imprisonment and probation the criminal is, in theory, educated to become a useful and contributing member of society. (For a fuller discussion of various theories of punishment, see Module 12.) These two views of the relationship of sanctions to the criminal are in tension with each other. The first seems to call for severe sanctions, the latter for constructive rehabilitative programs that may well be less severe.

There is also a tension between how sanctions relate to the criminal and how they relate to society and social welfare. An important and difficult job for any judge is to balance the welfare of society (its need to be protected from repeated crimes) against the welfare of the individual criminal (sparing the criminal from harsh, unusual, or unfair sanctions). There is also a tension between the welfare of society and the welfare of the potential criminal. Sometimes harsh mandatory sanctions are imposed by the legislature with a view toward deterring crime—for example, mandatory prison sentences for breaking drug laws. But this can work against the welfare of society. Judges may be moved not to convict people of these crimes, especially if they appear to be first offenders, in order to avoid applying the harsh sanction. But, when that happens, the welfare of society is jeopardized. The dilemma for the judge, however, is in balancing the danger to society against the welfare of the first offender. Our prisons, being what they are, are not places where you would send a person if you really had his welfare in mind.

To all of these tensions another must be added: the tension that arises when we introduce the wronged or aggrieved person into the picture. The aggrieved party has suffered some form of harm at the hands of the lawbreaker. There may have been loss of property (control of resources), loss of life or liberty, physical or economic harm, psychological anxiety, or social disadvantage. Whatever it be, there arises a grievance and, so, a claim for restoration. The wrongdoer is usually held responsible for making up this loss or rectifying the harm done. Ramkin appreciated this point in the case study. She saw the potential cost of damages should Jason Industries lose a negligence suit. The cost of restoration would be significantly greater than either the fine for noncompliance or the expenses of compliance. These damages represent efforts to make up to the aggrieved parties what they lost through the fault of the criminal.

In trials involving the potential to sanction the criminal by awarding damages or restitution to the aggrieved, a special tension exists. Too small an award would fail to adequately compensate the person who was wronged. Too large an award might be an unbearable punishment for the criminal. Further, for the good of society, the judgment must be universalizable. The judgment will set a precedent that others, not involved in the present case, will follow. If it is too high or too low to suit the circumstances of the present case, it may turn out to be an unfortunate precedent. Many practical problems of malpractice suits arise in such connection.

24:3.3 Special problems arise for those determining precisely how restoration is to be made in a variety of cases. It is easiest in financial matters, for the restoration can be on a dollar-for-dollar basis. Even here, however, two serious complications can arise. One is the difficulty of accurately measuring a loss, such as the loss of a work of art, an unpublished novel, or the loss of income that may result from libel. The other is the problem of collecting full restoration from a corporation that may go bankrupt, or from an individual who may lack resources to make the reimbursements. Other losses are even more problematic. Most civilizations no longer accept maiming or killing a criminal as a means of restoring to an aggrieved person what is lost through injury or through the death of a loved one. It is very hard to accurately fix a dollar value on the loss of a limb, the loss of sight, or on death. Insurance companies tend to establish fixed scales of compensations for such losses.

One of the problems involved in malpractice insurance is that people are awarded settlements for damages that are larger than individuals or insurance companies seem to be able to afford to pay. But this raises the problem even more clearly. How does one fix the financial compensation appropriate for sickness, injury, or death arising out of a criminal act, negligence, or malpractice? One useful approach is to distinguish punitive from compensatory damages. Compensatory damages are addressed to the loss that has been suffered. Punitive damages are meant to operate as sanctions, penalizing the wrongdoer for doing the harm. We may be able to establish a fixed schedule of punitive damages (sanctions). Measuring the compensatory damages will serve us up to a point. But some things such as life, liberty, health, and a loved one are impossible to translate into accurate dollar amounts.

Exercises for Module 24: Laws and Sanctions

1. *a.* Below is a list of statements, each of which offers either a predictive or a normative interpretation of some law. Mark each statement *P* or *N,* respectively.

_____ (1) If a pedestrian has his or her feet in the intersection, then the motorist may not drive his or her vehicle in such a way as to interfere with the pedestrian's progress.

_____ (2) If you hit a store in the downtown area, the cops are sure to bust you.

_____ (3) When you're on Route 30 between Otisville and Sonnensburgh, you'd better know that it's a speed trap.

_____ (4) No minor is permitted to contract for debts.

_____ (5) A person only does his legal obligation when he reports to the police any knowledge he has of a crime.

_____ (6) Sitting in jail for 30 days is just too steep a price to pay for a little fun one night.

_____ (7) The way the police tail an ex-con, that person's got to know jail's just around the corner for the smallest slip.

_____ (8) If the law is on the books, you ought to respect legal authority and obey it.

b. Suppose that a law prohibited the sale of heroin under pain of a $5,000 fine for each sale. State the normative interpretation of this law.

c. State the predictive interpretation of the law mentioned in *b*.

d. Without reference to any particular law, state the difference between the normative and the predictive interpretation of a law.

2. *a.* Define sanction by reference to the relationship of a sanction to legal wrongdoing and the relationship between sanction and burden.

   b. State the reasons cited to justify the imposition of legal sanctions. (24:5.1)

   c. State which of these reasons are directed toward the potential criminal, which toward the criminal, which toward the victim of the crime, and which toward society in general. (24:5.2)

Selected Answers to Exercises for Module 24

1. *a.* (1) *N.*   (2) *P.*   (3) *P.*   (4) *N.*   (5) *N.*   (6) *P.*   (7) *P.*   (8) *N.*

   b. Persons have a legal obligation or duty not to sell heroin.

   c. Persons who sell heroin will have to pay a penalty of $5,000 for each such sale.

   d. According to the normative interpretation, a law asserts what one's legal duty is; according to the predictive interpretation, a law asserts what penalties one will suffer for acting contrary to the law.

2. *a.* A sanction is a burden imposed upon a person for the wrong he or she has done in acting contrary to his or her legal obligation.

RESOLVING NORMATIVE ISSUES

PART

RESOLVING
NORMATIVE
ISSUES

VALUE DIVERGENCE AND CONFLICT

This cluster is devoted to the question, "To what extent and by what strategies is it possible to resolve value conflicts or normative tensions rationally?" This question is divided as follows: In Module 25 the typical kinds of *ethical* tension are set out. In Module 26 the typical tensions of *social philosophy* are set out. In both of these modules the emphasis is on conflicts *between* values. Then in Module 27 three strategies for rationally resolving normative conflicts are presented. The presuppositions of each, the plausibility of each, the limitations and strengths of each, and the problems to which each gives rise are then presented. The educational goal of this cluster is for you to understand the variety of normative tensions in ethics and social philosophy, and to learn the kinds of strategies available for rationally responding to these conflicts.

Preliminary Notes on Cluster Nine

Normative thought in both ethics and social philosophy revolves around a number of normative concepts, such as freedom, duty, justice, utility, and interest. The opening cluster of this book was devoted to providing you with certain central tools and distinctions for understanding these normative concepts more clearly. Throughout the book philosophical analysis has been continually employed, and the standard of universalizability has been invoked and explained. The distinctions between absolute and relative, objective and subjective, intrinsic and instrumental values have regularly been cited to clarify normative concepts and issues. We have attempted to clarify and to exhibit the value that people intuitively find in individualism, autonomy, security, rule-following, trust, community, respect, happiness, rationality, responsibility, and the explicit articulation of normative expectations in law. That each of these is valuable seems indubitable. Moreover, it seems clear that persons can pursue them with greater certainty once they have knowledge of just what each one is.

Up to now the main emphasis of the book has been on exposition and clarification of basic values. Along the way, however, we have noted two sorts of conflicts. (1) One kind of right may conflict with another kind of right, or one sort of freedom with another sort of freedom. In such cases it will not do to simply say that all people's rights or freedom ought to be respected, for the conflict implies some difficulty in respecting all of those rights or freedoms. (2) Conflicts may arise between one person and another. One person's freedom may have to be restricted in order that freedom for another can be secured. Scarcity of resources may imply that if one person's claim to justice is honored, then the very same claims made by another person cannot be honored. Here the conflict is not between one sort of right or one sort of freedom and another, for the same standard of justice or the same right is in question throughout. In such cases the conflict is between persons, not values.

We are now in a position to explicitly note a third sort of conflict. Whereas we have discussed rights, utility, happiness, freedom, and justice as relatively separate topics, it is entirely possible that pursuit of utility may conflict with the honoring of rights, or the doing of one's duty may be the source of unhappiness. That is, this third type of conflict is conflict between the varieties of values and concerns we have considered.

Throughout this cluster we will speak generally of tensions between different ethical theories or social policies. It is important that you understand the distinction between the two forms that tension can take. One kind of tension, the more moderate and sometimes easier to handle, is *divergence*. Whenever one set of reasons leads to the conclusion that one action should be taken while a second set suggests that a different action should be taken, the result is divergence. What you would do in following the first set of reasons is simply different from, but not incompatible with, what you would do in following the second set of reasons.

Consider an example: Sara, who has been living with a married man, Frank, might conclude on deontological grounds that she should urge Frank to seek neither an annulment nor a divorce. Then, on grounds of self-interest, Sara might decide that continuing her relationship with Frank could only hurt her in the end. She might decide that if she and Frank were never to marry, then she could not be satisfied with the relationship. From this line of reasoning, Sara might conclude that she ought to break off her relationship with Frank. Here we have an example of divergence. On deontological grounds Sara has concluded that she should admonish Frank not to seek an annulment or a divorce, and on egoistic grounds she has decided that she should end her relationship with Frank.

This example of divergence illustrates that divergence does not necessarily imply conflict. That is, it is possible for Sara *both* to urge Frank not to seek an annulment *and* to break off her relationship with him. When two sets of reasons lead us to divergent conclusions, it is often possible for us to resolve any tension by simply doing both of the recommended actions. Sara could both urge Frank not to get a divorce and break off her affair with him. Whenever the recommendations implied by two sets of reasons diverge without contradicting each other, only constraints such as lack of opportunity, lack of time, lack of resources, or lack of cooperation between involved parties will prevent one from following out both lines of reasoning and accepting both recommendations.

Sometimes courses of action not only diverge, they conflict. Different ethical theories or social policies can lead to recommendations that turn out to be logically contradictory to one another. That is, if you follow the one recommendation, you are thereby prevented from following the other. If Sara did consistently urge Frank to get a divorce and did marry him, then it could not possibly be the case that Sara, following deontological dictates, consistently refrained from urging Frank to get a divorce and did not marry him.

Essential conflict arises in cases where no matter *how* you go about following one set of recommendations, you are thereby prevented from following another set of recommendations. Essential conflict between recommendations is by definition inevitable and unavoidable. In many other cases of conflict, however, it is only the *manner* in which you act, and not what you are trying to accomplish, that leads to conflict. Working alone all evening will preclude spending the evening with your friends. But if your aim is essentially to work alone in order to get your work done, you can do your work perhaps in the afternoon and still spend the evening with your friends. On the other hand, if your aim is to work in the evening, then perhaps you need not be alone in order to do your work and you can spend the evening in the company of your friends anyway. It is often difficult to get people to define their goals with sufficient care to clarify what is really essential to their achievement as opposed to what is only coincidental or instrumental. Things that are only coincidental or instrumental can potentially be replaced in order to dissolve a conflict with another recommended action.

MODULE 25
SPECIES OF ETHICAL CONFLICTS

In previous clusters you have had occasion to examine ethical egoism, utilitarianism, and deontological theories of ethics. Intuitively you might well imagine that tensions can exist among the values of self-interest, utility, and duty. There are possible conflicts among the dictates of egoistic, utilitarian, and deontological positions. After reading Module 25, you should be able to

- Distinguish considerations of self-interest, utility, and deontology.
- Recognize the cluster of meanings that theorists have attached to the ideas of self-interest, happiness, and duty.
- Give examples of cases in which different ethical theories would imply diverging actions.
- Give examples of cases in which different ethical theories would imply conflicting actions.
- State abstractly the features of examples of values divergence and values conflict that lead to those values tensions.

THE CASE OF THE PERPLEXED FRIEND

"Come in, Sara, I'm Dr. Yontek. You mentioned on the phone that you were concerned about your friend. What seems to be the problem?"

"Well, ah, Doctor, you see, ah, I have this friend. She's a good person. Well, ah, ah, ..."

"Yes, what about her, Sara?"

"She's been living with a married man. He wants to marry me—I mean her! Oh, no. . . ."

"That's all right, Sara, I understand. How do you feel about marrying him?"

"Well—I would personally love it. Life with him would be fantastic for me. We have so much in common, you know. He's a fine father, and I'd want that for any kid I'd have. And with his kind of job, I'd never have to worry about money. I'd even be able to play the stock market like I've always wanted. I mean, if it were just up to me and I had only me to think about I would marry him today. But I can't!"

"What do you mean, 'can't,' Sara?"

"I mean I can't ask him to divorce his wife, and leave his children. Divorce would ruin them. She's a sweet innocent woman who adores her husband. Divorce will make her become hard and bitter. And the three children are only in grade school. They need their father. No! Too many people would be hurt if he got a divorce. Why should I make all those people unhappy and risk destroying the futures of those children? You know the statistics, Doctor. Kids from broken homes wind up getting divorces themselves when they marry. Doctor, what should I do?

"Well, Sara, it's not for me to answer that question for you. But have you thought about some options? You and he—what's his name?"

"Frank."

"You and Frank could take the children. Maybe with counseling his wife could make a more satisfactory adjustment. I realize these measures would not solve all the personal problems associated with divorce. But you do have some options."

"No I don't, Doctor. Divorce is wrong. It's against Frank's religion. He thinks he can get his marriage annulled by his church. But even if he could, I still think that marriage is forever and the annulment would not make me feel any better about it, even if it did help Frank feel better. He made a commitment, and his wife trusts him. I cannot bring myself to encourage Frank to get his annulment. Since I believe it's wrong, I would be asking Frank to do something that is wrong. And that's wrong too. Don't you see, Doctor, I'm stuck. What should I do?"

25:1.1 Egoism and General Utility. As Sara talks to Dr. Yontek, she presents a variety of reasons why she should or should not marry Frank. Notice the first set of reasons she gives, which argue in favor of her marrying Frank. She would find married life with him fantastic *for her;* she would be satisfied with the kind of father he would be for her children. She would be contented by his job security and satisfied at the prospect of investing in the stock market. Essentially in this paragraph Sara describes her own self-perceived self-interest. She tells Dr. Yontek how marrying Frank would, she believes, allow her to further that interest. Her thoughts are self-centered. She does not consider how happy Frank might be because of what they have in common. The kind of father Frank would make pleases her because it coincides with her ideal of what the father of her children should be, not because of any expressed genuine concern about her children's own welfare.

In contrast, the reasons Sara first gives against marrying Frank are of a general utilitarian sort. She brings into play the interests and welfare of Frank's present wife and children, not simply her own interests. She evaluates the probable consequences divorce would have on both the wife and the children. Risks are calculated and both short- and long-term consequences are brought into play. While, of course, the consideration of long-term consequences is quite compatible with ethical egoism, the reasoning in this passage is definitely not egoistic, since intrinsic value is ascribed to the impact of the consequences upon others besides herself.

The possible tension between egoistic and egalitarian utilitarian considerations is amply demonstrated in this portion of the case study, since these two sorts of considerations lead Sara to opposite, contrary conclusions. Abstractly speaking, there is bound to be tension here, because ethical egoism involves treating only one's own happiness as intrinsically valuable, whereas universal utilitarianism involves egalitarianism, that is, attending to everybody's well-being equally and regarding each person's well-being as intrinsically valuable. Thus, ethical egoism and universal utilitarianism obviously diverge, because utilitarianism understands the happiness of each person as intrinsically valuable, whereas ethical egoism understands the individual's well-being as alone being intrinsically valuable. Moreover, although a person's happiness may tend to coincide with his or her pursuit of egoistic purposes, this need not always be the case (especially if psychological egoism is false). For if psychological egoism is false, then persons are free to pursue non-egoistic purposes, and it may be that some people are sometimes happier if they act on the premise that there is equal, intrinsic value in the pursuit and achievement of each person's interest, even though the dictate of ethical egoism is, of course, that persons should pursue their own interests.

25:1.2 *Happiness and duty* also conflict at times. The final set of reasons Sara gives concerning whether to marry Frank have a distinctly deontological character. According to deontological ethical theory, as defined in Module 16, not only are some states of affairs intrinsically good, but some actions are intrinsically right or wrong and not just instrumentally right or wrong as they conduce to intrinsically valuable states of affairs. While the discussion of deontological theory was presented within the framework of a discussion about rights, deontological theories are not necessarily confined to human rights. The pursuit of justice, the enhancement of freedom, and the maintenance of personal integrity are other examples of goals that may be intrinsically right. At bottom, Sara's argument in the case study rests on Frank's having made a commitment and his wife's trusting him. Sara seems to be suggesting that it is keeping one's commitments and not violating the trust that others have in one that are intrinsically right and valuable. In this paragraph of the case study she does not focus on any further aspects or consequences of the keeping of commitments or the respecting of trust.

Such deontological considerations need to be distinguished from the desirability of happiness, which seems to be involved in Sara's earlier comment. In both her egoistic and utilitarian arguments, Sara seems to be concerned ultimately with what will make people happy. There her conflict is between what will make *her* happy and what will lead to the happiness of Frank's *wife* and *children*. It is important to see, however, that the deontological considerations Sara eventually offers do not rest on the hidden premise that people are necessarily happier when they keep their commitments or do not violate the trust that others have in them. It is possible that Frank would be happier marrying Sara and breaking his commitment to his wife. It is even possible that Frank's wife, after getting over the shock of being betrayed and divorced, would be much happier either living alone or remarrying someone far more compatible with her. Some would say that there is a happiness intrinsic to keeping one's commitments and not betraying the trust that others have, but even if one allows this to be called a form of happiness, it is clearly different from that of good times and pleasant experiences.

Deontologists have also criticized utilitarians for failing to be concerned about the distribution of happiness. Traditionally, utilitarians have attempted to state in quantitative terms how much happiness would be produced for how many people by alternative actions or policies. The right action or policy has then been understood as that most likely to produce the greatest happiness for the greatest number. Deontologists have objected that this conception leaves a very unhappy possibility open: the greatest happiness for the greatest number might be achieved by making some people very happy at the expense of others who would suffer great and undeserved misery, such as slaves or scapegoats. The deontological argument has been that to whatever extent happiness may be intrinsically valuable, its distribution, as well as its amount, must be considered. As long as a utilitarian holds that the greatest amount of happiness should be produced, he can accept the importance of distribution only in the following way: for egalitarian reasons, if two distributions produce equal happiness, then one could decide between *those* alternatives on the basis of the comparative evenness of the distributions.

25:2.1 Competing Values in Ethics. Thus far we have shown how the case study illustrates conflicts between the values of self-interest, happiness, and duty. The question is how to decide which is the most important value. To better understand the differences, we should examine the benefits that theorists have associated with each. We will, then, devote this section to a theoretical summary of the varieties of things that may come into conflict as problems of decision making in ethics arise. We will try to show why people have valued self-interest, happiness, and duty as they have. When divergence and conflict arise among actions dictated by these considerations, how is there plausibly something of importance at stake?

25:2.2   The pursuit of *egoistic self-interest* has been seen as a life of prudence, of foresight and planning, of taking care of one's needs, of not acting foolishly. The importance of self-knowledge has been emphasized, since the person who knows himself best will know best what his own interests are and will, thus, be advantaged in pursuing them. Efficiency and effectiveness have also been emphasized as virtues. For even if you know yourself well and know what your interest is, still you will be frustrated and dissatisfied if you cannot accomplish what is in your self-interest. Similarly, inefficiency will be a fault, for it means unnecessarily wasting resources in accomplishing one's goals.

Autonomy is generally valued highly by ethical egoists, since (a) rational deliberation is assumed to conduce to one's self-knowledge, effectiveness, and efficiency of action, and (b) freedom from constraint is essential to the pursuit of one's self-interest. Moreover, the development of autonomy is itself a part of one's self-development, and self-development in all respects tends to be highly regarded by theorists advocating the pursuit of one's self-interest.

25:2.3   *Happiness* has been viewed as the aim of human action by thinkers as divergent as Aristotle and John Stuart Mill. Such different thinkers have conceived happiness in very different ways, associating it with many different things. Human beings, as largely noninstinctual creatures, have a large variety of potentialities; they can learn to do and find happiness in a great variety of activities. In fact, most people have more potentialities than they can realize in a lifetime. Part of Aristotle's understanding of human happiness is the development that brings human potentiality to realization. He also understood the development of these potentialities into an integrated life as part of human happiness.

Happiness has often been associated or equated with sensory pleasure, and unhappiness with pain. The meanings of pleasure and pain, however, have not always been strictly sensory. For pleasure can mean contentment or satisfaction; pain can encompass anxiety and frustration. Since it is clearly possible that a human being can be fulfilled or frustrated, a theory that attempts to encompass such ideas is clearly superior to one that ignores them. One might also conceive of variety in human experience as itself a source of pleasure and thus happiness.

The definition of happiness has also been affected by the capacity human beings have for reflecting upon themselves, their actions, and their lives. A person can reflect both on himself or herself and on others. When such reflection takes place, a person may like or dislike what he or she sees or may be content with himself or herself and with others, or may even despise himself or herself or others. This has led to the suggestion that happiness means accepting oneself and one's world, whereas unhappiness means despising and rejecting oneself or others.

As persons reflect upon themselves, they may find that they have or have not made a careful and rational attempt to live up to their own highest ideals of human life and action. Thus if we think of a person of conscience as one who has made such an attempt, then we can understand the suggestion that the happy person is the person of conscience.

25:2.4 Doing one's *duty* has also been highly prized in human history. Kant is famous for emphasizing that to act out of duty is to act out of the only pure moral motive. One acts because it is right, independent of consequentialist concerns. In discussing deontological ethics we have already noted the connection between duties and respect for persons. Thus it is easy to see how a person of duty is conceived as virtuous for maintaining his loyalty to others and upholding the trust they place in him. Because the person follows the commitments he or she has made, his or her actions have a consistency that many have found admirable. The purity of actions has seemed noble. Here the idea of an action's being noble is that it is an action of principle, an action exhibiting consistency, and, therefore, an action in which one is true to the commitments one has made. It is an action in which one is, therefore, being respectful of oneself by maintaining one's own integrity or, in other words, achieving the integration of one's thoughts or principles with one's actions.

Autonomy also plays a crucial role in deontological ethics. The person who would act out of a pure sense of duty must be self-possessed and rational as only an autonomous person can be. In turn, much of the ground for the assertion that persons are deserving of respect consists in the beliefs that those persons are themselves at least potentially autonomous and that their autonomy is intrinsically valuable and worthy of respect.

Exercises for Module 25: Species of Ethical Conflicts

1. Below is a list of statements meant to justify various courses of action. Mark the reasons of self-interest *S,* the reasons of general utility *U,* and the deontological reasons *D.* (25:1.1, 25:1.2)

_____ a. When you've made a promise, you ought to keep it.

_____ b. Any other course of action would have benefited everybody else more than me.

_____ c. The law is worthy of respect in itself.

_____ d. We both were only trying to make everybody as happy as possible.

_____ e. I tried to reassure everybody because I could see they were very anxious.

_____ f. It would have been like lying not to tell the district attorney what I knew.

_____ g. If my testimony helps convict that criminal, it can't hurt, and it might help deter others from committing similar crimes.

_____ h. I figured that testifying could only help my reputation as a civic-minded citizen.

_____ i. My integrity was preserved, whatever happened to the others.

2. Below is a list of statements, each of which commends a value traditionally associated with either self-interest, happiness, or doing one's duty. Mark each statement *S, H,* or *D,* depending on which the value has been traditionally associated with. In the starred cases more than one answer is plausible. (25:1.1, 25:1.2, 25:2.3, 25:2.4)

_____ a. It's only prudent to think what you're doing to yourself in the long run.

_____ b. Her motives were purely principled.

_____ c. *A lot of planning and calculation goes into acting rightly.

_____ d. Telling people the whole truth just tends to make them discontent.

_____ e. She abused the trust they had placed in her.

_____ f. *Tom uses his own wits to make his decisions for himself.

_____ g. *You can waste a lot if you take the wrong approach to a problem.

_____ h. *A person has a lot of joy in knowing she's lived up to her ideals.

_____ i. A person who doesn't know what he wants is bound to make a fool of himself.

_____ j. Even though I didn't know myself what would happen, I spoke in such a way as to try to relieve everybody's anxiety.

_____ k. *There's a natural sense of fulfillment in developing your abilities.

_____ l. To the end, her loyalty never wavered.

3. *a.* Give an example where egoism and utilitarianism would divergent actions.
   b. Give an example where egoism and deontological theory would imply divergent actions.
   c. Give an example where utilitarianism and deontological theory would imply divergent actions.
   d. In each of *a, b,* and *c,* abstractly state the features of the example that give rise to the divergence.
4. *a.* Repeat 3*a, b,* and *c,* but supply examples in which the actions are conflicting.
   b. For each example, abstractly state the features that give rise to the conflict.

Answers to Exercises for Module 25

1. *a.* D.   *b.* S.   *c.* D.   *d.* U.   *e.* U.   *f.* D.   *g.* U.   *h.* S.
   i. S.
   For a discussion of self-interest see Cluster Two; general utility is covered in Cluster Three; and deontology is discussed in Cluster Five.
2. *a.* S.   *b.* D.   *c.* S, H.   *d.* H.   *e.* D.   *f.* S, D.   *g.* S, H.
   h. D, H.   *i.* S.   *j.* H.   *k.* H, S.   *l.* D.

3*d* and 4*b.*   Since utilitarianism is egalitarian and egoism is selfish, divergence or conflict can arise when what is in one's own self-interest diverges from or conflicts with the greatest happiness of the greatest number. (See Cluster Preliminary Notes.)

Since deontological theory is principled while egoism may be calculating, and since deontological theory is committed to respect for all persons whereas egoism is not, divergences and conflicts can arise on either of these grounds. (See Cluster Preliminary Notes.)

Since utilitarianism is consequentialist where deontological theory is principled, since utilitarians are committed to happiness as deontologists are not, and since deontology involves respect for every person whereas utilitarianism commends the greatest happiness of the greatest number, whatever may be happening to others, divergence and conflict are possible on each of these grounds. (See Cluster Preliminary Notes.)

MODULE 26
NORMATIVE CONFLICTS IN SOCIAL PHILOSOPHY

The normative questions of social philosophy are typically those of freedom, justice, utility, rights, law, and sovereignty. As with ethical tensions, tensions between values in social philosophy can arise between two species of the same value (say, between two criteria of material justice or two alternative concepts of freedom) or between these basic values. As with ethical tensions, tensions in social philosophy can take the forms either of divergence (25:3.1) or of conflict (25:3.2). In social philosophy, however, a special complication arises, insofar as sovereignty, or ultimate authority, involves the question of who has the authority to adjudicate and resolve tensions within a society. In turn, there is the question of whether the sovereign should exercise its authority through the law or through social customs and mores. As we shall see, social philosophy is also complicated by the question of whether the state's aim is to protect its citizens from harm or to promote positive benefits for them. After reading Module 26, you should be able to

- Describe the kinds of tensions in social philosophy arising between each of the following: justice, freedom, human rights, and social utility.
- Explain the pertinence of the concepts of sovereignty to such conflicts.
- Explain why these conflicts take different forms, depending upon whether the fundamental aim of the state is avoiding harm or promoting benefits for its citizens.

THE CASE OF WELFARE REFORM LEGISLATION

The Orchard City *Daily Trombone* recently published a summary of a draft copy of some proposed legislation. It solicited responses and counterproposals from its readers. Here is what it published:

"Portions of the so-called *Welfare Reform* bill now before the House would give full child support to welfare mothers for all their illegitimate minor children who (a) are alive as of the date the law takes force, or (b) are alive as of the date the welfare mother first becomes a resident of the state, or (c) are born to a welfare mother within 270 days of either of the above dates. All illegitimate children born after that time would receive half support. However, at the second illegitimate birth resulting from a second or subsequent pregnancy following that time the mother will be sterilized. (The procedure will eliminate reproduction but leave other sexual functioning unimpaired.)"

Here are some of the letters the paper received:

"Dear Editor: I support this legislation. We have to do something to make these women act responsibly. Maybe sterilization will force them to think a little about their morality. Yours, R.F."

"Dear Editor: Sterilization is an outrage. Why do we want to punish those women? It's not fair! You can't legislate morality. Besides, what if they tried to use contraception but it failed? Where is the justice here, I ask you? Why do we sterilize these women but let married women breed litters of children? Yours, J.B."

"Dear Editor: I believe this legislation is the only reasonable solution to a growing financial problem. We cannot afford more money for handouts, but we do owe the less fortunate people of this world an even break. So, okay. Support the ones we have, but that's it. No more. This legislation draws the line right where it belongs. Yours, C.G."

"Dear Editor: Our most treasured American possession is our freedom. This legislation would restrict my freedom. I have the right to have children just like anyone else. What gives the government the right to stop me, to threaten me with sterilization, or to withhold its full support from my child? I'm on welfare not because I want to be, but because I have to be. I have my rights, too. Yours, Anon."

"Dear Editor: If we suppose that our welfare pot is only so big, then we will have to be very careful about how we distribute its resources. We can only support so many children before we either run out of money or lower the levels of support so much as to make it meaningless. So, for the good of those whom we are supporting, we have to set limits on how many we support. Otherwise we deplete our resources and water down our welfare so much that everyone suffers. I support this law, but it does not go far enough. Putting new illegitimate children in foster homes would reduce total government costs and probably give the kids a better home environment too. We could even go further and put these kids up for adoption. Yours, Z.M."

26:1.1 Types of Conflict. The case study clearly illustrates some of the ways in which *internal conflicts* arise concerning fundamental values of social philosophy. By relieving the tax burden for welfare, the legislation would tend to enhance the effective freedom of the taxpayers at the expense of that of the welfare mothers and their children. Similarly, not taxing people, allowing them to keep the dollars they have worked for, might be deemed just from the point of view of a work criterion, while providing full payments to welfare mothers and their children would seem just on a need criterion. Without much trouble, you can probably imagine other cases in which there is a conflict between two species or forms of a given value. You probably can also think of cases in which there is conflict between persons concerning the same value. The issues of abortion, hiring quotas, and tax liabilities and exemptions can easily provide you with more examples of such internal conflicts (for more cases review the case studies that begin the modules in Clusters Six, Seven, and Eight). Conflicts often arise between the fundamental values of concern to social philosophers. We shall, in the remainder of this section, consider the wide variety of such conflicts.

26:1.2   Let us first consider conflicts between *justice* and *social utility*. When we think about social utilities, we are thinking about benefits minus costs. Many groups in society typically are very costly—for example, children, the elderly, and the handicapped. All of these groups may incur more costs, at least in the short run, than they generate benefits. Therefore, it will tend to be utilitarian to minimize these costs. That, of course, will mean minimizing the benefits to these relatively disadvantaged groups. Yet for one reason or another it may seem unjust to deny a full share of benefits to members of these groups. Often it will seem unjust simply on a need criterion. The educational needs of the young, the medical needs of the old, and the special care required by the handicapped can be easily documented. In some cases justice might be claimed by a work criterion. For example, it might be argued that the elderly, on the average, have worked hard enough that they ought to be able to avoid the cost of medical treatment during retirement. Their inability to afford that treatment might be used to indicate that they were not sufficiently paid for their labors when they were in the work force. Yet it is quite possible that, however deserved a treatment may be, its cost will be greater than any benefit derived from it. In such cases justice and utility conflict. Reviewing the letters to the editor in the case study, you should now be able to pick out further conflicts suggested by the letter writers between justice and utility as applied to the welfare reform legislation.

26:1.3   *Rights and freedom* can also be in tension in a society. Ultimately, one cost of many social programs takes the form of restriction upon persons' freedom. This, for example, is always true when social programs are paid for through public tax monies. As some of the letters to the editor argue, the payment of taxes constitutes a restriction of both negative and effective freedom. One's freedom to act is constrained, even though one's action is causing no harm to others, inasmuch as one is constrained to pay his or her taxes. Once the taxes are paid, of course, one's effective freedom is reduced by the amount of the tax payment.

In conflict with the undesirability of restricting freedom, however, we often find claims about human rights. In her letter to the editor, the anonymous welfare mother asserts her right to have as many children as she pleases. Similarly, the United Nations Declaration of Human Rights certainly implies the right of each of her children to a nutritious diet and the medical care required for good health. Yet for that right to be secured, it would seem necessary to impose the duty of securing it upon those able to do so. Such a duty, however, inevitably restricts their freedom.

26:1.4   We can easily continue to pair off the fundamental values at issue in social philosophy and show how conflicts can arise between them. There is no doubt that there is frequently tension between the values of rights and utility, rights and justice, justice and freedom, and utility and freedom. You may even wish to refer to the case study to see whether you can detect instances of these conflicts of values. We believe it appropriate, however, to examine the remaining possible conflicts within the context of a more broadly based consideration of the underlying social and conceptual factors that lead to such conflicts.

26:2.1 The Underlying Structure of Normative Social Concepts. Just what are some of the most basic reasons why such tensions tend so often to develop? Consider first the concept of social utility. When one attempts to measure social utility, one is concerned about an aggregate —that is, how great the balance of pleasure over pain, or happiness over unhappiness, is *throughout the whole society.* Consequently, questions of social utility pay no attention to the distribution of these benefits within society. In other words, it is quite possible that the greatest balance of pleasure over pain, or whatever, will exist in a situation where some unfortunate individual suffers a great imbalance of pain over pleasure. It is false to assume that because a society as a whole has a fine positive utilitarian balance, each member of the society sustains a similar balance. More likely, some will sustain a better balance while others will sustain a balance not nearly so good. For example, saying that our society is, generally speaking, affluent does not mean that there are no poor people or no economically disadvantaged groups in our society.

Questions of justice, however, are not about the aggregate but about the distribution of benefits and burdens. Moreover, talk of justice presupposes some criterion for the appropriateness of a given distribution. No similar consideration of a criterion is to be found in the discussion of social utility. Thus utility may come into conflict with justice either because the most general question of distribution is not addressed or because the more particular question of the deserts of individual persons is not addressed.

Conflicts between social utility and human rights can arise for similar reasons. Human rights are rights of each individual; it makes little sense to think of them as the rights of the society as an aggregate. (The rights of nations, if there are any, need not be identified with the basic human rights of individuals.) Consequently, the existence of a good balance for the society as a whole is no guarantee that the rights of each of its members are being honored.

It is important, though, to notice how considerations of rights are distinct from considerations of justice. This becomes clearest when rights are asserted to be indefeasible and inalienable. An indefeasible right is one that cannot be overridden by another consideration; an inalienable right, one that cannot properly be renounced. An indefeasible and inalienable right belongs to a person simply because he or she is a person. There is nothing special about him or her in virtue of which he or she deserves that right. Moreover, there is no condition under which he or she might not be deserving of it. Thus, whereas questions of justice are typically questions about what characteristics of persons make them deserving of some benefit or burden, any characteristics that give persons indefeasible and inalienable rights are, of necessity, conditions that all people meet. In this regard many theorists are inclined to speak of human rights as a basic floor, a minimum standard beneath which treatment of human beings may never permissibly fall.

There is a dynamic tension between freedom and all of the foregoing values: social utility, justice, and human rights. On the one hand the pursuit of any of these latter can imply restriction of freedom. To secure one person's rights may require imposing a duty upon another. To do justice or to achieve the greatest social utility, it may be necessary to require persons to act in certain ways, thus restricting their freedom. On the other hand, the pursuit of these values can also enhance and secure freedom. Sufficient funds may hire, train, and pay a competent police force to secure civil liberties. The more fully rights are respected, the greater the increase in effective human freedom. Paying workers their justly earned wage increases their effective freedom.

The problems of value-conflict resolution may be further complicated by the number of social values that come into tension. Any two, three, or possibly even all four, of utility, justice, rights, and freedom may come into play in given social circumstances, with each value tending to pull in a different direction. The case study illustrates such possible complexity in values conflict. These complexities may be more the rule than the exception in a society where the lives and interests of persons touch one another at many points.

26:3.1 Divergence, Conflict, and Authority. The question of sovereignty (who shall have the authority to rule) arises in human society for a variety of reasons. Because human beings have the capacities both to help and to harm each other significantly and because they must make significant choices, ensuring security and freedom is centrally important to human life. The question of sovereignty, however, has another source worth noting. Since tension does exist between fundamental social values, the problem arises of which value should prevail in any given course of action. The problem is especially difficult because decisions have to be made without perfect knowledge. If decisions are not made, sometimes the opportunity to act is lost, and so in effect a decision has been made, even if not formally. For instance, if no reform is instituted in welfare legislation, then automatically, without any formal decision, the same welfare legislation will continue in effect. Undeniably, decisions are going to be made one way or the other. When those decisions need to be made with less than perfect knowledge about a given subject, the question of who should have the ultimate authority to decide becomes especially poignant.

When it comes to questions of social policy, sometimes there is not only ignorance concerning factual matters but also uncertainty about how the tension between fundamental social values ought to be resolved. For example, in the case study we may both be (a) ignorant of what the consequences will actually be if the welfare structure is changed (will the welfare mothers stop having illegitimate children if threatened with sterilization?) and (b) uncertain of which fundamental social values ought to take precedence (the rights of the welfare children present and yet unborn vs. the freedom of the taxpayers, say). Even if one can successfully argue that having an established authority in such circumstances is desirable in bringing social stability, the question of who ought to have sovereignty is especially important in the light of the need to act upon, and decide between, fundamental conflicting social values.

26:3.2   Besides the question of who shall be established as legitimate authority, there is also the question of how that authority shall be exercised. Should the legitimate power invested in a sovereign be implemented through use of law or through the force of custom and socially accepted mores not covered by law? At this point social philosophical questions as to the legitimate purposes of the law come into play in the matter of values-conflict resolution.

26:3.3   Conflicting fundamental social values are made more problematical on still another count. There remains the question of whether the aim of the state is the avoidance of harm or the promotion of good. Reviewing the case study, you can see how these different aims will redefine the claims that citizens, on the basis of their rights, can make against the state. For example, if the state's goal is to help people avoid harm, welfare mothers can claim the right not to be sterilized, since that procedure would be considered a harm to them. If the state's goal is to promote social good, then on balance the sterilization of a few may be desirable. Similarly redefined is the conception of the justice owed to persons. The task of avoiding harm to the unfortunate and innocent children of the welfare mothers, say by providing them with adequate nutrition, medical opportunities, and public schooling, is a much smaller task than promoting their good by providing them with opportunities for further enrichment and travel and the variety of experiences that might add richness, pleasure, and potential happiness to their lives.

Exercises for Module 26: Normative Conflicts in Social Philosophy

1. *a.* Give an example of a situation in which conflict would arise between each of the following:

   (1) Freedom and justice.
   (2) Freedom and utility.
   (3) Freedom and rights.
   (4) Justice and rights.
   (5) Justice and utility.
   (6) Rights and utility.

   b. In each case abstractly state the features of the example that give rise to the conflict. (26:2.1)

2. *a.* Below is a list of problem situations that exemplify the ways in which the question of sovereignty gains significance. Identify each situation as one in which the following problems arises: (*PH*) people need protection from harm; (*SF*) the freedom of people needs to be secured; (*RI*) resolution of disagreement is necessary in the face of ignorance; (*RT*) resolution of disagreement is necessary in the face of value tension.

   _____(1) The occupants of cars disabled on freeways in the city of Troidee are being robbed.
   _____(2) Unemployment and inflation cannot both be reduced quickly.
   _____(3) Although gasoline may become very scarce, automobile companies are not sure they could build vehicles meeting a legislative requirement of 28 miles to the gallon in city driving.
   _____(4) Even though terrorists don't hurt the passengers of the

planes they hijack, they do delay the passengers in getting where they want to go.

 b. Explain why sovereignty is important to the resolution of each of
these conflicts. (26:3.1 and 26:3.2)

3. In discussing the welfare legislation mentioned in the case study,
Senator Prome Good made the following speech: "The people on
welfare in our state today are largely the children of the people we
had on welfare 20 years ago. Welfare reform legislation must reduce
the burden on the taxpayer by breaking this cycle. If the children
of welfare recipients were raised in an environment where they
learned to appreciate taking initiatives, we could break this cycle.
What do we want? Just to prevent people from starving, when they
could be headed toward a higher standard of living? I think that
most people who can work would rather work, and we should give
them that chance without penalizing them. Let's have all welfare
kids adopted into good working homes at birth, and put their
parents to work at jobs where they'll earn their own money."
(26:3.3)

 a. Explain how the senator spoke to the questions of (1) avoiding
harm, (2) securing freedom, (3) resolving disagreement in the face
of ignorance, and (4) resolving disagreement in the face of value
tension, all from the point of the view that the sovereign ought to
put the promotion of good ahead of the prevention of harm.

 b. After you have checked your answer, write a speech for Senator
Ava Harm containing statements that counter Senator Good's
speech on all four points.

Selected Answers to Exercises for Module 26

1. For more details about freedom, justice, utility, and rights, see Clusters
Four, Six, Two, and Five, respectively.
2. *a.* (1) *PH.* (2) *RT.* (3) *RI.* (4) *SF.*
3. *a.* (1) The harm of being in need of welfare assistance would be overcome by reducing the percentage of people requiring welfare.
  (2) The restriction on the taxpayer of having to pay higher taxes would
be reduced, increasing his freedom.
  (3) Without claiming to know, the senator urges action on his belief
that most of those who can work want to work.
  (4) Leading welfare recipients to a higher standard of living—since that
promotes their good—is given the priority over simply providing for
basic needs. Similarly, providing an improved environment for the

children is given precedence over avoiding the harm of disrupting the welfare families. (See 26:3.3.)

MODULE 27
MODELS FOR RATIONAL RESOLUTION OF NORMATIVE CONFLICTS

In Modules 25 and 26 we described the fundamental values of ethics and social philosophy and the kinds of tensions that tend to arise between them. We offered explanations of why those tensions arise, given the difference in the kinds of values involved. The problem remains, however: How can such tensions be rationally resolved? In our daily experience we are all too aware of nonrational and irrational ways of resolving these conflicts: (1) people ignore the issues, (2) they engage in deceptions, (3) they use persuasive, emotional language, capable of moving persons without providing them with sound reasons, and (4) they all too often engage in the use of force. But are there any *rational* alternatives to these procedures? Yes, indeed there are. They are effective but they are not perfect. They may not resolve all the value tensions, but they are useful in easing and resolving many of them. Similarly, they may work in some but not all circumstances. Nevertheless, even these imperfect procedures are of considerable worth as we try to resolve the value tensions in our lives and our society in rational ways. After reading Module 27, you should be able to

- Characterize each of the following three models for rational normative tension resolution: hierarchy building, problem dissolution, and compromise.
- For each of these models state what makes it plausible and what it assumes.
- For each model state its limitations, its implausibilities, and the problems that it does not fully handle.

THE CASE OF KUBULA, JARANKO

The news broadcast was barely audible through the crackle and static of the old radio receiver. But its message was clear. The city of Kubula was beset with riots and the country of Jaranko was on the verge of civil war once more.

". . . the soccer match had been played up by the government press as a match between Xororian Leftists and Polaried Rightists. It appears that the government hoped the game would settle the running feud. The government was wrong. A fight erupted in the second half. The crowd of 80,000 poured onto the field and joined the battle. Riots broke out along Lamumbuka Street, which separates Xororian and Polaried sectors of the city. Scores of people are dead, hundreds injured. The police seem unable or unwilling to stop the rioters and streetgangs. The military is already arriving in the city. A meeting between Xororian and Polaried leaders is in progress at this moment. This is Jean Flech, CNB news, Kubula."

Prime Minister Lukarta snapped the radio off. "There you have it, friends. It is all over the western news services. Every capital in the world knows we are at it again. And is it really so important? I mean, a game of soccer leads to riots, to a revival of the old prejudices. No. Please, friends, consider what is more important. Think of our nation, Jaranko. We need financial and medical aid to improve our economy, raise our people's standard of living, and cure diseases that have been controlled everywhere but here. Is it not better to put aside the old and pointless fights? Let us put down our arms, call back our guerrillas, and make peace."

"A pretty speech, Minister Lukarta, but no good. We cannot trust the Polaried nor their leaders. They are a band of thieves. Dogs who would take away our jobs and destroy our culture."

"You cannot trust us! What a joker are you! You are the ones who wish to change the laws, to destroy the old ways of structuring society. You call for "socialism" when what you really want is anarchy and governmental chaos. Swine!"

"Friends, please, please. This is not the way to settle our problems. Yelling, fighting. Soon you will be shooting even here in the high court chamber. Please, I beg you, show control . . . . Good. Now, perhaps we can erase the present tensions in the city first. Having done that much, we will save many lives. Then, later, when we have had more time to reflect, perhaps we can talk again about long-term solutions."

"We Polarieds agree. Too much blood is flowing down sewers. Let us ease back, stop the fighting, then talk."

"That is fine for you to say, but we Xororians are poor. You can talk and talk forever; but no reforms will come from talk. We need action. That is why we are in the streets. That is why we will stay there until the problem is solved. No! You cannot fool us with a smile and a promise to talk tomorrow. Let us talk now. Let it be on your conscience, Abalu, that while we talk people die. So let us talk quickly and let us solve our problem."

"Friends, please once again. At least a ten-hour truce, do you agree to that? Just ten hours to count the dead, tend the wounded, and try to reach accord."

"We accept a five-hour truce—a truce until noon. If no solution has been found, we will attack in force on schools, hospitals, and apartment houses."

"Five hours, we too accept. But now, let us begin. Minister, what do you propose?"

"Yes—well, friends, I propose that we discuss a compromise. The Polar-ieds will give up control of the court system and half the seats in the Senate in return for access to the Xororian-controlled labor unions. The Xororians may then have equal representation in the Senate, and equal representation in the unions. The government's executive ministry will assume control of the courts. What do you think?"

27:1.1 The Strategy of Hierarchy Building. The citizens of Kubula face a conflict between social stability and justice for their lower class. The social order that benefits the Polaried Rightists is apparently suppressing the Xororian Leftists unjustly. The threats of the Xororians to continue fighting are the result of their decision that social stability and the utility of the society as a whole are less important than the rectification of the injustices to them. Implicit in their thought is the idea of a hierarchy and its use to resolve or attempt to resolve a social problem. The Xororians perceive two values, social stability and justice, as in conflict. They are convinced it is impossible to achieve both. Being so convinced, they ask: "Which is the more important to achieve?" They then form a ranking from the most important on down:

(1) Justice, especially for the Xororians.
(2) Social stability.

The implication of the hierarchy is that, since justice is more important than social stability, at least in the current circumstances, and since the two are in conflict, justice, the higher value, should be achieved even at the expense of social stability, the lower value.

Put abstractly, then, the strategy of hierarchies amounts to this: it is assumed that two or more values cannot both be realized. Then it becomes appropriate to ask, "Which value should be realized?" The trivial answer, "The more important one, of course," is given substance by ranking the relevant values from most important to least important. From the ranking a decision may be drawn about the course of action to be followed.

27:1.2   Let us look at the *plausibility* of the strategy of building value hierarchies. In the case study the Xororians' use of a hierarchy is not very persuasive, because you can imagine all too easily that the Polaried Rightists would be inclined to form their own hierarchy and come to a contrary conclusion. The conflict would persist, and nothing would have been gained by forming two contrary hierarchies. If the formation of hierarchies is to be a useful model for rational conflict resolution, to formulate our ranking we need some objective criterion to which all parties could appeal and that all parties would accept.

The crucial question is what such a criterion might be. A simple example may help to illuminate the kind of criterion that hierarchy theorists have found promising. Suppose that two children go to hear Heifetz play the violin. Each child likes classical music, and after the concert each child claims to have liked the music very much and to have found it very pretty. Is there any way in which we can distinguish the quality of the two children's appreciation? Well, suppose that one child has no training as a musician, while the other child has already spent many years practicing the violin for two hours a day. That child, thus, is aware of the artistry and the technical precision involved in Heifetz's playing. On this supposition we can say objectively that the second child's appreciation of the concert is richer than that of the first. For while both children found the violin music pretty, the second child alone could appreciate the performance for its technical artistry. The other child, by hypothesis, was unaware of the technical difficulty of Heifetz's playing.

What can be extracted from this simple example? Essentially the second child's appreciation is *more encompassing* than the first; it involves everything that the first one's does, *but it also involves more*. Thus if one's action or one's social policy could be said to contain not only one desired value but another value besides, then it could thereby be said to be the better for it encompasses more values.

The nineteenth-century English philosopher John Stuart Mill, in his book *Utilitarianism,* asserted, "It is better to be a human being dissatisfied than a pig satisfied; better to be Socrates dissatisfied than a fool satisfied." This remark is easily interpreted as illustrating the concept of a hierarchy based on the richness of experience. Socrates is able to experience the environmental awareness and the sensations of which the pig is capable, but the pig is not capable of the self-awareness, the abstract thought, the rationality, the awareness of time, and so on, of which Socrates is capable. Socrates' experience is judged the better by Mill because it is richer and more encompassing.

One strategy for defining a hierarchy upon which to base decisions is to identify the policies or actions that encompass the greatest number of desirable values. Therefore, hierarchy theorists are very interested in the question, "What kind of action or what kind of social policy has the greatest or more encompassing positive value?" The description of such an ideal would allow them to determine what sort of action or social policy ought to form the top of their hierarchy. Theorists could then concern themselves with how actions or policies with less of these values might rank in relationship to each other as inferiors to the ideal. The basic plausibility of such hierarchical thinking is that richer actions or policies—that is, actions or policies containing all of the positive value of another plus an additional positive value—are to be valued more highly.

An alternative way of forming hierarchies to use in decision-making allows us to rank values instead of policies. This alternative way is not based on the assumption that some policies allow for greater *richness* but rather on the assumption that some values are *more fundamental*. For example, suppose that in Country X there is a labor union, some of whose members hold insecure jobs. These members are frequently laid off, and usually they cannot find other work. Country X has no welfare programs for those laid off; they must fend for themselves. The union, however, also has a group of rather wealthy, highly trained, much de- sired workers whose labor is always in demand. The union is thus faced with a problem. To its first group of members job security is very im- portant, because without a job they literally face starvation. To its second group of members job security is not really an issue, because they are confident they will always have a job. This group of workers wants the union to demand an increased number of four-day weekends for holiday trips as its highest bargaining priority.

The union, of course, wants to keep all of its members. Somehow, though, the leaders recognize that the concerns of the first group of workers are the more important. They express this importance as follows: "You can have a job without holiday trips, but you can't have holiday trips without a job."

Stated abstractly, the concept of a fundamental value is the concept of a value such that if it is not realized, then another, less fundamental value, cannot be realized, while at the same time if the less fundamental value is not realized, the more fundamental value can still be realized. Life, safety, and health could be said to be very basic values, because without them many other values, such as having leisure time, developing talents, and engaging in entertainment, cannot be pursued or are at least jeopardized.

27:1.3   The problem with hierarchical thinking is that conflicting values do not always neatly form hierarchies. That is, it is not always obvious or demonstrable that of two conflicting actions or policies the one guarantees a richer result or reflects a more fundamental value than the other. Often it looks as if they aim at ends that are divergent. If one action aims at peace and another at justice, it is not clear either that peace will involve justice or that justice will involve peace, or that one is the more fundamental.

It is important, however, that we do not overestimate the difficulty in developing hierarchies of values. The mathematical notion of a *partial ranking* can be employed. Consider an analogous situation in arithmetic. Suppose we wanted to rank the following from highest to lowest: 2, 16, a number between 1 and 5, 7, and a number between 7 and 10. Some things can be said. Sixteen is the highest; that is, it is higher than 2, higher than the number between 1 and 5, higher than 7, and higher than the number between 7 and 10. Similarly we can say that 2 is lower than 7, lower than the number between 7 and 10, and lower than 16. Thus we can rank some of the numbers from highest to lowest. Others, however, we cannot place in relationship to each other. The number 2 may be higher than the number between 1 and 5, but it may be equal to it and it may be lower. The number 7 may be either equal to or lower than the number between 7 and 10. Definite higher-lower relationships cannot be stated in these cases. The value of a partial ranking, however, is that some rankings can be definitely and objectively made, even if others cannot. Thus, by analogy, even though there may be cases where it is not clear which alternative is the richer or which value is the more fundamental, still the strategy of forming hierarchies will be useful wherever a clear and definite partial ranking can be made.

27:2.1 The Strategy of Dissolution. If we serve parsnips, Susan will be unhappy. If we serve eggplant, Roger will be upset. We have no other vegetables on hand. What shall we do? Clearly, given our supply of vegetables, there is tension between pleasing Susan and pleasing Roger. This tension, however, hardly seems inevitable. We could serve both vegetables and please both Susan and Roger. Or, when we went shopping, we could buy other vegetables that both of them like. There doesn't seem to be any necessity that either of them should be displeased by the food served.

Just as it is possible to serve both of two particular vegetables, so it is also possible to pursue both of two complementary, although divergent, aims. The Xororian Leftists are concerned that if a truce is established without negotiations being planned, then no negotiations will take place. But again there is no necessary incompatibility between a truce and negotiation. A plan for negotiations could be built into a truce plan.

Even when aims are not merely divergent but conflicting, it is possible that the conflict only arises because of *present* circumstances. It may be that in other circumstances the conflict would dissolve, and so it may be that changing present circumstances can lead to resolution of a current problem.

27:2.2   Let us consider the *plausibility* of the strategy of dissolution. Dissolution is a particularly promising way to handle tensions in situations involving alternative evils. When it seems that no matter which choice we make, we will choose something undesirable, the possibility of not having to choose at all, or the possibility of being able to choose a third alternative, is particularly attractive. Antagonistic parties, for example, may often feel that they can afford neither to trust, nor not to trust, each other. If they trust each other, then they are likely to be taken in and harmed; if they distrust each other, they will be unable to work together to restore peace and the possibility of prosperity for themselves. More promising is a third alternative: working closely with each other without trusting each other but with considerable safeguards to ensure that each side performs up to the other's expectations.

In general what underlies the strategy of dissolution of the conflict is the development of *alternatives that avoid the problem*. If tension is due to divergence without conflict, then it is possible to accommodate the divergence by doing both. If tension is due to undesirable sets of consequences of either of two alternative courses, while still a third or fourth course of action remains, then do neither of the first two. If a conflict arises between two aims owing to present circumstances, then change the circumstances so that, despite divergence, there is no longer conflict between the two aims.

In a word, then, this strategy for the resolution of value conflicts is built upon *flexibility*. It argues for flexibility at all levels. At a material level, the more resource and technological abundance a society or a person has, the easier it becomes to use resources in alternative ways or to create alternatives for people. At a personal level it argues in favor of persons' being clearly and distinctly aware of the ends they are seeking. Having a clear idea of one's goals allows one to distinguish them from the means that one is accustomed to using but that one may not need to use in order to accomplish those goals. The more flexible persons are to choose different means to accomplish their ends, the better the strategies of dissolution can be carried out. At a social level flexibility is again a virtue. Whether in developing new kinds of transportation systems or new kinds of laws, the flexibility provides a society with extra alternatives that turn conflicts into divergencies and ultimately dissolve tensions.

The strategy of dissolution also makes a virtue of foresight. Once the Polarieds and the Xororians are at each other's throats, it is difficult to restore peace, much less prosperity, to Jaranko. Keeping alternatives available, not making commitments one may be unable to keep, planning to ensure that divergent aims do not become conflicting but can be accommodated within a single plan—all of these are encompassed within the virtue of foresight so dear to the strategy of dissolution.

27:2.3 There are *limitations* to the strategy of dissolution. It seems inadequate to handle two main kinds of cases. In the first place, some conflicts seem to be unavoidable, especially given circumstances over which we have no power and thus under which we are forced to live. For instance, rights, as conceived of in the twentieth century, require a considerable abundance of resources if they are to be honored. Because of resource scarcity, honoring those rights may be impossible, or may require that human freedom be severely curtailed by a tightly organized, centrally controlled society and a government that constrains freedom in order to make society more efficient in its production.

Other conflicts are unavoidable because unwise promises or other commitments have been made. If the Polaried leaders have made commitments to their people, then there is something wrong in their not meeting the expectations they have created, even though meeting them does conflict with the right of the Xororian people to an improved standard of living.

Some theorists would argue that dissolution is also limited as a strategy because it does not build character. If it is honorable to keep your commitments, then it is desirable to develop the character traits that will enable you to keep them. Moral fortitude and nobility of soul are valuable, according to some theorists, not simply as means enabling persons to keep commitments but as ends in themselves. The ability to integrate principle into practice and to be confident and dedicated in following ideals is thought of as intrinsically good. With this thought in mind one may find the strategy of dissolution of conflicts suspect; a hierarchical approach may seem much superior. For whereas a hierarchical approach demands that the agent be morally firm and have the moral resolve to follow the highest principle through the gravest of conflicts, the strategy of dissolution continually attempts to prevent situations from arising in which moral resolve and fortitude will be needed.

27:3.1 The Strategy of Compromise. Throughout the case study Minister Lukarta advocates a third strategy for conflict resolution, that of compromise. He does so because no mutually acceptable hierarchy is detectable and the problem cannot be made to dissolve. Lukarta asks first that the present fighting be stopped and time be allowed for reflection on possible long-term solutions. This temporary truce would serve social stability, yet open some prospect for future negotiation on the matter of justice for the Xororians. The proposal goes some way, but not all of the way, toward trying to satisfy both of the principal immediate concerns at stake. A temporary truce is not lasting peace and stability, and postponed justice is not immediate redistribution of benefits and burdens. The other parties to the dispute are too hot, however, to accept this initial compromise proposal. The minister falls back to a proposal for a temporary truce of ten hours to allow for immediate negotiations. Both parties accept a similar proposal with a five-hour limitation. At this point the minister makes a proposal that would give both the Polarieds and the Xororians *a part* of what they have been seeking to gain through confrontation. As the price for stability the Polarieds are asked to give up control of the courts and half the Senate seats. On the other hand, the Xororian gains here do not secure immediate redistribution, and the Polarieds are to be granted partial control of the Xororian labor unions. The case study leaves us at a point where this compromise proposal remains to be tested in negotiation and possibly in action.

27:3.2   Let us consider the *plausibility* of the strategy of compromise—the strategy of providing something, but not everything, for everybody, or of providing some of each of the values, rather than realizing any one of the values to the exclusion of others. Like the strategies of hierachy building and of dissolution, the strategy of compromise has its presuppositions. First, since it proposes that everyone should be given something or that each of the values should be actualized in some degree, it assumes that the valuable commodities can be distributed in degrees. It assumes that a right or a freedom as well as a benefit or a burden can be actualized in degrees if not fully. The second presupposition is that no rational hierarchy is available either of the values that are in conflict or of persons whose interests should take first place. The first clause of this denial means that we cannot apply the hierarchy strategy. The second clause is, in effect, the assertion of egalitarianism, for if no person can be ranked higher than any other, then all persons must be ranked equally. The third presupposition is that the tension between the values cannot be dissolved. For if it could be, and thereby all that is valuable could be achieved or all that is undesirable avoided, then there would be no sense in agreeing to a compromise that would accept less. Compromise, then, is a last-ditch strategy, predicated upon the failure of both the hierarchy and the dissolution strategies.

27:3.3   Like the others, this strategy has *limitations*. The strategy of compromise involves two sorts of problems, one theoretical and one practical. Theoretically, the problem involves the presupposition that the contested values can be realized in degree rather than fully. If one is concerned about a benefit that enhances the quality of life but is not essential to a minimal standard of living or even to a good and satisfying life, then it is easy to see how such a compromise would be possible. However, suppose that one of the values in contention is regarded an indefeasible and an inalienable right. How well would Christians be satisfied with a compromise on their right to worship as they chose if it were proposed that they could worship any way they chose, provided that they did not worship on Sunday nor pray to Jesus? How valuable would freedom of assembly be if it were conditioned on never speaking critically about the rulers of one's country? In other words, it is certainly possible that when one compromises a value by achieving the realization of only part of it, the part realized will be insubstantial or of no real value or gain at all, especially in comparison to what was sacrificed in the compromise. As long as all parties are agreed that they are negotiating concerning relative desirables and undesirables, none of which they absolutely must achieve or avoid, there is room for negotiation and for compromise. In fact, however, not all parties may feel that there is such room for compromise. Theoretically, it is not clear that some rights and freedoms could be meaningfully compromised without being substantially destroyed.

A practical problem with the strategy of compromise is that it tends to blur the line between power and authority. In practice one is usually pushed forcefully toward a compromise that favors the more powerful, for they are much more able to enforce their will than are the weak. If fair compromise desired by the weak but unpalatable to the powerful is insisted upon by the weak, the powerful may become totally unwilling to grant even a small compromise that might have been initially acceptable to them. Thus, while the ideal of compromise says that each party will give something and it assumes that all the parties are equal, the realities of power in society suggest that all parties will not be treated equally and that compromise will tend, therefore, regularly to promote a degree of injustice in favor of the powerful.

Exercises for Module 27: Models for Rational Resolution
of Normative Conflicts

1. Characterize each of the following models for resolution of normative tensions: hierarchy building, problem dissolution, compromise. (27:1.1, 27:2.1 and 27:3.1, respectively)
2. Below is a list of assertions. Some are true of hierarchy building, some of problem dissolution, and some of compromise. Put a T or F

in each of the three columns in order to indicate whether an assertion is true or false in each view.

	HB	PD	C

a. This model will work only if there is no essential conflict in the situation.

b. This model will work if one of the values in tension is more fundamental than the other.

c. This model assumes that a rational solution is possible even if it is impossible for all parties to achieve everything they originally wanted.

d. This model can work even if there is an essential conflict between values that cannot be objectively ranked.

e. If this method is successful, no violence arises out of the resolution of tension.

f. This model is likely to work in favor of the powerful.

g. The workability of this model is improved when there is an increased variety of means available to achieve each goal.

h. This model requires the choice of one of the values in tension over the other.

i. This model works toward the full achievement of all goals and values.

j. This model works toward the partial achievement of central values.

3. Describe three cases such that each is best handled by a different one of the three strategies. Then state the characteristics of each of the cases that make it best handled by a particular strategy.

Selected Answers to Exercises for Module 27

2. *a.* F, T, F.   *b.* T, F, F.   *c.* T, F, T.   *d.* F, F, T.   *e.* T, T, T.
f. F, F, T.   *g.* F, T, T.   *h.* T, F, F.   *i.* F, T, F.   *j.* F, F, T.
Review the plausibility and limitations of each strategy in order to understand each one more fully.

3. Tensions in which there is no essential conflict can, at least with ingenuity,

be resolved in such a way that everyone can achieve all of his goals. If this is possible, it is more desirable than achieving only the prioritized goal or only some of one's goals to some extent.

If there is an essential conflict between values, at least in the situation, then if one value objectively has a higher priority than the other (s), the value with that priority should be realized and the other value(s) ignored or compromised to some extent.

If there is both an essential conflict and no objective hierarchy in accord with which one value is of higher priority than the other, then compromise becomes appropriate if the partial achievement of conflicting values is possible.

These comments suggest that there is an objective hierarchy of strategies. The hierarchy goes like this: first, try to dissolve the problem; perhaps all values can be realized or other options exist. But if essential conflicts arise, try building a hierarchy, trying to maximize the most important values. But if no objective ranking is possible, go to compromise.

INDEX